"Bravo! Given the 2016 Order of Celebrating Matrimony 2nd Edition changes to the 1969 1st Edition, *Rites of Passage: Preaching Baptisms, Weddings, and Funerals* provides a clear guide for new preachers and creative insights for the more experienced among us. Utilizing the proven strategy of connecting the Bible and the Liturgy to create a unique preaching for a particular assembly, this work approaches these rites with a variety of practical lens by which the preacher can create memorable and meaningful encounters with Jesus Christ. A true help for the busy priest or deacon, *Rites of Passage* will amplify the preacher's ability to deliver impactful homilies that will move people."

— Rev. Jeff Nicolas
  MDiv, Doctorate in Preaching (Aquinas Institute)
  Pastor of St. Bernadette Catholic Church
  Chaplain (Maj) KY Air Guard

"This book is a great find for anyone looking to explore new preaching strategies. As *Rites of Passage* makes clear, effectively preaching baptisms, weddings, and funerals requires that the homilist know well both the Word of God and those to whom he preaches. In the words of Pope Francis, 'A preacher has to contemplate the word, but he also has to contemplate his people.' To preach in a way as to be heard and understood, with particular attention to language and ritual, the homilist must take into consideration both the culture and context of those gathered in any given situation. Authentic evangelization leading to missionary discipleship is always founded on the Good News of Salvation in and through the person of Jesus Christ. I recommend this book to anyone who desires to encounter a renewed sense of Pentecost in better appreciation of preaching as an integral means of the sacramental grace made available in the liturgical rites."

— The Most Reverend Charles C. Thompson
  Archbishop of Indianapolis

"There are few texts for preaching in the contexts of baptisms, weddings, and funerals, and rarely are they combined in a single volume. This is a unique and comprehensive text—nothing of its kind exists—an outstanding work; a work that is long overdue, and one that is desperately needed. This is not just a text, albeit it is an excellent one that must find its way into the seminary classroom and formation programs for permanent deacons, but it is also a superb manual, reference, and working guide that will be marked-up, dog-eared, and highlighted by its every reader. DeBona, Schotchie, and Agnoli are providing an essential tool for all of us who preside, officiate, and minister at baptisms, weddings, and funerals."

—Deacon David J. Shea, DMin

"This is an informative, challenging, encouraging, evocative resource that offers new and experienced preachers many avenues into preaching the homily at liturgical celebrations rich in evangelization potential. The authors exhibit a sensitivity to the integration of biblical and liturgical texts with the human experiences given expression in the rites of Baptism, Marriage, and Funerals. Add it to your homiletics shelf!"

—James A. Wallace, CSsR, author of *Preaching to the Hungers of the Heart* and *The Ministry of Lectors* and editor of *Preaching in the Sunday Assembly*, is director of San Alfonso Retreat House, Long Branch, NJ

Rites of Passage

Preaching Baptisms, Weddings, and Funerals

Guerric DeBona, OSB

David Scotchie

Francis L. Agnoli

LITURGICAL PRESS

Collegeville, Minnesota

www.litpress.org

1   2   3   4   5   6   7   8   9

Library of Congress Cataloging-in-Publication Data

Names: DeBona, Guerric, 1955– author.
Title: Rites of passage : preaching baptisms, weddings, and funerals / Guerric
   DeBona, OSB, David Scotchie, Francis Agnoli.
Description: Collegeville, Minnesota : Liturgical Press, 2018. | Includes bibliographical
   references and index.
Identifiers: LCCN 2018007528 (print) | LCCN 2018032088 (ebook) | ISBN 9780814645437
   (ebook) | ISBN 9780814645192
Subjects: LCSH: Preaching. | Baptism—Sermons. | Marriage—Sermons. | Funeral sermons.
Classification: LCC BV4211.3 (ebook) | LCC BV4211.3 .D43 2018 (print) | DDC
   251/.1—dc23
LC record available at https://lccn.loc.gov/2018007528

CONTENTS

INTRODUCTION

Formation by Word and Symbol:
The Changing Contours of Preaching
during the Sacramental Rites

Guerric DeBona, OSB

The present volume on preaching baptism, marriage, and funerals has been organized in much the same way that my previous preaching commentary on the Sunday Lectionary, *Between the Ambo and the Altar*, has been laid out. The goal is much the same: to evoke that process of preparation for preaching that would involve first and foremost a contemplative and exegetical strategy with the Sacred Scriptures; then a movement to discover how these biblical texts might connect with the liturgy; and finally, how a preaching event might emerge in a variety of sociohistorical conditions based on these scriptural and liturgical textual encounters.

The authors of each of these sections dealing with the church's sacramental "rites of passage" sought a variety of textual and pastoral nuances for the celebration of each occasion. Among the three of us, my section on baptism was perhaps the easiest to manage, just by virtue of the limits of the possible biblical and liturgical texts and adjustments to pastoral occasions. At the same time, though, preachers are aware that there are a number of variants from which to choose when it comes to baptism, depending on the shape of the occasion. Father David Scotchie's section on preaching marriage brings with it a number of biblical choices for this rite of passage, but also offers a number of alternatives for celebrating the sacrament, depending on a number of situations—which are considerable. If the typical Catholic congregation is growing more and more diverse, the assembly gathered to celebrate a couple's union is all the more so, since this congregation will almost always count itself among different religious confessions as well as the growing (noninstitutional) evangelical community and the unchurched. Finally, Deacon Francis Agnoli occasions his strategy for preaching funerals with a wide variety of opportunities as well; the final rite of passage carries with it texts that necessarily address the seemingly endless human conditions of the funeral, among them the manner of death, the appropriateness of the text to the pastoral need of the bereaved, all in the context of celebrating the life of the departed. To this end, we hope that the wide variety of choices available for celebrating and preaching the funeral rite will give the celebrant and the bereaved a fitting opportunity to celebrate the life of the beloved dead. In all instances, we urge sensitivity for the sake of all those in attendance.

The three coordinates I recommend for contemplating the homily crucially depends on the sociohistorical horizon of the gathered assembly. By my reckoning, preaching becomes actualized when the Word is completed in the ears of those gathered. Therefore the central question for those preaching these seminal moments of transition remains always a live one: Who are those gathered to celebrate these sacraments of baptisms, marriages, and funerals to hear the Word proclaimed? Consider, if you will, some possibilities, past and present. Some of us might remember it still, like faded and discolored snapshots taken from an antiquated Polaroid camera preserved in a scrapbook: A young couple named Jim and Dorothy and married about two years have recently moved only a few miles from All Saints High School where they met; they are expecting their first child. After the child is born, they take her to the parish priest who officiated at their wedding and who has been pastor at St. Gabriel's for twenty years. She is christened Mary Louise. Relatives and friends gather at the family home, where Jim's parents have lived for thirty years. Mary Louise will be the first of several children baptized Catholic and raised in large Catholic elementary and high schools.

We turn the page. Mary Louise has been dating Robert, also raised Catholic for two years. He has just proposed. They tell their parents. They receive instructions from the new associate at St. Gabriel's. It is a large wedding because Mary Louise and Robert each have six siblings. They take a short honeymoon because Robert has to be back in town to work on a new engineering project.

We turn the page. Jim has unexpectedly died of a heart attack at the age of sixty-five. Since he has lived in Middletown, USA, for his entire life and been on the parish council and a eucharistic minister at St. Gabriel's, there is an enormous funeral. The neighbors rally with phone calls and visits to Mary Louise and the family. Everyone volunteers for a eulogy. Five priests concelebrate the funeral liturgy. Casseroles and cold cuts appear after the Mass and graveside service. Her friends, many of whom she has known since Catholic elementary school, comfort Dorothy.

These events represent the lives (and the parish neighborhood) of countless Catholics, many of whom helped to build the religious infrastructure that supported their seminal transitions in life in the church: from a babe in arms to a child of God in baptism; from a single adult to a life of marriage with children; from an earthly dwelling to the promise of a heavenly home. The Catholic school system and the parishes that supported them created a catechetical system and network of symbols, rites, and codes structured around a very familial sacramental system. Baptisms, marriages, and funerals were as much a part of Catholic life as regular attendance at Mass on Sunday. These were communal celebrations that provided situational meaning because the community itself was a tightly woven web of relationships, living in close proximity. "This is what we do here" could well be the subtext of thousands of Catholic parishes passing the church's familial rites of passage down from one generation to the next. But as is well known, the days when we celebrated these sacramental rites in the midst of a strong, highly integrated Catholic culture have vanished in America; and so necessarily are the ways in which we preach them.

Those who preach baptisms, weddings, and funerals in the twenty-first century can no longer presume that their congregations maintain a semblance of traditional religious and biblical literacy, to say nothing of a catechetical understanding of the church's sacramental life. Why? The reasons are complex and point to the gradual erosion of traditional forms of worship in the United States, meaning structures that initiate, catechize, and foster ongoing membership. There are a number of sociological reasons why Catholic religious membership has been on a downward spiral, which include the loss of a post-immigrant community life, the diminishment of the Catholic parochial school system, and the turning away from institutional religious expressions of contemporary America.[1]

---

1. See, for instance, Patrick W. Carey, *Catholics in America: A History* (Westport, CT: Praeger, 2004); James O'Toole, *The Faithful: A History of Catholics in America* (Cambridge, MA: Harvard University Press, 2008); Peter Steinfels, *A People Adrift: The Crisis of the Roman Catholic Church in America* (New York: Simon and Schuster, 2003).

Additionally, as our immigrant population increases and blesses our nation with diversity, those who are making these rites of passage have not been formed in European, traditional post-immigrant models but come to these important life transitions in paths quite different from the way our parents and godparents embraced these sacraments. In a certain sense, the people of God have been formed—but by a secular society with its own sets of values and expectations, well outside the pale of Catholic culture or, indeed, the sense of the "metanarrative" we call salvation history.

Our historical and social networks have been transformed considerably over the past several decades and require us to adapt our preaching to a particular cultural horizon. These new sociohistorical conditions are still emerging. The scrapbooks holding the still life of a bygone era have been stored in the attic; and in their place we find something moving, organic, and still changing, even as I write this. No longer limited to parishes or neighborhoods, millions gravitate to social media, or move to worship spaces far beyond the parish boundaries. Family systems are seemingly more complicated than ever and many of these relationships are fragmented. Ten-year-old Juan puts a DVD in the entertainment center and sees his single mother at the Easter Vigil receiving baptism and confirmation as part of a cohort of twenty in the RCIA last spring. Some months later, his half-sister, Rosita, who has a successful business halfway across the country and is now in her mid-thirties, has just uploaded a video of her wedding on Facebook. Her new husband, Rodney, has asked his older son by his first marriage to be the best man while the youngest one serves as an usher for the wedding at Blessed Stanley Rother Catholic Church. A year later, Juan and Rosita's birth father dies alone in an emergency room. A friend calls a parish priest and asks for a funeral at St. Bruno Catholic Church. A preacher will be asked to name the grace inside the sacramental life of the church in the midst of these diverse and often fragmented concrete circumstances of our contemporary life.

These contrasting scenes from the past and present represent two quite different cultural reflections of religious affiliation and expression; they are reason for us to rethink the role of liturgical, sacramental formation as well as the homily preached on this important occasion. The preacher at sacramental rites today stands in the midst of a very diverse and secular culture, celebrating the most consequential milestones in the lives of his parishioners. How, then, does proclamation of the Gospel become a meaningful, Christ-centered event for those transitioning in a sacramental rite of passage today? Preachers who proclaim a saving word for their congregations must be a "mediator of meaning," as *Fulfilled in Your Hearing* (1982) refers to the one who unfolds the homily at the liturgical assembly. "Like humans everywhere, the people who make up the liturgical assembly are people hungry, sometimes desperately so, for meaning in their lives. . . . Without ultimate meaning, we are ultimately unsatisfied. If we are able to hear a word which gives our lives another level of meaning, which interprets them in relation to God, then our response is to turn to this source of meaning in an attitude of praise and thanksgiving."[2] Whether we are at Sunday Eucharist in a large suburban parish, or celebrating a baptism on Sunday afternoon in an inner-city community, we do so as a particular historical congregation making meaning. That incarnational, sociohistorical horizon in a particular time and place holds a special place when it comes to a sacramental rite of passage, which is anything but an abstraction. Father James Wallace describes preaching at sacramental rites precisely in terms of an incarnation of the Word made visible, a divine response to the weary, to those who are hungry for "meaning." "The sacraments are encounters with the risen Lord; a primary function of our words is to make the presence of Christ palpable, to facilitate this meeting with Jesus. As a language event, the preaching is one of the integral components of the rite, crucial in bridging the gap between the Liturgy of the Word and the Liturgy of the Sacrament, between anamnesis and mimesis, between remembering what God has done in the paschal mystery of Christ and what we are presently engaged in doing as an act of realizing the presence of salvation in our midst."[3]

When it comes to preaching the sacraments today, then, how can we understand our proclamation to the people of God *using language as an event* that gathers and announces the enfleshment of the Word made visible? One way to construe preaching the sacraments is to begin to note the emergence of a variety of ways to interpret sacramental theology over the past fifty years or so; these theologies grant us a vital perspective on preaching so that we might *name grace in the present tense*, as it were, for those gathered to celebrate Christ among us. Generally speaking, when

2. USCCB, *Fulfilled in Your Hearing: The Homily in the Sunday Assembly* (Washington, DC: NCCB, 1982), 7.

3. James A. Wallace, CSsR, *Preaching to the Hungers of the Heart: The Homily on the Feasts and within the Rites* (Collegeville, MN: Liturgical Press, 2002), 78.

these theological speculations concerning sacramental theology have sought to discover an *experiential model* for celebrating the church's rites of passage, they help us unfold the task of *preaching as a formational moment*. When it comes to encountering these rites of the church, as Peter Fink suggests, "The focus of attention is on the liturgical enactment of the sacraments, rather than on sacrament as an abstract theological concept."[4] To take this proposition a bit further is to ponder precisely how meaning becomes mediated and embodied in a sacramental hermeneutic for contemporary culture. As the ancient precept has it, sacraments are for the people, *sacramentum propter hominem*. And as people change so is the rite culturally expressed and interpreted in and for the Body of Christ. Further, we know that Christ is present in the very act of celebrating the sacraments through rite, symbol, and language, since the risen Lord has passed these mysteries of salvation on to the church. Therefore the *Catechism of the Catholic Church* reminds us that when celebrated validly, the very elements of the rite itself signify the reality of the sacrament. Concerning the grace of baptism, for instance, the *Catechism* says, "The different effects of Baptism are signified by the *perceptible* elements of the sacramental rite. Immersion in water symbolizes not only death and purification, but also regeneration and renewal. Thus the two principal effects are purification from sins and new birth in the Holy Spirit" (1262).[5]

The *perceptible* elements of sacramental rites themselves suggest a hermeneutic of real presence that the preacher unfolds in an enculturated idiom for those gathered by extending the rite into proclamation. An experiential model of sacrament is good news for preaching, then, since it is an essential task of the preacher to name God's saving acts, even as the Word proclaimed in the assembly has revealed these mysteries. As

4. Peter E. Fink, SJ, "Sacramental Theology after Vatican II," in *New Dictionary of Sacramental Theology* (Collegeville, MN: Liturgical Press, 1990), 1110. For an excellent overview, see David N. Power et al., "Sacramental Theology: A Review of the Literature," *Theological Studies* 55 (1994): 657–705; Geoffrey Wainwright and Karen B. Westerfield, eds., *The Oxford History of Christian Worship* (New York: Oxford University Press, 2005); Paul Bradshaw, ed., *The New Westminster Dictionary of Liturgy and Worship* (Louisville, KY: Westminster John Knox, 2002).

5. *Catechism of the Catholic Church*, 2nd ed. (United States Catholic Conference—Libreria Editrice Vaticana, 1997). See also David N. Power, OMI, *Sacrament: The Language of God's Giving* (New York: Crossroad, 1999).

sacramental symbols and language of the rites draw the congregation into an incarnational reality of the risen Christ, the preacher unfolds meaning in the present circumstances, taking his cue from the very action of the sacrament itself. As Karl Rahner says in his discussion on the theology symbol, "The sacraments make concrete and actual, for the life of the individual, the symbolic reality of the church as the primary sacrament and therefore constitute at once, in keeping with the nature of this Church a symbolic reality. Thus the sacraments are expressly described in theology as 'sacred signs' of God's grace that is, as 'symbols,' and expression which occurs expressly in this context . . . As God's work of grace on man is accomplished (incarnates itself), it enters in the spacio-temporal historicity of man as sacrament, and as it does so, it becomes active with regard to man, it constitutes itself."[6] In other words, rather than deducing concepts embedded in an abstract understanding of sacrament, the one who unpacks the Word for God's people in the preaching event draws from the concrete experience of the Scriptures and the liturgy itself, together with an exegesis of the assembly.

With this critical stance in mind, preachers drink from the wellspring of the Scriptures proclaimed, together with the church's texts and teaching on the sacraments; we pass that overflowing sacred cup, freshly remembered, to those gathered around the Word. As part of the liturgy itself, the homily becomes not so much a text as it is an event-in-time that repositions and shapes the congregation. According to *Sacrosanctum Concilium*, the very experience of sacramental rite is formative. "Because they are signs they also instruct. They not only presuppose faith, but by words and objects they nourish, strengthen, and express it. That is why they are called 'sacraments of faith.' They do, indeed, confer grace, but, in addition, the very act of celebrating them most effectively disposes the faithful to receive this grace to their profit, to worship God duly, and to practice charity."[7] So if the sacraments embody the presence of Christ in his church, always constituting a concrete reality of a particular

---

6. Karl Rahner, SJ, "The Theology of Symbol," in *Theological Investigations Vol. IV*, trans. Kevin Smyth, 241-42 (New York: Seabury Press, 1966, 1974).

7. *Sacrosanctum Concilium* (The Constitution on the Sacred Liturgy), in Austin Flannery, ed., *Vatican Council II: The Conciliar and Postconciliar Documents* (Collegeville, MN: Liturgical Press, 2014), 59.

person in a sociohistorical community, then the church's preaching must enflesh this concrete experience for the hearer. Drawing on the theology of Rahner's notion of the human subject being constituted as a "hearer of the word," Mary Catherine Hilkert says that grace as the spiritual mystery "has to be manifested in concrete, historical, visible ways. God's presence is mediated in and through creation and human history, but that mystery remains hidden and untapped unless it is brought to word. The proclamation of the word and the celebration of the sacraments (Augustine's 'visible words') bring the depth dimension of reality—grace—to recognition and thus effective power."[8]

Preaching must *reorient the hearer to the Good News*, then, meaning that the one who speaks on behalf of the church to the gathered assembly makes the saving works of God in salvation history concrete to those who desire to live a deeper faith experience. While offering a word to the weary that will rouse them, the preacher reestablishes God's narrative of salvation through anamnesis in a world that has lost its collective memory. The preacher finds himself to be reflective of the risen Lord appearing to the disciples on the road to Emmaus. Though the followers of Jesus are downcast, the Lord (re)interprets the Sacred Scripture in light of God's messianic event in Christ who stands before their very eyes, waiting for the eyes of the blind and the ears of the deaf to receive a graced proclamation. "Then he opened their minds to understand the scriptures. And he said to them, 'Thus it is written that the Messiah would suffer and rise from the dead on the third day and that repentance, for the forgiveness of sins, would be preached in his name to all the nations, beginning from Jerusalem' " (Luke 24:45-47).

Those who have been dissuaded by doubts and fears are reshaped by the Word. To be sure, then, we take as our point of departure for preaching sacraments a mode that is distinctly pastoral, and driven by the church's mission. As *Gaudium et Spes*, the Pastoral Constitution on the Church in the Modern World (1965), tells us, "The joy and hope, the grief and anguish of the men of our time, especially of those who are poor or afflicted in any way, are the joy and hope, the grief and anguish of the followers of Christ as well. Nothing that is genuinely human fails

---

8. Mary Catherine Hilkert, *Naming Grace: Preaching and the Sacramental Imagination* (New York: Continuum, 1997), 47.

to find an echo in their hearts. For theirs is a community composed of men, of men who, united in Christ and guided by the holy Spirit, press onwards towards the kingdom of the Father and are bearers of a message of salvation intended for all men" (1). Preaching at the Eucharist as well as the sacramental rites opens up a space of longing for the Holy God, who forms and reforms us. I think we can presume, then, that preaching unleashes the Word among us in order that American Catholics might become what Sherry Weddell has called "intentional disciples." In this regard, "our personal response at the moment of receiving baptism or another sacrament is only the beginning of a lifetime of responding in faith to God's grace. If we don't intentionally seek to continue to grow in our faith, the initial grace we received can be thwarted."[9]

Finally, it is worth a final reiteration that this volume is designed to be useful in the cultural milieu of a variety of hearers, engaging a pastoral mission suited to a particular time and place. The Sacred Scriptures and the liturgical texts are in dialogue with God's holy people. As Pope Francis reminds the church, "The preacher also needs to keep his ear to the people and to discover what it is that the faithful need to hear. A preacher has to contemplate the word, but he also has to contemplate his people. He needs to be able to link the message of the biblical text to a human situation, to an experience which cries out for the light of God's word."[10] Preaching the rites of passage, or proclaiming Christ's living presence through the sacraments, must meet the faithful where they are—sometimes fragmented, often confused, searching for the God who already seeks them. It is for them, the people of God, that this text has been envisioned.

9. Sherry A. Weddell, *Forming Intentional Disciples: The Path to Knowing and Following Jesus* (Huntington, IN: Our Sunday Visitor, 2012), 113.

10. Pope Francis, *Evangelii Gaudium: The Joy of the Gospel* (Frederick, MD: The Word Among Us Press, 2013), 115.

PREACHING BAPTISMS

Guerric DeBona, OSB

The following section of the present volume is designed as a preaching companion for the revised *Rite of Baptism for Children*,[1] according to which, "after the reading, the celebrant gives a short homily, explaining to those present the significance of what has been read. His purpose will be to lead them to a deeper understanding of the mystery of baptism and to encourage the parents and godparents to a ready acceptance of the responsibilities which arise from the sacrament" (45). The RBC is very succinct as well as directive regarding the homily at baptism. If the preacher is strategic in following the overall arc of the guidelines in the rite, the homily will give new life to those gathered about God's work of redemption as that saving act becomes disclosed in their midst through the sacrament of baptism.

Let me say more about a strategy for the homily. I have laid out a dynamic for preaching in the pages that follow in a way that mirrors what I have already suggested previously in the three-volume commentary on the Sunday Lectionary, *Between the Ambo and the Altar*. The approach is a simple one: understand through study and *lectio divina* the biblical readings; then begin to make connections between the biblical and liturgical texts; and finally, develop a preaching tactic from these conversation partners. When it comes to preaching baptism, there is, of course, a wealth of symbols and liturgical language to draw out the biblical readings. In his excellent overview of preaching within the celebration of the sacraments, James Wallace, CSsR, says that the sacramental rites "are events of divine-human communication which effect transformation by offering

---

1. *Rite of Baptism for Children*, English Translation Approved by the National Conference of Catholic Bishops and Confirmed by the Apostolic See (Collegeville, MN: Liturgical Press, 2002). All references are to this edition, also referred to as RBC.

meaning rooted in the life, death and resurrection of Jesus Christ, the Word of God."[2] Practically speaking, there will be occasions in which the celebrant (and family) may prefer to use one reading; other opportunities may occur when the baptism will benefit from two. So I have created a commentary in these pages that accommodates both liturgical circumstances. The first four of these selections deploy one gospel reading, while I have paired two readings with ten others. I hasten to add that, as with *Between the Ambo and the Altar*, each tri-part commentary is designed to be suggestive and idea provoking. And I will underline that description especially when it comes to the section titled "Strategy for Preaching." I have included a focus sentence that might follow a reading that best suits the biblical text, the liturgical language, and the hearers. My overall hope is that the preacher will not necessarily follow my ideas as much as my strategy for preparing the homily by first interrogating the biblical text then recognizing the liturgical features with which that Scripture might be in dialogue. Finally, the preacher must attend to the needs of the listeners, especially when it comes to leading them to "a deeper understanding of the mystery of baptism." By my reckoning, the process of preparation for preaching expands with the generous association between texts that already share common features. So the liturgical texts for the celebration of baptism and the readings that the church has suggested for inclusion in the rite are dialogue partners; that conversation thrives by designed and imaginative association with one another.

If we presume that the overall goal of the homily is to draw the hearer more closely into the web of divine mystery as that encounter is disclosed in baptism, then I will here suggest a kind of checklist of attributes for the homily. Prospective preachers at baptism will have their own emphasis on these characteristics, to be sure, and these will vary according to pastoral need. But I present here a short list of features that might characterize a typical baptismal homily. These are, incidentally, in no particular order. The baptismal homily should: be **C**atechetical; **H**onor the biblical text; be **I**mage dominated; and be **L**iturgical and **D**iverse in its reach. These characteristics (conveniently) spell out the anagram CHILD.

---

2. James A. Wallace, CSsR, *Preaching to the Hungers of the Heart: The Homily on the Feasts and within the Rites* (Collegeville, MN: Liturgical Press, 2002), 76.

Catechetical

Most dioceses mandate a period of preparation for the couple present-ing their child for baptism. The guidelines for the RBC specifically link this religious education of the parents as a duty for the pastor who is to gather groups of families together in preparation "by pastoral counsel and common prayer" (5). So the homily will draw on a catechesis and prayer formation *already* established by a portion of those gathered and can deepen the experience of their understanding of the sacrament (as well as their commitment to raise the child in the faith) through an encounter with the Scriptures and the language and symbols of the liturgy. I would say that it is crucial that when it comes to catechesis and preaching, the homily does not simply rattle off some abstract theological sayings about the sacrament of baptism; rather, the preacher should attempt to deepen an understanding of what is *already present*. Echoing the *Catechism of the Catholic Church* that doctrine ought to be deployed in a systematic and organic way, *Preaching the Mystery of Faith* observes that "catechesis in its broadest sense involves the effective communication of the full scope of the Church's teaching and formation, from initiation into the Sacrament of Baptism through the moral requirements of a faithful Christian life."[3] Certainly, there are abundant areas of doctrine that might be explored, not only from the perspective of the parents and godparents but also for the hearers who have gathered with them to celebrate this sacrament of initiation; for example: questions such as how baptism incorporates the newly baptized into the church by sanctification from original sin, making the neophyte a child of God; exploring the mystery of Christ's own baptism as a witness to the incarnation; responding in faith to the new reality of this baptism by faithfully engaging the church's teaching in dialogue and witness. These subjects and more are topics for catechetical preaching. That catechesis will be more effective, as we shall see shortly, when church doctrine becomes supported by the biblical and liturgical aspects of the homily.

3. USCCB, *Preaching the Mystery of Faith: The Sunday Homily* (Washington, DC: USCCB, 2013), 23. See also *Catechism of the Catholic Church*, 2nd ed. (United States Catholic Conference—Libreria Editrice Vaticana, 1997), 5.

Honor the Biblical Text

The instructions in the RBC say that the homily is to lead those present into a "deeper understanding," which cannot occur without a prayerful encounter with the biblical readings. Much like the Sunday homily, preaching for the sacrament of baptism springs from an encounter that is voiced through the Scriptures. The preacher is the first among hearers, listening attentively with the whole church, together with this particular gathered assembly witnessing to the Christian sacrament of initiation. Above all else, the word of God is living and active, transforming the lives of those who hear, as St. Benedict advises his monks, "with the ears of the heart." Quoting his predecessor, Pope Francis reminds the church that "[a]ll evangelization is based on that word, listened to, meditated upon, lived, celebrated and witnessed to. The Sacred Scriptures are the very source of evangelization. Consequently, we need to be constantly trained in hearing the word. The Church does not evangelize unless she constantly lets herself be evangelized. It is indispensable that the word of God 'be ever more fully at the heart of every ecclesial activity.' "[4] It is critical that the Scriptures engage those present by unfolding God's activity in Christ, of which baptism is a symbolic witness. That does not mean, of course, that the homily becomes a kind of heady, abstract dissertation. No, the Scriptures are pathways to a deeper understanding of the mystery of faith, a gifted encounter with divine revelation that has been passed on to the church. In turn, the ecclesial community remembers the works of the Lord and the joy of the risen Christ active in the lives of God's people. Whether there are one or two readings, the biblical witness contextualizes the present circumstances of the celebration of the sacrament in the local church by communicating the working of the divine plan throughout history. Salvation history is present here and now. By attending to the readings and how they are applicable to the lives of those gathered, the preacher will be able to "bring the hearers to a more explicit and deepened faith, to an expression of that faith in the liturgical celebration and, following the celebration, in their life and work."[5]

---

4. Pope Francis, *Evangelii Gaudium: The Joy of the Gospel* (Frederick, MD: The Word Among Us Press, 2013), 128.

5. USCCB, *Fulfilled in Your Hearing: The Homily in the Sunday Assembly* (Washington, DC: NCCB, 1982), 27.

Images

It should come as no small surprise that the use of images is crucial to the development of any homily. We know that the more concrete the language, the more the homily will be retained by the hearer. "Language is often abstract, but life is not abstract. Teachers teach students about battles and animals and books. Doctors repair problems with our stomachs, backs and hearts. Companies create software, build planes, distribute newspapers; they build cars that are cheaper, faster, or fancier than last year's. Even the most abstract business strategy must eventually show up in the tangible actions of human beings."[6] In addition to the principles of rhetoric that suggest concrete language in the homily, the preacher takes his cue on the use of imagistic language, symbols, and metaphors from the Bible and the liturgy. Consider the images that are deployed in many of the biblical readings commonly used for the celebration of baptism: water from a rock; new heart versus stony heart; water flowing from the temple; buried with Christ; baptized into one Body; clothed with Christ; bond of peace; living stone; anointed on head with oil; dwell in the house of the Lord; radiant with joy; heavens being torn open; the kingdom of God belongs to such as these; he is one; he came to Jesus at night; born of water and the Spirit; a spring of water welling up to eternal life; rivers of living water will flow from within him; he smeared the clay on his eyes; I am the true vine; you are already pruned; immediately blood and water flowed out. If we take our initiative from Scripture itself, then the homily will be a bounty of images. Further, the ritual of baptism is itself a fragrant and tactile series of gestures linked with the biblical witness and meant to communicate God's love to those assembled. From the cross traced on the head of the child at the beginning of the rite to the anointing with the oil of catechumens to investing with the white garment and to the passing of the lighted candle and chrismation, the sacrament of baptism is a feast of images. These visual moments of human contact incarnate God's word among us in sacrament. The homily might use these very images or extend the sacramental imagination in a variety of ways for the benefit of the hearer.

---

6. Chip Heath and Dan Death, *Made to Stick: Why Some Ideas Survive and Others Die* (New York: Random House, 2007), 99–100.

Liturgical

The language of the liturgy is always a suitable conversation partner for the homilist; all the more so when preaching inside the sacramental rites. When paired with the Scriptures, the dialogue between the word of God and the church's ritual language becomes irresistible for the preacher. The liturgy extends into time and space, or what the Scriptures have revealed in mystery, gifted story, and symbol. The church's language puts sinews on those strong bones, breaking into our comfortable worlds and reorienting us to God's future. Just as an example of the way the RBC recalls the Scripture, we could note the many instances that the Blessing and Invocation of God over Baptismal Water recalls the readings just proclaimed and accounts for the Scripture in contemporary and transformative ways for those gathered. If Mark 1:9-11 has been proclaimed, there are abundant interpretations to mediate meaning for the assembly, with the help of this excellent liturgical text invoking God's sanctification. The Blessing and Invocation is a salutation to the gift of water as a tributary of sanctification, "a rich symbol of the grace you give us in this sacrament." The allusions to water as receiving the Spirit of God at the "very dawn of creation . . . making them the wellspring of all holiness"; or the waters of the great flood as a sign that would "make an end of sin"; or again, the waters of the Red Sea through which Israel was led out of slavery and was "an image of God's holy people, set free from sin by baptism." All of these flashpoints in salvation history speak to the christological theophany on the Jordan: "In the waters of the Jordan your son was baptized by John and anointed with the Spirit" (91). This text, as so many treasures in the liturgy, points to a reality in the gospel that might be expanded in the homily before the *Blessing* actually occurs. I will underline here as well that glossing these liturgical texts in concert with the biblical readings provides a powerful catechetical moment: the unfolding of the incarnation and the beginning of Jesus' adult ministry in a trinitarian moment in the theophany at the Jordan; Jesus, truly God and truly man, has sanctified the waters for all humanity by the will of the Father and the working of the Holy Spirit. Finally, the liturgical language functions in harmony with the biblical text in order to remind the congregation that the homily is "by definition a profound ecclesial act."[7]

---

7. *Preaching the Mystery of Faith*, 30–32.

Diversity

We know that more and more baptisms are celebrated with diverse communities; this pluralism is all to the good for the good and the growth and prosperity of the church and its mission. Our culture in America is at a critical juncture when it comes to racial and class divisions, as well as policies and attitudes toward immigrants and migrants. Much of these attitudes, especially those governing race and immigration, are driven by fear and, frankly, excessive nationalism. Those who preach will certainly encounter diversity in their hearers, but it is well to remember that the church was founded in the midst of diversity at Pentecost. For Pope Francis, "Differences between persons and communities can sometimes prove uncomfortable, but the Holy Spirit, who is the source of that diversity, can bring forth something good from all things and turn it into an attractive means of evangelization. Diversity must always be reconciled by the help of the Holy Spirit; he alone can raise up diversity, plurality and multiplicity while at the same time bringing about unity."[8] This blessing of peoples of mixed cultures and backgrounds is expressed in several ways. Those gathered for the celebration will be various in everything from age to language. Although the homily will be relatively brief (about 5 minutes, for instance) compared to Sunday preaching, a wide net for evangelization is cast in order to catch the multiple experiences of the listeners. An older population will have a tough time grasping rapid-fire contemporary images for which they have little or no reference point. For those in the congregation who are either unchurched or attend any church less frequently than a few times a year, ecclesial references are not going to go anywhere. Then there is a language barrier, especially in parishes with growing Hispanic/Latino communities. In the latter congregation, it is absolutely necessary to make all feel welcome because hospitality, the welcoming of the neophyte into the church community, is a foundational principle of the sacrament of baptism. Ideally, the language will be a bridge, not a hindrance, to building a sacramental community. If we do not attend to the diversity and blessing present in the gathering of diversity itself, then the ritual of baptism, which pours out upon a neophyte divine hospitality in God's word and communicated by ritual, will not be effectively communicated. As *Preaching the Mystery of Faith* reminds

8. *Evangelii Gaudium*, 99.

us, "Good preaching honors the experience of immigrant families and sympathizes with the challenges of adapting to life in the United States. In this regard preaching must reflect insight into the Church's evangelizing mission, which requires cultural discernment based on gospel values that go beyond those of any particular culture."[9] How the preacher regards the assembly of those who have come to witness the baptism is critical to the celebration.

1. John 3:1-6

Readings from the Ambo

With its dramatic turn centered on Nicodemus's encounter with Jesus by night in a quest for understanding, John 3:1-6 remains a centerpiece for the unfolding mystery of Christian baptism and initiation into the church community. Nicodemus (and the Woman at the Well of Samaria, his foil later in chapter 4) provides John with a showcase for the Lord's disclosure of the presence of God in mysterious signs in the midst of darkness because "[h]e himself understood it well" (John 2:25b).

As the text tells us, Nicodemus was a Pharisee and a leader of the Jews, but singled out as a particular and somewhat forward-thinking character among the elders. For instance, we later learn that when there is discord among his peers concerning Jesus' identity as the Messiah, it is Nicodemus who questions the rash judgment of the chief priests and other Pharisees when he says, "Does our law condemn a person before it first hears him and finds out what he is doing?" (John 7:51). Toward the end of John's gospel, it is Nicodemus (recalled as the one who "had at first come to Jesus by night") who brings a preposterously lavish "mixture of myrrh and aloes weighing about one hundred pounds" (John 19:39) to anoint the crucified Jesus. Nicodemus's search for the Lord by night, then, becomes part of a larger tapestry in the Fourth Gospel, deploying the interplay between light and darkness that the author has used as a dominant image from the beginning (cf. the Prologue) and running throughout the text. That a leader from the Jewish community seeks clarification in the midst of darkness reminds us that the Light—Jesus himself—doubles for the revelation of that which will overcome the night of sin and evil. More particularly,

9. *Preaching the Mystery of Faith*, 40.

it is the revelation of the kingdom of God (an expression more common in the Synoptics than in John's gospel) to Nicodemus that becomes the ultimate disclosure of the Light, since seeing that apocalypse appears to be the very reason for being born again from above: "Very truly, I tell you, no one can see the kingdom of God without being born from above" (NRSV). Along these lines, we might recall that the invitation to "come and see" was linked as well to discipleship early in the gospel when Philip invites Nathaniel to come and see Jesus, who, in turn, promises the young man from Cana in Galilee that he "will see greater things than this"—a vision of the Son of Man (John 1:45-51).

Jesus' encounter with Nicodemus, then, establishes some literary characteristics that will haunt John's gospel: plays on words, irony, misunderstandings, and some character development absent from the Synoptics. In a sense, Jesus' meeting with this Pharisee is like the dawn illuminating the night, attempting to break through the shadows of morning. Nicodemus's presence later in the gospel reminds us of how slow the process of the knowledge of coming to see the kingdom of God in Christ really is, since, when the question of Jesus' identity occurs later in chapter 7, the Jewish leader more or less defaults to a question about the Law. Jesus' admonition to the member of the Sanhedrin to be "born from above" (*anothēn*) in the earlier chapter does not appear to be absorbed by Nicodemus by chapter 7. In chapter 3, the conversation suggests something like a dialogue of misunderstanding based on a new way of seeing things that has yet to unfold for one still in relative darkness. Nicodemus, therefore, is not unlike the crowds who, later in the Bread of Life Discourse, misunderstand the new way of seeing the kingdom: How can someone be born again from his mother's womb? How can he give us himself to eat? These questions betray the fundamental blindness at night that John seeks to expose to the sun: the presence of darkness or misunderstanding while standing in the presence of the true Light. To grasp the dance between darkness and light, ignorance and knowledge, falsehood and truth, is to recognize the invitation to conversion at the heart of the sacrament of baptism. Those who are baptized are initiated into the light of Christ: they are, quite literally, the Enlightened.

Connecting the Bible and the Liturgy

Jesus' meeting with Nicodemus and the disclosure of the vision of the kingdom of God for those born anew is a text that marvelously interfaces with the RBC for reasons that should be fairly obvious. It is not a coincidence that the (re)naming of the children becomes the first order of the way the rite wants to reimagine this new addition to the Christian community. As he has explained to Nicodemus, the Lord wants to alter our way of seeing things by giving us another language, the language of the kingdom; it is not a system based on nature, or a pragmatic identification. But Jesus has handed the church a new alphabet of the kingdom, enabling us to speak differently, even as the mouth of the newly baptized will be opened for proclamation at the end of the rite itself. Furthermore, there is a new condition, linked with the new name for each of the neophytes: baptism, being born anew is the inheritance we have from the New Adam, since they are now children of God. The RBC advises that the celebrant may choose other words for the dialogue with the parents concerning the naming of their children, but the questioning might mirror the search by night so emblematic of Nicodemus's dialogue with Jesus. Indeed, the conversation between the two represents a very human journey toward God, a searching for meaning in the midst of emptiness: the open heart seeking a new understanding, with a new name now so that a new way of living in the new order of creation might be born anew.

Those who rename their children are also charged with the light of guidance. The celebrant tells the parents and godparents, "Receive the light of Christ," even as they are asked to carry on what has already occurred in baptism when the children have been "enlightened by Christ." The child has been given the light of understanding in the midst of community, the family of humankind. "This light is entrusted to you to be kept burning brightly." The parents and godparents become agents of the church, microcommunities that will eventually blossom into larger portions of the human family. In a very real sense, they are "sponsoring" or witnessing for the rest of the church community who are now part of the children's family. Yet the sobering implication here of the burden of such guardianship is clear enough. Parents and godparents are to "keep the flame of faith alive" in those who have now been enkindled by the sacrament. Hence, the meaning of the candle should not be lost on those who will discharge this responsibility of sponsorship: they are entrusted with helping the child see a new vision by the light given to them, requiring them to be born anew and see that God's word is a lamp for their steps, a light for their path. Therefore, parents and godparents are crucial symbols in and of themselves, torches burning in the night that hope to set ablaze the vision of the gospel that is the light of the Christian faithful. In a certain sense, the parents and godparents might find a thoughtful parallel with Nicodemus as an elder searching and guiding not only for himself but for Israel. Guardians carry the light in the ongoing revelation of truth in the midst of darkness.

Strategy for Preaching

The first few chapters of John's gospel—with special attention to chapter 3—are the ideal site into which the preacher might probe the mystery of baptism. In fact, these chapters are so rich that they also provide an apt catechetical instrument for parents and godparents when it comes to instructing these guides for the newly baptized well *before* the rite. Additionally, among those gathered in the early pages of the Fourth Gospel are fascinating characters who enflesh the exploration of the human subject's search from darkness to light, marginalization to community, apathy to faith. Nicodemus comes to the Lord not only as a member of the Pharisees and leader in the Jewish community but as a kind of Everyman haunted by the darkness and searching for the light of Truth. Therefore the focus sentence for this homily on John 3:1-6 might be that the children are brought to the light of baptism this moment as the Lord rescues them and us from the powers that bind us.

The net cast here in preaching this passage in the context of baptism is necessarily broad in its reach. The hearers will be parents and godparents and other family members, perhaps young couples who are themselves searching for the light of understanding when it comes to raising a child by faith. We know that raising a child is not an easy task these days—as if it ever was—but the Scriptures and the rite are not simply texts with formulas for a ritual of initiation; no, they are consoling messengers in helping to shed some light on accompanying a child throughout life with understanding, love, and mercy. Here, an introduction could position Nicodemus as something like a guardian or parent in Israel, since he is longing for rebirth not only for himself but also for the nation as an elder in the Sanhedrin, the people of Israel. Clearly, he seems to have come to an understanding of Jesus' identity slowly, and when he does so it is as an elder or older family member grieving, delivering at Jesus' burial an overabundance of oil and spices.

That introduction, which draws on the loving Christian sponsorship of the parents of those (or the one) to be baptized, moves us nicely into the body of the homily, which could begin with: The Lord has claimed those to be baptized as his own and made them children of light. (A very brief excursus from the *Catechism of the Catholic Church*, 1213–84, on baptism could follow with a theological explanation here and, crucially, be accompanied by a visual image or short story dealing with something like initiation to support the doctrine.)

But the homily, like the rite itself, does not end there. Parents and godparents have only just begun their search with their children, and so they are entrusted with the light to keep that search burning. A reference to the baptismal candle and its connection to the pascal candle would be appropriate in this context. An illustration would go a long way to complete this thought: Can you imagine taking your children on a camping trip in a dark forest without a lamp, or even a match to light a lantern? So the church has given us a bright light taken from the Easter candle: let this be our guide along our journey with Christ.

Now: a caveat, if you please. When it comes to dealing with images of light and darkness, these strong words are not an invitation to polarize or project pet peeves onto the congregation, small as it may be. Those who wish to represent contemporary culture as utter darkness ought to remember that we are all part of this culture that we are called to illuminate through Christ's presence. There is nothing in the gospel we have just heard to indicate that Nicodemus or Israel or their culture remains part of some dark underworld, although this member of the Sanhedrin remains associated with the mystery of the night when he brings the lavish gift of spices to anoint Jesus' body in John 19:39-40. He is a seeker. Much like those gathered to celebrate baptism, he is looking for the Lord in the midst of obscurity and even death, holding only a fragile candle as he does so.

2. Matthew 28:18-20

Readings from the Ambo

There are a few things to observe as we begin to unpack this very last portion of the Gospel of Matthew. The first of these is that this commissioning of the eleven disciples comes from the "authority" (Greek:

exousia) Jesus has claimed as the risen Lord, which he now passes on to the disciples. Matthew uses *authority* in specific ways throughout his gospel, notably in his confrontation with the religious leaders who, as in Matthew 21:23, ask Jesus by what *power* (i.e., authority) he does these things. Therefore, the events leading up to this call to mission have been a vindication for Jesus' authority as Son of God and a fitting climax to the *exousia* handed over to the risen Lord of heaven and earth: *all authority* has been given to him. Indeed, Matthew departs from Mark's very stark depiction of the disciples' postresurrection encounter with the empty tomb with a much more dramatic scene, also full of power of the risen One. "[A]s the first day of the week was dawning, . . . there was a great earthquake," while the angel rolled back the stone to announce that the Lord has been raised, confounding the stupefied guards and urging Mary Magdalene and the other Mary to tell the other disciples that Jesus has been raised from the dead. There is an electric, even sensational quality to Matthew's account of the resurrection that will draw the priests and the elders into a conspiracy with Roman guards to bribe them in order to falsify testimony that the disciples stole the Master's body during the night. Matthew wants us to see Jesus' triumph as the risen Lord and the call to mission of his disciples as the final word of God's power over worldly and religious authorities. A new age has broken into our human history.

It is that tension between heaven and earth that grabs our attention with the opening line, "All power in heaven and on earth has been given to me." As God's Regent, the risen Jesus now has assumed dominion over all creation. We might recall that Jesus has arranged to meet the eleven disciples on the mountain, the traditional locus of God's own authority as it was handed over to Moses in the Law. Now once again, the commissioning of the Eleven emerges from God's imperial authority, a mission to claim the world for divine power. Some scholars have suggested that Matthew's emphasis on Jesus' claim to authority comes precisely as an opposition to Roman imperialism and its own sway over the empire. After the resurrection, however, a new power has been unleashed that will colonize the children of God into another empire under the Law of Love. Jesus tells the disciples to teach them "to observe all that I have commanded you." The new Law is now handed over, the covenant renewed.

How will this be mission be accomplished? Baptism. This is not the baptism of John, as we know, but rather one that will account for the new order of creation, a discipleship "in the name of the Father, and of the Son, and of the Holy Spirit." So Jesus has given his followers a new relationship to live into, one that will sustain them, perhaps because "they doubted" (28:17). As if to reinforce this new world order of Father, Son, and Holy Spirit, Jesus tells his disciples that "I am with you always, until the end of the age." The final words of the gospel, then, concern promise and presence, an enduring legacy of God's reign to trump earthly powers, even in the midst of persecution. The call to mission in this passage obviously becomes the focal point. Jesus' summons comes as if he is a general rallying the troops, the Lord gathers his disciples; they are drawn to him not for the sake of perpetrating violence and subjugation, but to hear the sublime teaching of the Master to his disciples. We are left with this commission from one who has *exousia* from the Father. His followers are waiting to be born anew into this divine reality, something of a sequel to Matthew's gospel that is both ongoing and filled with God's new relationship with creation.

Connecting the Bible and the Liturgy

Jesus' sending his disciples into mission in the world has its most important and obvious liturgical connection with those who have gathered for baptism. The reality of the commission to bring a new relationship to the world based on Christ's teaching and commandments is clearly underlined when the baptism occurs for "several children," since these witnesses stand in testimony to Christ's authority unfolding in the actual liturgical time itself. Further, each of those to be baptized is welcomed into the Christian community with its distinctive sign of victory and authority. The officiating minister says, "My dear children, the Christian community welcomes you with great joy. In its name I claim you for Christ our Savior by the sign of his cross." From this moment on, the die has been cast; the imprint bestowed that will reach its culmination in the immersion into the life of the Trinity when the children are plunged into the saving waters of baptism will soon unfold. The command of the Lord to his disciples on the mountain is about to be engaged.

But this commandment to partake of the life of the triune God is not left to the priest or deacon alone. No, the parents and godparents are enlisted to hear the commissioning of the eleven disciples to the world and become cooperators with the grace that is about to be poured on those to be baptized. As the minister says, "I now trace the cross on your foreheads, and invite your parents (and godparents) to do the same." What has just occurred in symbol by the tracing of the cross on the heads of the children will be highlighted by the gospel about to be proclaimed, a ratification of the faith of the parents and godparents who have brought their children to these saving waters. We should not miss this particular invitation to the parents and godparents as a call to mission; they are, in fact, missioning their child(ren) with the sign of the cross and setting up the family as a microcosm of the church with its own call to evangelize.

There is more to say about this most crucial and ubiquitous sign in Christendom. If the sign of the cross is first traced on the head of the child, the Trinity will be invoked again (most importantly in the actual baptism itself). Indeed, the RBC emphasizes the ongoing power of the Trinity as well in the Blessing and Invocation of God over Baptismal Water when it invokes the Father who gave us "the gift of water" and made it holy throughout sacred history; when it recalls that the "Son willed that water and blood should flow from his side as he hung upon the cross"; when it asks the "power of the Spirit [to] give to the water of this font the grace of your Son." The Blessing and Invocation quotes Matthew 28 and then, as if in direct response to Christ's command to baptize, says, "We ask you, Father, with your Son to send the Holy Spirit upon the waters of this font. May all who are buried with Christ in the death of baptism rise also with him to newness of life." Finally, the presence of the Trinity is reaffirmed once again in the threefold profession of faith of the parents and godparents. Indeed, based on the language of the rite that runs throughout the text, we might say that Jesus' command to baptize all nations "in the name of the Father and of the Son and of the Holy Spirit" inhabits and embodies the congregation that has gathered for this sacrament. So when the culminating moment occurs when the child is submerged into its holy waters, baptism for the child has made present what the congregation knows already to be true: that the Trinity is a guiding presence in which we live and move and have our being, a living baptism that has taken hold of those witnesses gathered for testimony of the sacrament right then and there.

Strategy for Preaching

There is a certain generation of Catholics for whom the sacrament of baptism is a rather isolated ritual, without much claim on either the family or the larger community of the one to be baptized. Attentive filmgoers will recall the magnificently ironic ending of Francis Ford Coppola's *The Godfather* (1973) in which the rite of baptism of Michael Corleone's son becomes artfully segmented and crosscut in a montage style, together with the graphic murders of his enemies. That is a wonderful but tragic commentary on a baptism that becomes inverted in its connection with the world and evangelism. Seeking to bring the sacrament out of an isolated, even superstitious, ceremony with very little claim on the behavior of the baptized, the Second Vatican Council's strong emphasis on the priority of baptism as the gateway to Christian life has initiated a new way of thinking about this sacrament of initiation, especially its relational character and the inevitable call to mission it calls the neophyte to engage. The conclusion of Matthew's gospel presents the preacher with an opportunity to highlight the indelible mark of mission for the entire community, with those to be baptized as the primary symbol. Those gathered, then, reflect deeply on the nature of their own baptism as well as the indwelling of the Trinity, which is at the heart of the mystery of Christian life. So the focus sentence for this homily could be something like this: As we come to witness to the new life of those baptized, the church asks us to consider our own relationship with the Trinity, which guides the faithful and calls us into mission each day.

The point of departure for the homily might be precisely a point of departure: a trip we were asked to make. Maybe it is a business trip or something as simple as a shopping excursion for the family. But there have been times in everyone's life when we are called to accomplish something for another. (Some brief examples might follow.)

Baptism launches us into a lifelong mission to witness to the life of Christ on earth. (What this looks like, with examples to fill it out.) We have been given an extraordinary gift—we call that supernatural grace—to sustain us on our journey. We will, like these children, find rich resources in our own human family to help us along the way. Think back, parents and godparents: Who were significant instruments in your own Christian awakening over the years? (Examples that are specific enough to evoke memories in the congregation.) God finds instruments to do his work, even as you have been the divine workers in bringing the children to these saving waters.

So we do not act alone—far from it. It is the community of the Beloved that finds its animation in the Trinity that keeps us moving. (Perhaps a very brief explanation of the Trinity's importance in the life of the baptized Christian, using examples from the RBC, supplemented by a quote from the *Catechism of the Catholic Church*.) We are not alone, but Christ dwells in us, and his Spirit calls out to the Father in us until the day of our death. And when we receive the Eucharist throughout the course of our lives, we are further sustained on our journey to mission. Who knows who or how many these children will bring to Christ? (A few possible examples.) Let us make no mistake: God's power is at work in us all, and even now that Sprit is stirring in these children as Christ builds his sacred home.

3. Mark 1:9-11

Readings from the Ambo

Mark's account of the baptism of Jesus by John in the Jordan is quite stark, especially since, unlike the other Synoptic Gospels, the author has absorbed no birth narratives that would introduce Jesus into this pivotal moment in his life. At the same time, the present passage is rich in significance for a variety of reasons, which will soon become apparent enough.

It is John the Baptist who first introduces us to Jesus and also the one who parses the work of baptism for us. Immediately before this selection, John says that he has baptized with water but foretells that one "mightier than I is coming" who will "baptize you with the holy Spirit." Therefore John establishes a vital link between his own baptism of water and the work of the one who is to come who will baptize with the Holy Spirit. From a literary perspective, the hearer now waits in suspense to learn more clues concerning the identity of this powerful, promised new baptizer, and what he will be like.

And so the stage has been set for Jesus' entry immediately following this short preparation by John. The passage then goes on to reveal Jesus as precisely the embodiment of both the baptism by water and the Holy Spirit; both realities have claimed him. Jesus is baptized in the Jordan and then, "On coming up out of the water he saw the heavens being torn open / and the Spirit, like a dove, descending upon him." It is useful to note that there is a subtle but crucial difference between how this epiphany in the Jordan is disclosed among the Synoptic writers. Matthew 3:16 agrees with Mark that Jesus alone glimpses the rending of the heavens and the Spirit alighting on him. But in a departure from the other Synoptics, Luke reports this occasion of the Spirit's manifestation as a dove as an objective fact, as if viewed from one of the bystanders nearby, or even from another, more omniscient perspective. The distinction bears a lot of a weight for exegetes because if the Baptist is correct that the one who is coming will baptize with the Spirit, then that promised one must himself sense his unique call into mission by the Spirit as Son. This understanding of the Lord's mission greatly affects our understanding of how Christology unfolds in Mark's gospel. Jesus' sensing the Spirit's intervention unveils his unique call to ministry. So Mark's emphasis on Jesus' point of view when he emerges out of the waters of baptism remains crucial for our understanding of how the one who will baptize with the Spirit senses his relationship with the Father and the Holy Spirit, the Sanctifier, and implicates Christ's own distinctive and utterly unique call to baptize by the Spirit and power.

The baptism scene would not be complete were it not for the ratification of Jesus' baptism and mission by the voice that came from the heavens, "You are my beloved Son; with you I am well pleased." Here again, there is some ambiguity surrounding the point of view in this scene, this time concerning the voice from heaven. The address here is in the second-person singular, underlining the intimate quality of the encounter between the divine call from heaven and Jesus' baptism. So, on the one hand, we could claim that Jesus alone heard the voice that has called him "Son," since this is a continuance of the previous point of view when "he saw the heavens being torn open." At the same time, we could ask legitimately: How does the narrator know any of this information if this epiphany occurs from Jesus' perspective alone? The voice from heaven refers to Jesus as the "beloved" (*agapétos*), which raises, I think, another question: How did Jesus become the Beloved, since he has just appeared on the scene? The hearer of Mark's gospel might already be anticipating a similar query when Jesus faces someone in his hometown of Nazareth, in Mark 6:2, who asks, "Where did this man get all this?" The passage before us, then, hints at a kind of prehistory concerned in the baptism of Jesus with the voice from heaven, the Spirit, and Jesus himself. The baptism of Jesus is, then, in a certain sense, literally an originating moment par excellence, a new creation in which the voice of God speaks the Son into being, and in which the love of the Creator discloses his Firstborn by water and in the Spirit. So the theological implication is that Mark's gospel will orient itself around the Son's reordering of creation, a healing of what was lost and disfigured. It is the Lord who will baptize with the Spirit, who groans us into completion, as we await the redemption of our bodies. These fascinating narrative divergences in the baptism scene and shifts on points of view alert us to an important perspective in Mark's gospel that initiates the readers into a relationship with the Lord. The *hearer* (or reader) becomes a new creation by discovering a foundational experience with the Beloved. At the very least, the narrator's perspective suggests a privileged point of view on Jesus' call to ministry, something that potentially creates an alliance between the hearer and the Lord from these early portions of the gospel.

Connecting the Bible and the Liturgy

There is a substantial relationship that the Markan passage establishes with the so-called Explanatory Rites following the baptism. The biblical selection witnesses to Jesus' own unique relationship with the Father and the Spirit as the "beloved." Now those assembled to celebrate the baptism of their child(ren) can discover the special new relationship that has been won for the new Christian(s) after he or she has emerged from the waters of rebirth. The symbols and language of the Explanatory Rites are rich territory indeed, but I will focus only on three as a window into understanding the biblical text and the sacrament of baptism in an expansive way.

First, before the Anointing after Baptism, the celebrant says, "God the Father of our Lord Jesus Christ has freed you from sin, given you a new birth by water and the Holy Spirit, and welcomed you into his holy people." With this statement, the celebrant declares the newly baptized as beloved, taken up in a radically new relationship with God. Echoing the biblical passage, the heavens have opened and the voice of the Father has bid welcome to the one who is *agapétos*, beloved of God. The newly baptized, now free from sin, has become a child of God and brother or sister with Jesus himself and with the fellowship of "his holy people."

Second, the connection with Jesus and the Spirit establishes itself yet further during the anointing itself. The chrism of salvation becomes the outward sign that this person is now the temple of the Holy Spirit, sharing the life of Christ. "As Christ was anointed Priest, Prophet, and King, so may you live always as a member of his body, sharing everlasting life." It is notable that the language for this rite says that "He now anoints you."

That the child is beloved there is no doubt because God has anointed the neophyte with the trifold identity of Christ himself and so will bear that image until the day he or she dies. This anointing suggests the dignity of the newly baptized, sharing in the very person of Christ the Priest, Prophet, and King, all of which are identities associated with the ritual of anointing with fragrant oil. We might well imagine Pope St. Leo the Great in the background here, echoing his famous phrase, "Christian, remember your dignity!"

Third, the Clothing with White Garment underlines the connection with Christ and his own baptism because the new Christian has become "a new creation, and have clothed yourself in Christ." The use of white underlines the purity that is associated with Christ the Beloved Son and the sinless One. That clothing for the beloved implicates him or her into the new order of salvation with heaven and everlasting life as its goal. "See in this white garment the outward sign of your Christian dignity. With your family and friends to help you by word and example, bring that dignity unstained into the everlasting life of heaven." As Jesus received the waters of the Jordan to baptize with the Holy Spirit and with fire, so now the new Christian, clothed with dignity, is sent into the mission of maintaining Christian dignity, a kind of constant remembrance of the baptismal moment throughout earthly life. Hence, baptism has called both Jesus and the newly baptized child into the mission of salvation—to baptize with fire.

Strategy for Preaching

The scene in which Mark portrays the baptism of Jesus in the Jordan begins to suggest the christological meaning behind Jesus' mission, as well as his identity as Beloved Son. The breaking open of the heavens reveals not only the mysterious voice from heaven but also Jesus' consciousness of the Father's claim on him as Son, together with the Spirit's role in their communion. The preaching of a baptism that employs this passage might focus on the way in which Christ has made the neophyte a "new creation," and participates now in a sacramental way in the very identity of the Beloved Son. So the focus sentence here might be: All those who come to the waters of baptism emerge from those waters as a new creation, beloved children of God.

I think that an appropriate introduction could engage the hearers in a recollection of unconditional love—or its absence—in our culture.

What are the signs of unconditional love that mark our time? Sadly, it would seem from the unhappiness of society at large (examples could follow) that there are a great deal of people who feel not only conditionally loved—but unloved altogether. Consider the countless narratives of love and its loss and gain in popular culture, and yet we still inhabit an alienated society. As much as we spin the talk about loving one another, even among Christians, millions wake up in despair and go throughout their lives empty.

If we await the recognition that we have become a new creation in baptism, then we wait no longer. The waters of baptism are an outward sign of God's love for his Beloved Son, and the Spirit's relationship with them both. (Recall the scene.) Give some brief examples of Jesus' encounter with the Father in the course of Mark's gospel (transfiguration stands out as an illustration), depicting the Son as faithful witness. We share those same waters of the Jordan with the Lord, who made them holy. He is our brother, the Beloved of the Father.

As a marker of our sharing as beloved sons and daughters, these newly baptized children will be anointed in the fellowship of God's holy people. We will smell that chrism for a long time, and they will be imprinted as the beloved for a lifetime. They will share in Christ's identity as Priest, Prophet, and King. What a wonderful mystery we have before us! Christ has come to claim our beloved children and make them his own, like himself. The new Christian harbors Christ as a dwelling place, a precious abode to be nurtured and brought to full stature in the inner self, as Paul suggests in Ephesians 3:16.

Here is a good time to emphasize the white garment, which is a sign of the new creation and an invitation for the Christian to present this white robe to the Lamb on the Day of the Lord. Normally, those to be baptized are already wearing their baptismal garment (although they typically receive a miniature white cloth tunic), but there are a few circumstances in which the children will be clothed entirely anew after baptism. Frankly, in my estimation, if the liturgical symbol is to function fully and well, this completely new clothing in white should be preferred. The preacher could ask the hearers to notice the garments of white as a sign of transformation. These newly baptized will never wear such a garment again; it will be packed away and stored. But that should not be the case with the life of the new Christian. Indeed, the new creation that the baptized have become will afford a lifetime of growth and relationship with God.

The unconditional love of God will be a touchstone to a further development, since they have now a "dignity unstained," which awaits the coming of the kingdom. As that kingdom approaches, all the baptized here will hear again: "You are my beloved . . . with you I am well pleased." Such is the call of the Bridegroom, Christ the Lord, when we are called home to feast at the wedding banquet and clothed again in white—this time with the white funeral pall.

4. Mark 10:13-16 (Especially for Use with Several Children)

Readings from the Ambo

The passage depicting Jesus blessing little children, often sentimentalized in pious religious art, represents a strong and challenging invitation to understanding the dynamics of the kingdom of God. When this passage in Mark occurs in context, immediately following 10:1-12, we can see that the "hardness of heart," or *sklerokardia*, represents a fatal counterpoint to the characteristics Jesus praises in little children. It was stubbornness, obstinacy, and lack of openness that, Jesus says, caused Moses to permit divorce under the Law. On the other hand, Jesus' invitation to little children suggests a prioritizing of the little ones of humble heart and even privileging them as disciples who inherit the kingdom. Why? Because they have not yet been hardened by the kinds of experiences that walled up the hearts of their ancestors. Jesus showcases children as precognitive witnesses to the kingdom, as innocents unjaded by hardness of heart.

The passage's applicability to baptism, particularly when the rite is deployed for several children, becomes fairly obvious. The biblical scene replicates the baptismal moment in which the children encounter Christ in the sacrament of baptism in an a priori sacramental experience. We might argue that "Let the children come to me" represents the call of infant baptism, a belief in the Catholic tradition that the sacrament's efficaciousness engages the participant through grace and not conscious assent. The children are passive recipients; they are symbols for those gathered who now represent the voiceless blessings on the threshold of the Messiah. And so the passage reminds us that "[p]eople were bringing children to Jesus that he might touch them." The bringing of children to Jesus represents an act of faith on the part of these folks from "Judea and beyond the Jordan." We might recall that it was precisely this southern part of Palestine where people gathered also to be baptized by John. And so now a new encounter has emerged, not only in repentance in anticipation of the kingdom but to see it in its present manifestation through the one who will baptize by fire. In one of Mark's ironic turns, it is the disciples who become a hindrance to those wishing to bring their children to the Lord, when they "rebuked them." Perhaps these disciples, like those Jesus references in the previous pericope, have *sklerokardia*. They are oblivious to the unblemished hearts of children that Jesus clearly prioritizes.

From the point of view of those gathered to celebrate the sacrament and hearing this gospel, it is the adults (parents and godparents) who are responsible for introducing the children to Jesus, quite literally, at this sacramental moment. In regard to those who today bring their children to this same Christ, it will be their task to present an ongoing catechesis for the newly baptized child that will allow the blossoming Christian not to be hindered in the encounter with the Lord. Additionally, Mark deliberately calls our attention to the importance of Jesus' physical touch (*haptomai*), emphasizing the laying on of hands. Moreover, these gestures should not be lost to those gathered for the sacrament as witnesses; they are remarkable moments of physical touch involved in the rite, beginning with the signing of the children with the cross all the way through the *Ephphetha* or Prayer over Ears and Mouth. Human touch becomes the mediating symbol of Jesus' own blessing of the children, an aspect of the baptismal liturgy that I will emphasize very shortly.

Receiving the kingdom then becomes literally within our reach as we celebrate this sacrament. Christ's embracing and blessing of the children in Mark's gospel places those gathered—most especially the treasured witnesses of the baptism itself, the children—at the forefront of grace. Far from inaccessible, Christ is not just a messenger of the kingdom, but the very kingdom itself. The assembly recalls its own baptism, even as the sacrament itself unfolds.

Connecting the Bible and the Liturgy

According to directions for celebrating the ritual in the United States, the *Ephphetha* or Prayer over Ears and Mouth of the newly baptized may be performed at the discretion of the minister. Its positioning after the parents (or godparents) receive the light of Christ suggests that the child has a direct and unique call to mission. The opening of the ears and mouth of the child signals the call to evangelization, already made symbolically explicit in the handing on of the light to the child's guardians. The *Ephphetha* becomes further amplified, for obvious reasons, when it is done not only for one but for several children during the rite of baptism. Many are called even in our very midst to speak the Word even to the hard-hearted and weary.

The *Ephphetha* prayer alludes to the strong biblical roots that, like the gospel's showcasing Jesus' encounter with children, become an intimate encounter between humanity and the Divine, even a vocational call. Perhaps the most illustrative example to note here comes when God calls Isaiah to prophecy in 6:6ff. The prophet seizes the opportunity of enlightenment brought about by the touch of an angel holding blazing amber. "Then one of the seraphim flew to me, holding an ember which he had taken with tongs from the altar. / He touched my mouth with it. 'See,' he said, 'now that this has touched your lips, your wickedness is removed, your sin purged.' " The opening of a new identity carries with it an unmistakable purification for the work of God, a liberation from sin for the sake of divine mission. In the context of the gospels, we might recall Jesus' restoring the hearing of the deaf man in Mark 7:34. "[T]hen he looked up to heaven and groaned, and said to him, '*Ephphatha*' (that is, 'Be opened!')." The New Revised Standard Version translates the Greek verb as "sigh," but it is really a "groaning" (*stenazō*) toward heaven, as the New American Bible has it; with that, we can sense the larger landscape of creation at stake here: this encounter depicts not a simple or a single cure in the region of the Decapolis, but names the restoration of *all* creation with a deep compassion. This same verb is at the root of Paul's famous declaration in Romans 8:22 that "all creation is groaning" (*sustenazei*) as it awaits redemption. As Christ's healing ministry discloses the power of God to defeat and vanquish the scars of a world broken by sin and death, we might see him in Mark 7:34 as groaning on behalf of all creation, something that he will accomplish in its fullness on the cross. In the context of baptism, then, "Be opened" reminds us of the new order of creation called to hear God's voice directly (unlike Adam who hides himself in shame in the Garden of Eden) and to preach the good news that the Lord has liberated his people. Still further, this new order of creation finds an echo with the neophyte's clothing with the white garment.

Now clothed in Christ, the biblical and liturgical tapestry of the church weaves and displays God's eternal plan for all creation in sacramental mystery: that nothing will be lost and that all things will be restored in Christ Jesus. Indeed, those present at the baptism might find themselves, like their biblical predecessors at the curing of the deaf man, astounded and zealously proclaiming God's wonders, swelling all the more amid the several children who have been baptized.

That restored humanity is called not only to celebrate but also to be the prophetic witnesses who announce the Good News is the challenge that the *Ephphetha* prayer places before us. Here, the gathered assembly takes its cue from the newly baptized, now called into mission. At the same time, these baptisms witness to a collective call to the prophetic role of the assembly, a profound and abiding witness of the Body of Christ in the world. The neophytes will take their place in this Body of Christ, making the words of the Lord in Mark 10:13-16 all the more poignant: "Let the children come to me; do not prevent them, / for the Kingdom of God belongs to such as these." The newly baptized are *tomorrow's* witness of the kingdom in the assembly of the faithful.

Strategy for Preaching

Preachers would do well to remember to access the natural symbols unfolding before them. The most obvious and important of these gifts is the liturgical assembly itself, which, as *Sacrosanctum Concilium* reminds us, is one of the ways Christ is present at the liturgy. Consequently, the homily for the baptism of several children becomes a vital presence, a grace to be named, when preaching to a congregation celebrating this sacrament. Indeed, the gathering of children awaiting the sacrament of baptism witnesses to the human cry for restoration *today*, healing and union with the Body of Christ. (This is probably the first time anyone suggested that children's cries during a liturgy was not only a good thing but a welcome symbol!) As such, they are a blessing for those who have gathered to celebrate their initiation into the church. Therefore the focus sentence for preaching could be something along these lines: The children come once again to encounter the Lord, and he will bless them with his very living presence and call them to mission by opening their ears and mouths for the Good News. Let me say, parenthetically, that I am deliberately creating a small organizational feature in this focus sentence that will play to the preacher's advantage. This focus sentence structures itself into three sections around which the homily might be organized.

1. *The children come once again to encounter the Lord.*

   a. The homily would immediately begin to name the grace before those who have gathered by using the names of the children that have already been announced by the parents at the beginning of the rite in response to the question, "What name do you give your child?" Naming of the children by the preacher not only acknowledges their presence but draws the parents and godparents into the homily in a very personal way, since they have named the child. In a certain sense, the parents and godparents are allowed to take ownership of the responsibility for the baptism of their child, uniquely named by them. Therefore they have come before the Lord to be blessed.

2. *So will the Lord bless them by his very presence here in this baptism.*

   a. A brief review of the fundamental principles of the sacrament of baptism might follow; this theology mirrors the blessing Jesus bestows on the children in the gospel: it gives them his very presence.

   b. Certainly, there will be obstacles for these neophytes along the way, growing up in a world we cannot even begin to imagine. A consoling reference along these lines is the anointing with the oil of catechumens and the related texts. Those difficulties will be so much smoother if we allow our good example to unfold before them. (Perhaps some specific mention of the corporal works of mercy might be useful, or naming some parish outreach.) Christian life that is faithful and witnesses to peace and justice in the society makes a pathway to Christ. We are creating a road of discipleship in partnership with the church for the kingdom of God.

3. *Therefore the Lord will call each of them into mission by opening their ears and mouths for the Good News.*

   a. That proclamation has already begun in the loosening of these young mouths and the unsealing of these sensitive ears for the word of God. They will form a chorus of the eucharistic assembly, drawing us all closer to the Body of Christ.

b. We have asked in the *Ephphetha* prayer to open a path for the Word so that baptism will continue to live in the world as a witness to God's powerful works. These young children will become at this very moment God's agents of transformation, a grace in the world by their love. And so we, the Body of Christ, bless them and love them even as we send them forth into mission for God and the church.

5. Exodus 17:3-7; John 4:5-14

Readings from the Ambo

It is not difficult to imagine why water became a kind of mega-theme for the biblical writers. A desert people will thirst in ways that those of us in the comfortable West will have little substantial comprehension. So as the chosen people make their way through the barren desert out of Egypt and camp at Rephidim (derived from the Hebrew word meaning "to be refreshed" or to "find water"), they are understandably angry with God and Moses (clearly dramatized in the first few verses of chapter 17, but omitted in this selection). It would appear that almighty God has not provided an essential life source for the journey of liberation from Egypt.

Assuming his very difficult role of leadership, Moses is stuck in the middle between God and the people. The people bring a legitimate argument to Moses, which biblical scholars understand technically as a lawsuit. The Hebrew word *rib* designates the legal genre of this argument, introducing the people as plaintiffs against the defendants (God and Moses) for leading them into a promised piece of property that turns out to be literally not what they bargained for. The peoples' claim is that they were sold an empty piece of real estate and were deceived by its value. There is something almost comic about the way this passage unfolds, as if a naïve group of people got together and were sold a bridge in the middle of the desert or bought real estate on a nonexistent island. At the same time, the tragic and legal implications go deeper when they come to see that there is no water in this wilderness to sustain life.

But then comes the surprise that addresses both physical and spiritual thirst. Moses strikes the rock before witnesses (the elders) and they have their water. But the deeper issue is posed by the biblical author when the place is named Massah and Meribah because "the children of

Israel quarreled there / and tested the LORD, saying, / 'Is the LORD in our midst or not?'" So this test in the desert concerns God's real presence, which discloses itself first through water. An unmistakable deeper sign of the presence of the Holy is the reference to Mount Horeb where God tells Moses that he "will stand before him." (Here we might recall that on Mount Horeb was the initial sign of God's revelation to Moses in chapter 3 before him in the burning bush, unveiling his mercy to the Israelites.) Additionally, as if to underline the place of divine presence, later in chapter 17 Israel defeats Amalek as Aaron and Hur support Moses' arms and staff in order to secure divine power.

John 4 also begins with a request for water and ends with a sign of divine presence. The encounter with the woman at the well in Samaria forms a fascinating connection with Exodus 17 for several interesting reasons. Ignoring Jewish conventions (and probably, geographical common sense), Jesus crosses into the Samaritan city of Sychar and speaks openly to a woman at the heat of midday. Her thirst (and *his*, which often goes unmentioned by scholars) mirrors the Israelites in their own journey in the desert. But Jesus intends to reignite that desire for more than a quench for thirst: he pushes the Samaritan woman to discover the need for *living* water that will lead to eternal life. Like Nicodemus, the woman is searching for something substantial and unable to find it. I read the "five husbands" she has had in the course of her life not as a moral correction about loose living, but signaling failed relationships. No wonder she is thirsting at midday! The woman has not had a life-giving human encounter for reasons that go unsaid. This encounter at Jacob's well, however, will be different; it metaphorically invites us to conceive of the promise of a mystical marriage between flawed humanity and the Lord of eternal life who enkindles within us a desire to thirst deeper than we can imagine. We are at Jacob's well, after all, the place of the passing on of great inheritance; it is where Jacob purchased a plot of land and gave it to his son, Joseph (Gen 33:19; 47:22). Jesus intends to probe deeper into a substantial encounter with the woman. He does so by first revealing his own thirst, clearly a foreshadowing of Christ's longing to be quenched on the cross later in John's gospel (19:28). That the gospel unfolds this story with a Samaritan woman demonstrates the universality of the call to holiness in which God shows a desire to love all people. Finally, the woman's encounter with Jesus nicely prepares her for mission and evangelization because this woman, like the apostle Andrew in a previous passage (1:41), believes that she may have had a messianic encounter with someone who told her prophetically everything she had done.

Connecting the Bible and the Liturgy

In the Renunciation of Sin and Profession of Faith, the RBC makes an explicit connection between water and the presence of God. "By water and the Holy Spirit he (she) is to receive the gift of new life from God who is love." Emphasizing the connection between water and the Holy recalls Exodus 17:3-7 as well as John 4:5-14: water is a sign of God's new life in his people, even as the earliest lines of the book of Genesis speak of God's Spirit hovering over the face of the waters. The one to be baptized is thirsting for God and through the parents and godparents yearns for the living water of eternal life. At the same time, God is thirsting in love for those who long to be satisfied with the divine presence.

The invitation to the waters of baptism, then, is crucially linked to a deepening faith that begins and ends in God's presence; that presence is indelible, marked eternally, and will be further deepened over the course of years first by parents and godparents and then by the neophyte who will be drawn into the "full stature of Christ" (Eph 4:13) and no longer be an infant. To this end, the parents and godparents make it "their constant care to bring him (her) up in the practice of the faith. See that the divine life which God gives him (her) is kept safe from the poison of sin, to grow always stronger in his (her) heart" (93). So the parents and godparents are implicated in the act of baptism and drawn into mission by faith and love. Their primal thirst already having been quenched, they come to the waters. Not coincidentally, the minister interrogates the parents and godparents, probing the condition of their own thirst, even as they renew their own baptism in the Renunciation of Sin and Profession of Faith (93).

The Renunciation of Sin and Profession of Faith positions the parents and godparents as believers, witnesses exploring their own deep wells of living water leading to eternal life. The church clearly desires to raise the consciousness of the responsibility of Christian guardianship, while at the same time deepening the faith of the baptized: it is as if Moses once again is striking the rock in the desert and out of God's rich presence an abundance flows; it is a gift made greater by the Giver of all good gifts.

In this regard, the woman at the well thirsts because God has already bestowed on her a desire for eternal life. The living water that forever satisfies springs forth to provide for those even outside the circle of the chosen people. Christ has chosen her, even as he has chosen those to be baptized and the parents and godparents to drink deeply from the fountain of his wisdom and presence. The Preface for the Third Sunday of Lent (Year A) highlights the gospel's encounter between Jesus and the Samaritan woman when it says that "he had already created the gift of faith within her and so ardently did he thirst for her faith that he kindled in her the fire of divine love." In a lovely reversal mirrored in the Scripture passage itself, the Preface showcases the Lord's thirst for the faith of those who seek God; and he does so by fire: he kindled in her the first sign of divine love with parents and godparents similarly sparked by the pascal candle's flame; that gift is passed like an Olympic torch and passed on by faith to the newly baptized for the sake of the kingdom.

Strategy for Preaching

The overall strategy of preaching on this occasion might involve moving those gathered from a vicarious or remote experience of physical thirst to an awareness of the soul's longing for God. It is, after all, the prayer of God's people to echo the psalmist when he says, "My soul thirsts for God, the living God" (42:3). A common reality shared by all, this longing and thirsting could be explored briefly in the introduction and then move toward the deeper reality of that thirst and its connection with baptism in the body of the homily. The preacher could also invite the congregation to tap into the "rock" of their own baptism that is struck anew at this celebratory moment of the sacrament for those to be baptized. The focus sentence, then, could be something along these lines: We all thirst for living water and the Christian pilgrimage is nothing less than a discovery of our baptism so that our faith grows deeper for the sake of God's children entrusted to us and the coming kingdom.

Here is a general outline for a homily:

Introduction:

I had a seminarian in class once who capitalized on an ingenious slogan from the advertising world and made it a Christian mantra: "Obey your thirst." Some of us will remember that slogan popularized by a sports drink a decade or so ago. What could be more common than thirst in the human experience? If we do not have enough water to sustain us, we perish.

I. That is why we are here: to celebrate our common thirst for God and to see that longing satisfied for N. _____ at the church's rock in the desert.

    a. Biblical references as examples of the thirst that can be teased out in Exodus 17:3-17 and John 4:5-14.

    b. Scripture speaks for all of us to be satisfied by God.

II. So Christ causes us to go into the well of our own baptismal waters to remind us of our commitment to him and his commitment to us as an everlasting presence. Remember Jesus also thirsts for our love individually and as a church.

    a. Preface for the Third Sunday of Lent.

    b. Renunciation of Sin and Profession of Faith.

    Each day we refresh our faith with the life-giving waters of renewal.

III. We know that we have struck water in the desert when we share that gift of faith with others in joy.

    a. Story or illustration would be useful here of someone who encounters something so exciting they cannot keep from speaking about it (obvious parallel is the Samaritan woman).

    b. Our ongoing refreshment will be watching and loving the newly baptized N._____ grow into faith.

    c. The child of our own commitment to continually thirst for God is embodied right before us. What more of a profession of faith could the church ask of its members than bringing to this fountain one newly clothed in Christ?

6. Ezekiel 36:24-28; John 3:1-6

Readings from the Ambo

Ezekiel may strike some as the strangest and most eccentric of the Hebrew prophets, yet his voice is emphatic, astonishingly colorful (fueled as it is by ecstatic visions), and charged with God's powerful presence during the time of Israel's exile in Babylon in 593 BCE. Throughout the book of Ezekiel, the prophet names the hopelessness of Jerusalem, the darkness of exile, and the rampant idolatry of the nations. Chapter 36, which is late in the book, actually shows signs of renewal, although not without the prophet pointing out the loss of leadership in Israel that caused God to bring down a curse on the shepherds who neglected their sheepfold. In this regard, God forges a new alliance with his people literally on the edge, leading them anew across a river of salvation into sanctification. God will take over the role of the Shepherd.

The present passage provides a dominant metaphor with which to understand God's leadership of transformation, and the symbol finds an intense richness especially in a cultic context. Ezekiel was a priest and so the prophet concerns himself with the particular images of cultic pollution, regrettably engaged by Israel's faithless behavior mingled with idolatry. So one of the many things at stake in Ezekiel 36:24-28 concerns God's restoration of a divine right, meaning a return to orthodoxy, or right worship. That return is not a matter of rubrics but of transformation that only the Holy may accomplish by restoration in absolute divine freedom. Indeed, one senses throughout the book of Ezekiel that God's strength is global (note the catalog of nations who find a prophesy against them, beginning in chapter 25) and the pursuit of the chosen people both fierce and righteous.

When it comes to sketching out the plan dealing with the pursuit of the people of Israel and the delivery of divine promises to their nation, there are five traits that emerge in the context of the restoration:

1. Promise of restoration of the homeland. God will search out Israel, dispersed among the many peoples and call them one people.

2. That this gathering from wandering involves purification from sin, symbolized by a ritual cleaning in water.

3. Israel will have a new heart and a new spirit. Dry bones (cf. chapter 37) will come together in the midst of the desert and will arise anew, filled with a life-giving spirit.

4. This new spirit will renew the covenant so that those who have been gathered, sanctified, and renewed will follow the law of the Lord with one heart and mind.

5. Anticipation of the future homeland mirrors a familial environ-
ment, one that traces its own ancestry to the historical lineage of
the patriarchs.

The renewal of the relationship between God and Israel reorders the
chaos, shame, and dispersal of the exile. It is as if God is turning back
the clock and allowing the chosen people to begin again through divine
mercy. It should be clear that Ezekiel is not nostalgic for the old order and
promising something like the good old days for those who are hanging
up their harps by the waters of Babylon. No, Ezekiel's promised terrain
is a *new* vision from God, a *new* purpose and a *new* birth for a people
who have been led astray. So when Jesus tells Nicodemus in the famous
lines of John's gospel that "unless one is born of water and Spirit / he
cannot enter the Kingdom of God" (3:5b), he is recapitulating God's call
to Israel in Ezekiel: the renewal comes during the night of our wandering to reorder us into divine light by water and the Spirit. The Promised
Land, with God as Eternal and Good Shepherd (cf. John 10:1-21) of one
people, becomes the kingdom of God. In some sense, Nicodemus himself is in a kind of exile, having come to Jesus by night and in secrecy.
Although mostly a member of the Sanhedrin, Nicodemus will remain
somewhat marginalized outside institutionalized Judaism until the end
of John's gospel (19:39), bringing a mixture of aloes and myrrh weighing
in at the impossible amount of 100 pounds. Jesus invites him to consider
being born *anōthen*, which can mean either "from above" or "again." The
purpose of such rebirth, according to Jesus is to see the kingdom of God.
That new land, of course, is the place where God has gathered the exiles,
having been purified from sin and a new vision made possible by those
born of the Spirit. Jesus addresses himself to an open-minded member of
the religious establishment in order to reframe a tradition grown heavy
with legalism and religious intolerance; it awaits new birth.

Connecting the Bible and the Liturgy

At the conclusion of the rite of baptism there is a procession to the
altar, unless the baptisms occurred in the sanctuary. As the lighted candles
are carried for the child (or the children) the celebrant stands in front of
the altar and addresses the parents, godparents, and the whole assembly.

The point of this procession and its gathering around the altar suggests a movement of multiple points of light, alighted afresh from the paschal candle; this holy fire guides the newly baptized, a symbol of those who hold Christ as the Light in the midst of darkness, that place of exile. The procession ratifies what has just taken place and moves the newly baptized into the community of the faithful. The song or acclamation for this moment could be taken from the *Songs from Ancient Liturgies*, specifically 243: "Holy Church of God, stretch out your hand and welcome your children newborn of water and the Spirit of God."[10]

This short song aptly demonstrates both the capacity and the responsibility of the local church to gather as one Body in Christ and welcome through water and the Spirit the newly baptized. Such a gathering is a foretaste and vision of the coming kingdom. Appropriately enough, immediately following the words that name the baptized as children of God and anticipates future celebrations of reconciliation, Holy Communion, and confirmation, the Lord's Prayer follows. Indeed, "thy kingdom come" is an acknowledgment of a promised vision that is ours to receive after our wanderings. Much like God's renewal of the covenant with Israel, the one who has been baptized now begins anew; it is all future. Free from original sin, he or she accompanies the Lord on a lifelong journey to the peaceable kingdom. Restored in promise, gathered in from wandering, renewed at the font of the church's Rock, and guided by the covenant of love and the Christian's ongoing participation in God's kingdom, the new Christian is now received into the hands of the church, which shepherds the faithful until the one Great Shepherd appears again in glory to claim his flock.

Strategy for Preaching

The prophet Ezekiel allows for a blueprint of sorts for preaching when he expresses God's intention to rescue his people from the wanderings of exile and bring them back to a promised land. With both readings in mind, though, the focus sentence could speak more generally about the plan and vision God has for his people: God has gathered his people, sanctified and renewed them for a new birth into the kingdom. These three divine actions form an outline for the structure of the homily.

10. *Rite of Christian Baptism for Children*, 161.

As always, the introduction ought to lead into the body of the homily by gathering and focusing the listeners. And while on this topic of the introduction, I will mention parenthetically that if the introduction does not labor to introduce the homiletic body *strategically*, then the preacher is not using the short amount of time allotted for the homily for breaking open the word at baptism effectively. When preaching short homilies, every word counts. In this particular instance, it makes sense to envision an introduction that invokes God as a vigilant and active agent in the lives of the people. Those proactive characteristics of divine agency are certainly suggestive of how both Ezekiel and Jesus understand God in the present selection in the readings. Consider this as an introduction.

There are a lot of ways of gathering folks together these days. Our boss may schedule a meeting for us on our calendar; the children could have a Christmas show at the school for the proud parents; friends may invite us to dinner. But I would guess that there are few instances where a child—or a group of tiny infants—has been able to gather a group of people as diverse as this one. Just take a look at us: we have come from everywhere! Baptism has a way of bringing people together as the Church of God, the *ekklesia*, because God continues to gather the Christian assembly together by water and the Spirit.

Now to the body of the homily:

I. The prophet Ezekiel speaks for a God full of zeal and eager to gather the chosen people out of exile.

    a. Very short synopsis or description of exile, including loss of identity.

    b. Contemporary illustration of alienation. (I would not dwell on this feature too long in the context of a baptism, but enough simply to illustrate the point that exile is not only an event endured by Israel but one that the community of love suffers while it awaits the kingdom of righteousness and peace. Note contemporary examples of refugees and immigrants, often referred to as "aliens").

II. Baptism shepherds and sanctifies us into God's kingdom of love and care.

    a. To be "born again" is a popular phrase, but we commit to being children of God at our baptism.

   b. Our light from Christ guides us out of darkness as we await the coming kingdom (allude to Conclusion of the Rite).

III. So we are set on our journey to the kingdom with a new vision.

   a. Hymn text (243): the church leads us in teaching and sacraments out of darkness into the light of truth.

   b. Visualization: the newly baptized (named) involved in future Christian actions of social ministry, teaching catechetics, ministry to the sick.

   c. One candle for parents/godparents, but we all share the pascal candle and its mystery of light.

7. Ezekiel 47:1-9, 12; John 7:37b-39a

Readings from the Ambo

This selection from the book of Ezekiel fits snugly into the larger section of the divine restoration plan for Israel beginning in chapter 40 with the vision of the new temple. The priestly character of the prophet as well as the cultic character of the renewal of worship in Israel is underlined throughout these chapters. But the architecture of the new temple, including its gates, its measurements, together with its sacred furnishings and practices helps us to visualize what is at stake in the restoration. Further, Ezekiel images the Lord's return (chapter 43) and receives detailed instructions concerning a completely reiterated cultic law, after which emerges a depiction of a seemingly endless stream of water.

Perhaps more than any other qualities, abundance and excess characterize the sacred stream portrayed in this chapter; it signals that God's restoration of Israel has banished the curse of exile and replaced this dislocation with an ever-flowing stream of water in the desert. We should take this as divine largesse, even as it is a sign of purification. Taken as a whole, the passage invites us to see just how overwhelming the water becomes to the prophet as he expresses his ecstatic vision of the sacred waters. What began as a stream then becomes ankle deep, then knee deep, then waist deep, then unnavigable, except by swimming. The water seems to possess a life of its own, extending its powers to rejuvenate and to sanctify. As the new water makes salt water fresh, "[w]herever the river flows, / every sort of living creature that can multiply shall live, / and there shall be abundant fish . . ." We cannot fail to sense God's re-creation of the earth in a kind of prelapsarian landscape that has somehow eluded death and decay. "Along both banks of the river, fruit trees of every kind shall grow; / their leaves shall not fail, nor their fruit fail." It is the water of life, flowing from the sanctuary, that brings about abundant fruit that "shall serve for food, and their leaves for medicine." The water flowing from the sanctuary is incalculably deep in its ability to rejuvenate, sustain, and give new life.

This new territory has become sacred to the Lord and is now a symbol for worship. The perimeter of this new geography has been set by God himself, the exiles having been reestablished in a land not of their making or a territory seized by war, but reordered by God. In a sense, the Lord is redrawing the boundaries of exile, as if to erase the margins of Eden that formerly blocked the exiles' return. This topography of a new postexilic paradise becomes clearer in chapter 47, when God assigns territories to the twelve tribes of Israel. In a gesture to cast a definitive mark on this new Israel, the gates of the city are named after the twelve tribes and the city itself will be called "The Lord Is There" (cf. chapter 48). Divine presence is the guarantee that the exile is over.

John's gospel makes a vital and crucial connection with chapter 47 in Ezekiel. In John 7:37b-39a, Jesus himself becomes the sacred river of living water, giving life to those who believe through the Spirit. We have already seen the Samaritan woman in chapter 4 demonstrate her thirst for living water. Now Jesus' exclamation to come to the life-giving waters of his own person suggests that the Lord has become a sacred river to his people. We know that the great world religions often identify rivers as sacred and healing. Pious Hindus, for instance, know that all water is sacred, especially the rivers of the Ganges, Yamuna, Godavari, Sarasvati, Narmada, Sindhu, and Kaveri. But in John's gospel, Christ has named himself as a river from whom all who thirst may drink in the light of faith. The personification of the sacred waters will take on new meaning later when water and blood flow after Jesus has died on the cross (19:34), signifying the sacramental character now bestowed on the Lord's sacrificial offering of himself to the Father for humankind. Finally, the Johannine community reimagines the (destroyed) temple as Jesus himself, which has been raised up after three days in the tomb. The new temple of Jesus' body becomes the ultimate new geography with transcendent boundaries for the Christian believer.

Connecting the Bible and the Liturgy

After the Prayer of Exorcism and Anointing, the celebrant invites the congregation to move to the baptismal font using these (or similar words): "My dear brothers and sisters, we now ask God to give this child new life in abundance through water and the Holy Spirit." The request is straightforward and powerful. I would like to underline a phrase that has particular relevance to the readings. "New life in abundance" is a key touchstone with the Scriptures. Ezekiel's prophetic utterance in chapter 47 is nothing if not a vision of excess, a descant on a melody of life that overflows to nourish, restore, and heal. In the sacrament of baptism that will be celebrated, we are meant to see the waters not only as a ritual bath but as a sign of God's power and love in lavishness to restore humanity to innocence lost. At the same time, the sign of God's saving grace in baptism discloses a divine love beyond all telling precisely because of the measureless quality of its infinite care. As Ezekiel gradually wades through the sacred waters, the prophet is over his head in the river's capacity to overwhelm him completely. In this regard, Christ becomes irresistibly present to his people in the sacrament of baptism as the font of living water for which all creation longs. He alone confers this power on humanity by the will of the Father and the labor of the Holy Spirit. To encounter the Lord in baptism, then, grants us the Spirit so that "[r]ivers of living water will flow from within him" (John 7:38).

Ezekiel's vision of the new temple becomes present, even as the one to be baptized prepares to become a temple of the Holy Spirit. According to the RBC, the celebrant touches the water and says, "We ask you, Father, with your Son to send the Holy Spirit upon the water of this font. May all who are buried with Christ in the death of baptism rise also with him to newness of life." The invocation of the Blessed Trinity, then, foreshadows their presence in the baptismal formula itself, reminding the congregation that the living God has "breathed on the waters, making them the wellspring of all holiness" (Blessing and Invocation of God over the Baptismal Water, 54). The congregation cannot fail to see the connection of these now living waters with the life and person of God in Christ Jesus. "Let anyone who thirsts come to me and drink" (John 7:37). The promise of Christ to be an abundant source of life to his people begins here with the temple of his body, "a cornerstone rejected by builders" but a sacred river willed by God for healing and new life.

This same Christ will clothe the one to be baptized with his own person, be buried with him and also rise. In a very real sense, the one approaching the baptismal font comes to this new temple, having been ushered out of exile as sin's captive. Baptism is the restoration of another temple, an interior one that becomes the house of the Holy Spirit. To come to these waters, then, suggests more than purification. Christ has made new again, by water and blood, a holy and sanctified people capable of true worship in the Spirit. In so doing, he has also raised up his church, which awaits him as a bride until he comes again. So the Spirit and the bride say, "Come, Lord Jesus."

Strategy for Preaching

In her pioneering and influential work, *Purity and Danger: An Analysis of Concepts of Pollution and Taboo* (1966), cultural anthropologist and theorist Mary Douglas sheds light on why some cultures practice highly rigorous purity laws and practices. "Dirt is matter out of place" is perhaps the most famous phrase from Douglas's study.[11] There is undoubtedly a purification aspect to baptism, but to dwell on the cleansing feature of the ritual alone misses the point as well as its scriptural inheritance. Yes, washed clean from sin. But there is more. Baptism moves us into the community of the church by virtue of God's largesse, a graced love that is baroque in its abundance. So the focus sentence for these readings that points us in the direction of God's generous love might be something like: Baptism submerges us over our heads in God's love, where Christ dwells with us forever.

A good introduction would move immediately into examples of water that overwhelms us. After all, the medieval church's baptisteries, such as the one at Pisa, were famous for their enormously gracious spaces. It is true to say that the waters of baptism were meant to kill. A brilliant contemporary illustration of this reality is Flannery O'Connor's short story "The River" (*A Good Man Is Hard to Find*, 1955). But any introduction that reminds the congregation of the experience of Ezekiel being overwhelmed by water

11. Mary Douglas, *Purity and Danger: An Analysis of Concepts of Pollution and Taboo* (New York: Praeger, 1966), 35.

would be useful. Ultimately, that image will be tied to a later allusion to Jesus' invitation to come to him as the living water.

The body of the homily would then begin to unpack for the congregation a consideration of the way that the church has now committed itself to embrace the one to be baptized. What might this look like? The first issue to be confronted is *un*learning that God and the church exist as a series of rules and punishments. The Scriptures suggest otherwise (draw this out). And then this reality could be undergirded with some illustrations or extended images. This association of visuals could be connecting the life-giving relationship with the church (the word "relationship" is a key aspect here) that begins at baptism. So God's embrace looks like a mother bathing her newborn infant in warm sudsy water; a family reunion where the members form a circle with arms linking each other; an older sibling feeding a parent in bed during a protracted illness. The old self has died and the new self reborn.

Then: that means recommitting ourselves to Christ even as he has embraced the newly baptized. We are literally taken up into the care of God no matter where we have been or where we think we are going (allude to Israel's exile, perhaps, or Christ's invitation to come to the living waters he provides, or the role of guardian when it comes to parents). Our own Act of Faith, Hope, and Love relives the story of creation by seeing the waters of baptism as a continual blessing that bestows Christ's very presence on us. We have seen a whole people move out of exile into the waters of salvation. Although there may be only one or a few neophytes in the rite of baptism, the whole congregation may recall how the homily has moved them into the sacred waters of God's word. That word continues to purify and sanctify the church as we deepen the promises at our baptism day by day.

8. Romans 6:3-5; John 19:31-35

Readings from the Ambo

As is well known, Paul's letter to the Romans represents the theological pinnacle of the apostle's writing. The letter is a masterpiece of theological sophistication and rhetorical skill marshaled for a Christian community already present in Rome and who Paul would eventually join, albeit in chains. A major thread that runs throughout the intricate tapestry of Romans is Paul's famous theological argument for justification, which he takes up initially in chapter 3:21-31 by asserting that we have been justified by faith because of God's righteousness. "But now the righteousness of God has been manifested apart from the law, though testified to by the law and the prophets, the righteousness of God through faith in Jesus Christ for all who believe."

For Paul, faith in Christ justifies humanity apart from the law, a comforting reality to a group of Jewish-Christians struggling to understand how the law of Moses would be reconfigured in the context of the post-Jesus event. So Abraham becomes the iconic witness of being justified by faith for reasons that should be obvious ("our ancestor according to the flesh") when understanding Paul's rhetorical strategy and theological understanding. Abraham's faith made him righteous before God apart from the law, "Therefore, since we have been justified by faith, we have peace with God through our Lord Jesus Christ, through whom we have gained access [by faith] to this grace in which we stand" (5:1-2). Although we may have inherited Adam's sin and condition (5:12ff), "how much more will those who receive the abundance of grace . . . come to reign in life through the one person Jesus Christ" (5:17).

The theology of justification plays out in a particular way through baptism. The verse that introduces the present passage from Romans (6:3-5) puts the question directly: "How can we who died to sin yet live in it?" (6:2). Then he uses baptism as the focal point for this death to sin and dying with Christ: "We were indeed buried with him through baptism into death, / so that, just as Christ was raised from the dead / by the glory of the Father, / we too might live in newness of life" (6:4). This "newness of life" is a key to understanding the theological implications of this important passage. Living in this new reality after we have been buried with the Lord in baptism speaks not only of being re-created in Christ but also conforming to his resurrection, "[f]or if we have grown into union with him through a death like his, / we shall also be united with him in the resurrection" (6:5).

What does that look like? That "death like his" is portrayed vividly in John's gospel (19:31-35), which uncovers the mystical aspect of the Lord's death in an outpouring of blood and water from the Savior's dead and wounded body. As a Johannine sign of sacramental gift for the church, the blood and the water flowing from Jesus' side have come to represent the Eucharist and baptism, a literal unfolding of Paul's theological understanding of Christ's death: it is in union with Christ that the Christian community participates through water and blood, the consummate act of God's righteousness, the handing over of Christ, for our justification. Parenthetically, it might be said that the Johannine author's emphasis on the graphic reality of Jesus' death might be an attempt to thwart any attempts at gnostic or docetic representations of God never really dying in the flesh. But the very visual nature of the depiction of Christ's death in John 19:31-35 allows us to lean into the participation in the "death like his" and underlines Paul's emphatic claim of Christ's death and burial; this is a circumstance that leads to our participation by justification through faith, together with the Christian's own death in the waters of baptism, which also brings new life.

Connecting the Bible and the Liturgy

The revised RBC offers the possibility under certain circumstances for the sacrament to be a qualified, church-sanctioned catechist/administrator. If blessed water is available, the rubric allows an invocation (143). The latter portion of the blessing partners rather well with the aforementioned Scriptures and makes a nice connection, regardless of whether or not the celebrant is a catechist or an ordained minister, since the texts are meant to be conversation partners for reflection and preaching.

"You have created this water, and made it clean, refreshing, and life-giving." After hearing the gospel (John 19:31-35), the congregation would be poignantly aware that the water that has been made life-giving is not only before them in a baptismal font but flows dramatically from the wounded and dead Savior's side. Indeed, Christ himself has made the waters holy through his own baptism (cf. Matt 3:3-17; Mark 1:7-11; Luke 3:15-16, 21-22) and now water and blood come forth from his side so "that by the power of the Holy Spirit / it may give your people a new birth" (143).

At the same time, this new birth also meant death to sin, according to Paul, so that we might be justified in Christ Jesus. In so doing, the community of faith becomes members of the mystical Body of Christ, heirs to the kingdom and so may be called children of God. The invocation underlines the connection between death in baptism and the members of his Body when it continues, "When these children are baptized into the mystery / of Christ's suffering, death, and resurrection, / may they be

worthy to become members of your Church, / your very own children"
(143). For Paul, there is no question of becoming worthy; they are not.
Rather, they are justified by being buried with Christ so as to share in
his resurrection. Their faith is the faith of the church itself and has been
symbolically ratified by the parents and godparents: its testimony comes
in the evangelical witness and proclamation for the one to be baptized.
This action justifies the righteousness made sacramental in the life-giving
waters of Christ Jesus. The Eucharist will be the ongoing site of celebration, the mystical banquet, so that their justification might unfold for all
eternity. So the invocation begs the Father to grant those to be baptized
not a justification by the law, but a celebration based on God's righteousness in Christ. "Father, may they rejoice with Jesus your Son and the Holy
Spirit." It is as if all humanity has been embraced by the Father in Luke 15,
having returned shamefaced as prodigals to a celebration in our honor.
Embraced in the everlasting forgiveness of God and divine righteousness, the doors of the hall swing wide to welcome the newly baptized
into the celebration. The congregation's act of faith in acknowledging
God's gratuitous actions for our justification is "Amen." This "so be it"
is an affirmation of the Father of all blessings from the people of God, a
corporate act of faith soon to be made explicit in the Renunciation of Sin
and Profession of Faith by the parents and godparents.

As another conversation partner or as a sung text during the celebration of the rite, a brief but moving text might be used from the *Songs from
Ancient Liturgies* (161). I am thinking of 244, which nicely pulls together
some significant elements of the scriptural readings: "Rejoice, you newly
baptized, chosen members of the kingdom. Buried with Christ in death,
you are reborn in him by faith." We know that celebration is characteristic
of the Christian redeemed by the blood of Christ and justified by faith.
The RBC suggests that our appropriate response to God's righteousness
is celebration. That can only mean inviting the congregation to rejoice
with the newly baptized, together with the parents and godparents. The
water and the blood that flowed from the Savior's side have signaled not
only Christ's death but our own, even as we are reborn in faith.

Strategy for Preaching

The doctrine of justification by faith in Christ Jesus as Paul articu-
lates it in the letter to the Romans strikes me as a uniquely contemporary

challenge for the preacher, especially for American culture. We are a practical people whose life theme probably comes close to what Ralph Waldo Emerson envisioned in his famous essay "Self-Reliance" (1841). A spirit of the pioneer haunts America even in the twenty-first century; a pragmatic and individualistic rule of law tends to justify our daily existence. Theologically, we tend to be Pelagians or semi-Pelagians. We cannot imagine anything we did not earn. In this regard, baptism as a font of complete and utter justification by God's righteousness through grace is indeed something of a strain for our culture. Any preacher who comes to the ambo thinking otherwise might want to take a good look at the congregation. I once encountered a parishioner who was absolutely incandescent with anger after Mass over "those freeloaders" on the government (otherwise known as the poor and the unemployed). I am not sure what provoked the outrage. This homily on baptism will undoubtedly be a test of conversion for the faithful, even believers, who think that by their own efforts they have somehow purchased just a little bit of justification before God. And so the focus sentence for us could be: Baptism is a gratuitous, unconditional gift from God, which calls us to respond in faith. Indeed, the very fact that these are helpless infants more than suggests the reality of God's grace.

Sounds nice, doesn't it? But allowing the assembly to participate in unfolding its theological implications is another matter. Undoubtedly, the witness of the sacrament itself will carry those who participate in the celebration to some degree, but the preaching must address an American ideology that strives for a quid pro quo attitude. I dare say that there will be some that even view baptism itself as a kind of work that needs to be done, an item on a checklist that is expected to be performed. This contemporary stance that is suspect of a gift is the challenge of the introduction, especially when it comes to the economy of pragmatism as it runs headlong into grace. It is really hard to imagine a gift for free, to say nothing of sacrificial love. But these conflicts could be and should be raised in the introduction in order to prepare the congregation for the body of the homily.

I suggest that the main portion of the homily occur in two parts. The first concerns the strangeness of God's graciousness in baptism; the body of the homily might contemplate the central icon that confronts us on this happy occasion: the blood and water flowing out from the wounds of Christ. This divine action was anything but pragmatic and presents a complete contrast to a world that expects something for, well, something else. God's self-gift and self-emptying versus "the art of the deal." So this baptism is the height of God's expression of love, even in the midst of our pragmatic culture.

1. Christ's life of self-gift buries us with him in baptism so we do not have to worry about doing or accomplishing anything (cf. Invocation, 143).
2. That means an act of faith rather than an act of self-seeking.
3. A short story or illustration about self-gift.

Then: no wonder Paul accounts Christians justified in baptism (Rom 3:3-5). Love does that: it overwhelms, overcomes, and overtakes us with generosity.

1. Analogy: God's falling in love with humanity is like looking at a baby: we cannot take our eyes off him or her. (Example of the child or children about to be baptized.)
2. Our response to divine love is faith-filled celebration. In the Eucharist Jesus' blood is poured out for the church. We rejoice and say "Amen" in faith.
3. The witness of the sacrament of baptism orients us toward the future, where we are in God's hands, justified and redeemed.

9. Romans 8:28-32; John 6:44-47

Readings from the Ambo

The present Scripture passage taken from the letter to the Romans carries a particular and important meaning when seen in the context of the entirety of chapter 8, in which Paul explores God's plan for all humanity. Paul has already delivered his magisterial theological exposition of the doctrine of grace through faith in Christ Jesus who alone justifies. It remains now for chapter 8 to bestow an ordered confidence, as it were, in a life of the Spirit, which will override any question of sin's dominance in

God's reign. Indeed, scholars note chapter 8 as a profound comfort after the anguish of the previous chapter (7:22-25), where Paul seems close to despair: "For I take delight in the law of God, in my inner self, but I see in my members another principle at war with the law of my mind, taking me captive to the law of sin that dwells in my members. Miserable one that I am! Who will deliver me from this mortal body? Thanks be to God through Jesus Christ our Lord."

The last line professes gratitude that will expand throughout chapter 8 where its contours become a kind of ecstatic hymn to God's unfathomable wisdom: "For those who are led by the Spirit of God are children of God" (v. 14). Those Jewish-Christians living in Rome and mindful of their own salvation history were undoubtedly comforted by the present passage in the middle of chapter 8: "We know that all things work for good for those who love God, / who are called according to his purpose." In the context of Christian baptism, then, those who are called are about to move to the font of living water precisely because "those he foreknew he also predestined / to be conformed to the image of his Son." Indeed, baptism sacramentally conforms the neophyte to Christ's image, while leading him or her to the life of faith and so be justified and, in turn, glorified. Further, in his letter to the Colossians, Paul will be even more explicit about the restoration of humanity back into *imago Dei*, the original imprint from the Creator. He admonishes the church at Colossus, telling them not to lie to one another, "since you have taken off the old self with its practices and have put on the new self, which is being renewed, for knowledge, in the image of its creator" (3:9-10). He goes on to claim that this renewal dissolves the boundaries of nationality, religion, and class because "Christ is all and in all" (v. 11)!

Conforming to Christ has come upon the one to be baptized because God has drawn the neophyte into the mystery of the divine self, the unfathomable gift of the Spirit, which is even now at work. Paul takes justification in Christ, then, to its logical conclusion since we who have been justified in Christ have been taken up in him, meaning we have also been glorified or *edóxasen*. Now a word about Paul's use of *edóxasen* here. We might normally think of glorification as something we do for God in the context of praise and thanksgiving. But Paul understands the new creation to be glorified with and through Christ. Therefore, "If God is for us, who can be against us?" (v. 31). And those who are baptized are heirs together with Christ and therefore "will he not also give us everything else along with him?" (32).

The Johannine passage that I have paired with the Pauline reading from Romans underlines the theological and foundational cornerstone of our being taken up in Christ by the will of the Father. Those to be baptized are drawn by the Father, even as they come to the life-giving waters. John 6:44-47 comes to us in the larger context of the "Bread of Life" discourse in which Jesus confirms to his disciples (and the shock and scandal of his unwilling contemporaries) his nourishing eternal presence. Here again, sacrament becomes the fire on Mount Horeb, drawing Moses out from the wilderness into the presence of the Holy. The life of the baptized then transforms absolutely: an encounter with the living God, a conformity to the presence of Christ; it is the site where a life of faith, hope, and love unfold inside the mystery of the one who has destined the neophyte as an adopted child, now justified and glorified in Christ.

Connecting the Bible and the Liturgy

The celebration of the sacrament of baptism is a profound invitation to the whole Christian community to remember God's plan for sanctifying creation, groaning for completion in Christ. Indeed, from the claiming of the child as part of the church at the beginning of the rite of baptism until the blessing in the Holy Spirit at the conclusion of the sacrament, we sense that the assembly itself, together with the newly baptized, has been sanctified in witness and then missioned with a blessing. After the mother and father of the child(ren) are blessed, the celebrant asks God "to pour out his blessings upon these sons and daughters of his. May he make them always, wherever they may be, faithful members of his holy people. May he send his peace upon all who are gathered here, in Christ Jesus our Lord" (105). In Paul's language in Romans, then, we who have been justified by this sanctification in Christ have also been glorified as witnessed by the one who has been newly taken up in Christ and become a child of God. As the child has now been incorporated into the Christian community, the Body of Christ, the Christian assembly becomes one Body, one spirit in Christ.

Along these lines, a further dialogue partner in the church's liturgy that occurs outside the rite of baptism proper might be useful in making a connection with the present readings. I am thinking in particular of the Preface for Eucharistic Prayer IV, which offers some rich invitations to ponder God's ongoing sanctification of the human family, while acknowledging God as the source of life and the one who "made all that is, / so that you might fill your creatures with blessings / and bring joy to many of them by the glory of your light." This is the promise proclaimed by Paul that those God has justified will find joy "by the glory" of God's light. Indeed, Eucharistic Prayer IV goes on to praise the Father for sending the Holy Spirit "as the first fruits for those who believe, / so that bringing to perfection his work in the world, / he might sanctify creation to the full." We sense in these lines a very active God, bringing creation to completion through Christ and in the labor of the Holy Spirit. The action of the epiclesis follows immediately to "graciously sanctify these offerings." Those offerings are bread and wine, transubstantiated into the Body and Blood of Christ, but that sanctification extends to the assembly as well, gathered in praise and thanksgiving; they are now taken up into the glory of the passion, death, and resurrection of Christ who speaks the word of thanksgiving to the Father. That conformity to Christ as one body becomes further clarified in the second epiclesis, which underlines the assembly's participation in Christ's gift: "Look, O Lord, upon the Sacrifice / which you yourself have provided for your Church, / and grant in your loving kindness / to all who partake of this one Bread and one Chalice / that, gathered into one body by the Holy Spirit, / they may truly become a living sacrifice in Christ / to the praise of your glory." This prayer to the Father to sanctify those gathered echoes the eschatological promise of Jesus in John 6:44-47 when he says, "No one can come to me unless the Father who sent me draw him, / and I shall raise him on the last day." The second epiclesis asks that the assembly be taken up into that one Body of Christ, to the glory of God.

Strategy for Preaching

Every day I become more and more convinced that we live episodic lives, cut loose from the mooring of history and sacred memory. The United States, from the White House to Wall Street, resembles reality TV or clips from YouTube. Memories are short and history evaporates into Tweets or Instagram. Indeed, historical memory seems to only have a claim on us if its details are linked to some sensational event or gossip. The fact is that technology has canonized the present moment so that we can cyberspace our way through life, capturing a moment that will be obsolete in an hour. Relationships are bound to be catastrophes when we are overwired. I can "friend" you on Facebook and "defriend" you tomorrow if you do not "like" me. Is this any way for mature adults to live their lives?

I do not wish to belabor this point or to be dystopian. We have enough pessimists in our society. But preachers should provide their congregations with a certain realism about living in the world as a Christian community in conversation with "the signs of the times." Religious institutions—especially its preachers—are uniquely positioned to call the community back into *sacred and collective memory*, most crucially in the Judeo-Christian tradition to recall our place in salvation history. Indeed, Paul's chapter 8 in Romans means absolutely nothing without a sense of understanding God's own mission as we understand it from Scripture and tradition: God loved a creation out of nothing, brought it to a being that was good, very good, and redeemed it definitively in Christ from the decay of sin. Then God will bring his creation to glory in completion at the end of the ages. That narrative configures the baptized because of the righteousness of Divine Providence who has willed the justification of those to be caught up in Christ's glory. So how does the preacher reposition the episodic world of the assembly gathered for baptism in a focus sentence? Maybe like this: Our loving God has brought all of the baptized into life in Christ, and through the Spirit we are not only justified but continually sanctified until the end of time.

I use the word "reposition" very deliberately to suggest the importance of the introduction. Abstract clichés about sanctification in chapter 8 in Romans or truisms about faith and eternal life as if to gloss chapter 6 in John's gospel do very little to reorient the people of God out of a place of wandering—episodic living—into the narrative space of salvation history. As always, we begin where the people are, not with lofty deductive statements about how things are supposed to be. That rhetoric may have worked once but now requires more inductive strategies. Guided by the baptismal event that those who have gathered have come to witness, start inductively and small and move toward the larger picture. For instance, how about beginning the micronarrative of the life and sanctification of the patron saint that the family has chosen for the one to be baptized? These biographies offer a visualized and intimate portrait of justification that God has moved to glory.

After the introduction, the homily could then express a theological affirmation of the ongoing work God is accomplishing in the church and the sacraments through sanctification of its members. Baptism is the primary example here (illustrated by Rom 8:28-32 and Col 3:10) while the Eucharist nourishes by building up faith, hope, and love in a relationship with Christ born at baptism (John 6:44-47). We are drawn continually into the fire of divine love as we, together with all creation, long for completion.

The preacher might then draw from the language in Eucharistic Prayer IV, as noted earlier, or similar prayers in the rite, such as those deployed in the final blessing. These prayers unfold for the congregation the progressive work and labor of the Holy Spirit in sanctifying the Body of Christ. Here, the preacher invites the congregation to see baptism as the church's sacrament that leads the Body of Christ to be glorified. That ongoing work calls the newly baptized, as well as the baptized assembly, into a deeper faith so that "whoever believes has eternal life."

10. First Corinthians 12:12-13; John 15:1-11

Readings from the Ambo

Paul's seminal discussion of the Body of Christ and its diversity of membership fits squarely into his discourse in chapter 12 of 1 Corinthians and its design for an architecture of spiritual gifts. "There are different kinds of spiritual gifts but the same Spirit; there are different forms of service but the same Lord." That seems plain enough; Paul is interested in healing factions and bringing the Corinthians in line with orthodox worship and table fellowship, previously discussed in chapter 11. But there is more. In chapter 10, Paul alludes to this same powerful metaphor in his discussion of the sharing of the breaking of bread: "Because the loaf of bread is one, we, though many, are one body, for we all partake of the one loaf" (v. 17). Additionally, in his central discourse on the Law and the righteousness of faith in the letter to the Galatians, Paul uses baptism as a way to argue unity in Christ. "For through faith you are all children of God in Christ Jesus. For all of you who were baptized into Christ have clothed yourselves with Christ. There is neither Jew nor Greek, there is neither slave nor free person, there is not male and female; for you are all one in Christ Jesus" (3:26-28). A key feature to note here (something of an echo to Col 3:10) is the introduction of baptism as a way to understand unity in Christ. This divine reality with whom the newly baptized have been clothed extinguishes the demarcations of race, class, and gender. In the end, the unity Paul expresses is never accomplished by human efforts alone. No, the Christian community is perfected in a sacramental way by being drawn into an encounter with Christ in both baptism and Eucharist.

The metaphor of the Body of Christ provides Paul with a fitting image to illustrate the necessary unity into which all have been baptized. In John 15, Jesus describes himself appropriately enough to the disciples as a single body—albeit a living vine with many branches. The mystical tradition in Christianity will purchase this particular relationship of the vine and the branches as a way of understanding contemplative prayer. The vine gives life to the branches in silence, even as they feed from the source of their very being. But the image of the vine and the branches also extends Paul's discussion of the one Body from the perspective of sacrament as well, and begins to suggest that to be one with the Body means also being sustained by the Body. The vine nourishes the branches, even as the bread feeds the members who have become grafted onto its vine.

Once baptized, the member is irrevocably part of the Body and so the members continue to partake of the source, the very Person of the living vine. So these two images, so basic in biblical theology, disclose an essential way in which the life of the baptized unfolds: by participating in Love's sustaining fruits, together with other members, we are knit together in an unbreakable unity, complemented by diversity. The vine engages a lifelong—indeed, eternal—relationship of love with its members. "Whoever remains in me and I in him will bear much fruit, / because without me you can do nothing." Jesus forges a vital link between baptism and the Eucharist. It may well be that there are branches grafted on the vine, but they may fall away. The Lord pleads for the faithful to remain there, otherwise it "will be thrown out like a branch and wither; / people will gather them and throw them into a fire / and they will be burned." The invitation is lifelong discipleship in one Body, one Vine, which bears fruit in mission. Keeping the commandments—the Law of Love—is a sacred and relational aspect of Christian discipleship, which, especially in John's gospel and Paul's theology, remains nonnegotiable.

Connecting the Bible and the Liturgy

Perhaps the most apt demonstration of what occurs in the readings thematically will be the very circumstances of those who are gathered to celebrate the rite of baptism. From a liturgical point of view, unity of gesture begins to suggest what is at stake when we speak of the one Body in Christ. Unlike the celebration of the Eucharist, in which the assembly will be composed of either the baptized assembly or those waiting for the sacrament (such as those in the RCIA), the persons in attendance in this celebration will be witnessing to diversity, but not necessarily linked in common baptism. They could be friends or relatives of the family who are there in a simply loving and supportive role. Perhaps raising the consciousness of the congregation to their own gifts—whatever they may be and from whatever tradition might be represented—could be best accomplished in a common song or sung refrain, depending on the size of the congregation and their ability. One voice speaks to one Body out of unity.

If those gathered are small in number, the RBC offers some lovely gospel refrains from which to choose. One notable selection comes from the letter to the Ephesians, which invites the assembly to contemplate the unity expressed in baptism and, indeed, their own oneness with the Lord and God of all creation. "There is one Lord, one faith, one baptism, / one God and the Father of all" (201). This verse from Ephesians is an appropriate prelude to John 15:1ff and Jesus' relational claim on the community of love as a vine supporting its branches. If there are musicians present, there are many popular hymn tunes that could support the celebration and underline the importance of unity. Here again, the congregation is asked to affirm its unity in Christ as a way to witness the one baptism. In a sense, these signs of unity of the congregation are signs of faith; it is the Spirit that has drawn this assembly into one, regardless of religious persuasion or any other identity. In this regard, if there is a hymn—either classic or contemporary—it might be placed not simply as a background jingle when something else is going on. Rather, I think a useful and purposeful placement could be just after the general intercessions. That placement is regardless of whether this celebration occurs at the Eucharist (and the hymn accompanies the preparation of the gifts). After all, the Body of Christ has just voiced its intentions as a corporate self to the Father. The hymn underlines the unity already expressed in the prayers offered by the congregation. And still further, the acknowledgement of the One Lord, Jesus Christ, serves as a confirmation of the assembly-as-witness, even as the parents and godparents are led to the baptismal font for the celebration of the sacrament.

Finally, a short text that acknowledges all present might be another dialogue partner, especially if there is no opportunity for singing. At the conclusion of the Rite of Baptism for Several Children (C), the celebrant expresses the church's intention to ask God to bless all those present. This final prayer of blessing is quite neutral in respect to traditions or other affiliations and could be helpful if there is a diverse congregation with little or no religious background. "May God, who loves all people, bless all the relatives and friends who are gathered here. In his mercy, may he guard them from evil and give them his abundant peace" (70). This is a blessing for all people of goodwill who have come to celebrate the sacrament for the sake of the parents and their child. There is a common humanity that is shared at this gathering, an underlying unity with the God of all creation.

Strategy for Preaching

As I have suggested earlier, the celebration of the sacraments—especially baptisms and weddings—brings together a diverse group of people united for a common purpose. That diversity can be a cause for rejoicing, even as those gathered are united in Christ. In a pluralistic society, though, there will be present at both baptisms and weddings a whole range of faith commitments as well as the unchurched, meaning those with no religious affiliation of any kind. That mixture of people is all for the good because the Vine is a life-giving source to all branches, even those who do not realize they are tangentially connected to him. The celebration of the sacrament of baptism should evangelize without proselytizing, awaken rather than alienate, catechize without coercing. The metaphor of the vine and the branches might stir up for the congregation a recognition to be connected more deeply to the source of all life. So the focus sentence for this homily could be something like: God has drawn us together in our diversity in this celebration of baptism and unites us as a unique family.

Consider, if you will, a colorful introduction where folks have gathered for a common purpose. I am thinking of concerts, sporting events, and such. I was reminded recently of the Coney Island Polar Bear Club founded at the turn of the nineteenth century by a health enthusiast. Yes, there is nothing like a dip in the Atlantic Ocean in midwinter to draw people together! It is hard to resist a smile when those committed to the plunge into icy waters emerge triumphant, quickly receiving a large towel from family and friends.

The waters of baptism are not icy, but they have drawn us all together for God's purpose. We welcome all to celebrate this sacrament with us, the baptized as well as those who do not share our faith. We have all come to these waters in friendship and love.

Then:

I. Possible illustration: names of family and friends who have come from afar, especially if this is a baptism for several children.

II. The parents and godparents of N. _____ will be wrapping their child in a warm white cloth, when the infant emerges from these waters. But all of us who have gathered here will provide the support and love necessary to build a human family, a membership in Christ. A human being cannot survive without the love and support of a network of branches on a vine. No wonder Jesus chooses this metaphor to encourage his disciples to stay close to him as a source of life.

III. Paul has a little more sober advice to the Corinthians and gives us a model about how to live together, even in our diversity. That will involve most especially gratitude for the gifts we all possess together as a family.

    a. There will be points of resistance to living as a family and a community, even under the best of circumstances. We could be either a common Polar Bear Club, coming together for a common human purpose. Or we could be polarized in our politics, religion, and society.

    b. As a culture, we might start to ask: How can we come together as a pluralistic society for a common purpose?

IV. Baptism has a lot to teach us in this regard because it is a sacrament that is utterly relational. It is into Christ and the Christian community that N. _____ has been baptized.

    a. The Eucharist, which is food for the pilgrim church, is inextricably linked to the baptized because that sacrament of Body and Blood sustains the branches that have been grafted here onto the source of life, the Life-Giving Vine.

    b. We who are gathered here, then, do so in love. Where there is love, there is surely God present. All of us are committed to the peace that comes from Christ. We desire to keep love safe as the greatest of gifts. Without love, we are nothing, as Paul reminds us. Let that love wrap our new Christians in a warm, gigantic towel this day and show him/her/them the love of all God's people. "Show us, O Lord, your kindness and grant us your salvation" (Rite of Baptism for Several Children, 42).

11. Galatians 3:26-28; Mark 1:1-9; Psalm 23:1-3a, 3b-4, 5, 6

Readings from the Ambo

Paul's understanding of the Mosaic law is complex and his treatment of its aegis over the people of Israel conditioned by God's entrance into history in Christ. The concluding portion of his arguments in this selection from Galatians concerns the Spirit's activity in the life of those who follow the law; it underlines the emphatic role that a relationship with God claims on those who believe.

Generally speaking, I think that a helpful way of comprehending Paul's teaching in our day in regard to the law and the Spirit is to remember his own illumination on the way to Damascus, in which he encountered the Person of the risen Lord. Indeed, Paul thinks of himself as an apostle (and not coincidentally, the tradition names him the Apostle to the Gentiles), even though he was outside the historical circle of Jesus of Nazareth. Therefore, Paul will account his relationship with the Lord beyond space and time. That Paul enters into another sphere claimed by the Person of the risen Christ describes what is at stake with his conversion. He literally sees anew, having been blinded by the presence of the one whose followers he has persecuted. In his own conversion, then, Paul demonstrates the failure of the law to possess him the way the Lord does now, and his new understanding of the Spirit becomes dominated by the abiding presence of the risen Lord.

If we were looking for a way to voice this Pauline conversion it might be Psalm 23, which becomes the lens through which he sees everything. "The Lord is my Shepherd" and not the law is my Shepherd. The Lord has created a bond much greater than the letter could possibly do, even the sacred letter forged by God through Moses. It is Paul's desire, therefore, that all who are baptized are immersed into a new relationship in the same Spirit of Christ. "Through faith you are all children of God in Christ Jesus. / For all of you who were baptized into Christ / have clothed yourselves with Christ." This *relationship* with the risen Christ transcends all things, making the green pastures of the sheep guided by the Shepherd both level and nourishing; all enjoy the same company of the Lord—Jew or Greek, slave or free person, male or female. Additionally, this egalitarian stance not only repositions the Christian by virtue of a relationship but also offers a design for order not based on class or gender. In the twenty-first century, it is difficult to grasp how radical such a claim is in the midst of a first-century Mediterranean culture, a highly structured patriarchal society with distinct divisions of labor, class, and gender.

So the work of the Spirit that dwells in the baptized becomes disclosed as a trinitarian moment in Mark 1:9-11. The disclosure in the Jordan at the moment of Christ's baptism is itself an iconic representation of the Son and the indwelling union of the Holy Spirit. The promise of baptism makes all those who have been submerged in the new waters made holy by Christ vessels of sanctification, children of God and brothers to the one Lord who abides in the newly baptized. After all, this is not the baptism of John, which was about repentance; this is the new order: Psalm 23 becomes the new anthem for the Christian community, especially so for the newly baptized, now restored and resting in green pastures. The Spirit of the Lord is no casual visitor but a living and active presence, celebrated in the outpouring of new life upon new life, inviting friendship with God as children.

Connecting the Bible and the Liturgy

When Paul speaks exhaustingly of the Spirit, he does so to encourage the Galatians to live out of a new reality: the presence of the Lord. The gifts God bestowed on the beloved in baptism, purchased by the living water sanctified by Christ, establishes an irrevocable seal that binds us to a covenantal relationship with the living God. That covenant is not unlike the one God made with Israel, with one important exception: this baptism will erase boundaries of distinction between Jew and Gentile.

As a kind of sacred coda on the rite, the Blessing and Dismissal (105) recalls the work of the Spirit, this time at work in the congregation at large; the celebrant begs the Father to bless those gathered and sends them forth; it is a recollection of the baptismal promises now reinvigorated in the celebration of the sacrament. Indeed, the very blessing of almighty God, the Father, Son, and the Holy Spirit, echoes the action of the baptism that has just been celebrated, pouring out the blessing of God's generous gift on all those gathered to go in peace. In a more specific way, the congregation is reminded of its own collective identity as the community of the baptized, as those who were "clothed" in Christ with a garment that is ever new, making all who receive it children of God. I am thinking here particularly of the benediction that occurs after the blessing of the mother and father: "By God's gift, through water and the Holy Spirit, we are reborn to everlasting life. In his goodness, may he continue to pour out his blessing upon these sons and daughters of his. May he make them always, wherever they may be, faithful members of his holy people. May he send his peace upon all who are gathered here, in Christ Jesus our Lord." The individual has become incorporated into the church of all those "gathered here in Christ."

Those who have been already baptized and join in the celebration of the newly baptized are reminded that they were re-created anew in the Spirit "in Christ Jesus" since they have died to themselves and now live in him. Like Paul, the scales and blindness of sin that once covered our eyes have fallen away. Psalm 23 also comes to mind here with the renewal of a relationship with the Great Shepherd of souls as a church. The gathering of the baptized precisely as an assembly will continue the formation work of the Spirit begun at baptism. As I have mentioned in a previous instance in this volume (#9), an additional connection in this regard is one of the many versions of the "second epiclesis" prayer occurring in the celebration of the eucharistic liturgy. This portion of the eucharistic prayer reminds us that the Holy Spirit continues to labor in the work of sanctification for the faithful, that the assembly has been taken up in Christ, together with the gifts of bread and wine so that "we might live no longer for ourselves but for him" (EP IV). Consider the unity expressed by Paul in Galatians and the second epiclesis in Eucharistic Prayer III. "Look, we pray, upon the oblation of your Church / and, recognizing the sacrificial Victim by whose death / you willed to reconcile us to yourself, / grant that we, who are nourished / by the Body and Blood of your Son / and filled with his Holy Spirit, / may become one body, one spirit in Christ." The prayer emphasizes the new relationship we have in Christ in the Spirit, now sustained in the eucharistic food we have been given. Do we have to look any further for a Father who provides for his children? For a Shepherd who cares for the flock? Paul's erasure of distinctions becomes even further clarified when we see that the unity of the Body is made holy in the presence of the Spirit. The living and active presence of God has come upon Jesus in the Jordan, has been recalled in this baptism for a new child of God, all of it a witness to the Spirit that has poured itself out like water for the sanctification of the church, making us aware of the Spirit's activity in the members of Christ's Body.

Strategy for Preaching

There are few opportunities as demonstrable for deepening the faith of the baptized as when the faithful gather to celebrate this initiation into the Christian faith. Whenever the assembly comes together as the Body of Christ the faith of the baptized can be and should be augmented by preaching. And naming the grace of baptism for all of those assembled as well as the neophyte constitutes good preaching. The homily, then, invites the assembly—especially the parents and godparents, who have a unique role to play—to see what the Holy Spirit is doing *now in the present moment*, acknowledging an intimate encounter with the Spirit that Jesus himself beheld at his own baptism in the theophany at the Jordan. The focus sentence might be: The power of the Holy Spirit never rests but is present even now in our midst and in our hearts in these waters of baptism. Baptism also allows the preacher to explore the theological, catechetical, and liturgical issues of collective worship and the forging of one Body in Christ. It is perhaps an obvious point to mention that although Paul does not mention the Body particularly in the Galatians reading, the second-person plural form would suggest a collective: "Through faith you are all children of God in Christ Jesus." Faith gifts for the children of

God a new relationship not only with the Holy but with other baptized members of the community.

One possible introduction could be a brief retelling of Paul's conversion on the way to Damascus, with an emphasis on his new identity as an apostle born of the Spirit of the risen Christ. The homily may then tease out levels of conversion. Some Christian denominations speak of being slain in the Spirit's power. But we have all been slain in the Spirit already, right? We have died with Christ and now are children of God. The attention could now move toward the child(ren) and the work of the Spirit. God has come to him/her in a way that we cannot possibly imagine. Well, we do not have to imagine it: we are here witnessing the Spirit by our very lives as a baptized assembly.

I. Yes, even now the Spirit has drawn us together as one. What does that feel like?

   a. Examples: covered by a sleeping bag when camping in the fall with friends; diving into piles of fallen leaves when we were children and hiding in their shelter with family members; refreshed by the Spirit's power as water covered us at baptism: we can imagine that now because we are swimming in this font together!

II. That is the labor of the Spirit that continues to sanctify and cover us with God's power to be children of God—together as a church.

   a. Examples: second epiclesis.

   b. The Lord is my shepherd—could we change it to our shepherd?

   c. We are sent forth together (cf. Blessing of the Congregation).

III. The grace of baptism loves us into being as one church, one Body in Christ.

   a. N. _____ is loved by parents, godparents, and this congregation. But nobody loves him/her more than the Great Shepherd, who covers him/her with the warm arms of love.

12. Ephesians 4:1-6; Mark 10:13-16

Readings from the Ambo

Mark's gospel gets us into the thick of discipleship with this particular selection, a most appropriate one for baptism. Beginning with chapter 8, verse 31—when Jesus discloses his future passion, death, and resurrection—following Jesus becomes more and more arduous. This is the road to Jerusalem, and there is no turning back for the Lord. There have been invitations to take up the cross, a bewildering transfiguration, a futile attempt on the part of the disciples to heal a boy possessed by an evil spirit, which causes the Teacher to rebuke and castigate them as a "faithless generation," asking them, "[H]ow long will I be with you?" (9:19). Then there is the dispute about who is greatest, advice to enter the kingdom lame rather than in sin and thrown into hell, and teaching on divorce. Finally, Jesus twice endorses children just before the present passage. What a collection of mishaps to prove that discipleship is hard stuff!

The contrast could not be more obvious between the clueless disciples who want to be at the top of the ladder of success on the one hand, and the least in the kingdom whom Jesus prefers on the other. Indeed, the example of the child in their midst is a correction to the disciples' notion of the kingdom itself; it is not the territory purchased by power, or even a symbol of human strength, but the reign of selflessness and love. And so the emblematic person with no status, the poor, is indicative of a sojourn in which "many that are first will be last, and [the] last will be first" (10:31). When the disciples lack the faith to perform cures or exorcisms, the Lord draws on the most vulnerable, unimportant nonentity in first-century Palestine—a child. With children prioritized in our culture as cute and playful creatures, it is hard to imagine that children had no status at all in antiquity, unless they were the male progeny of the ruling class. So in a sense, Jesus surrenders his own authority and allows the witness of the least in the kingdom to speak silently as a symbol, to articulate what the disciples have been missing all along. In the end, the example of a child could not be more practical for Jesus' purpose: Receive me as like this one—without the need to be great.

Paul has very honest words from prison to the church at Ephesus, especially concerning efforts to be maintained in unity and peace. There is an echo of Jesus' example of a child when Paul asks the community to live a life worthy of their calling "with all humility and gentleness." These virtues must necessarily be in place in order for the community to participate in the "one Body and one Spirit." In the letter to the Ephesians, Paul proposes a development of his theology in a way that will eventually own a wider reach than the occasional behavioral circumstances of the local community. Unity, for instance, concerns not simply living in peace but has theological ramifications; we belong to the Lord precisely because of the call we have received, and so this relationship has consequences: bearing with one another through love, striving to preserve the unity of the Spirit through the bond of peace: "one Body and one Spirit . . . one Lord, one faith, one baptism; / one God and Father of all, / who is over all and through all and in all." We have moved from an admonition to a cosmic claim about God, the Father of all.

To be baptized, then, makes the child a member of the Body of Christ, who is the head, and joined in a relational way to other members as they build one another up in mature love. In so doing, the baptized grow into what Paul calls later in Ephesians, "full stature of Christ" through the mutual sharing of gifts (4:13).

Connecting the Bible and the Liturgy

It must be obvious that the rite of baptism is filled with gestures and words and symbols that orient those gathered toward discipleship. By my reckoning, among the numerous examples of liturgical gestures that we have already discussed in this volume, perhaps the most poignant occurs early on when the priest or deacon announces a kind of separation from the comfortable womb of the natural family. At the same time, the church becomes the new womb giving birth by water and the Spirit, even as the children of God gather in welcome. Addressing the child, the celebrant says to him or her by name, "[T]he Christian community welcomes you with great joy. In its name I claim you for Christ our Savior by the sign of his cross. I now trace the cross on your forehead, and invite your parents (and godparents) to do the same."

The way of discipleship has literally been drawn on the one to be baptized, who will carry the cross throughout the course of a lifetime. This discipleship reorders the natural world where a Darwinian survival of the fittest or interests in economic and social power hold sway. The question "who is greatest?" or an interest in self-aggrandizement has no currency in the kingdom of God. Instead, the "first will be last, and [the] last will be first." The new reality is all the more obvious at a baptism, since the child has been "claimed" not by natural birth but by a supernatural relationship with the Savior. The family has been enlarged to include the family of faith, or whoever does the will of the Father, even as the parents and godparents witness the unfolding of this new reality.

It is hard to ignore the natural symbols of the parents present during the claiming of their child(ren) for the church. The parents surely are unselfish vessels of God's will as they bring their child(ren) into the expansive community of the church, so that they might be incorporated into the one Body, into the head who orders all things in himself. Far from preventing the little ones from entering into the midst of the Lord, the parents' presentation of their children in baptism begins to suggest the theology of the family that does not stay enclosed and self-satisfied. Rather, the family unit is continually open to the larger community, radiating creativity for the sake of the kingdom. Those who have gathered as family and friends and parishioners are also natural symbols. With those who have come attendant at the celebrant's welcoming the child in their name, the newly baptized already becomes knit together in the community of love, as those gathered welcome him or her into their midst. This gesture of human hospitality to the one who is about to be baptized anticipates the supernatural welcome by God, which occurs when the child is plunged into the mystery of the Trinity itself, the apogee of the perfect community. There are a number of ways that the liturgy might support the crucial link between community and the new discipleship that is unfolding. The RBC recommends that if there is a procession to the place in the church where the Liturgy of the Word will be proclaimed, an outpouring of the call to discipleship and its mandate to Christian love and unity might be sung as an expression of gratitude of the one Body, speaking a word of thanks, as the faithful strive "to preserve the unity of the spirit through the bond of peace and love."

There are any number of biblical witnesses that might serve as sung processional hymns as those gathered move to the Liturgy of the Word. Since we have emphasized the church as a womb giving new birth, a psalm that comes to mind is Psalm 84, "How lovely your dwelling, / O Lord of hosts! / My soul yearns and pines / for the courts of the Lord. / My heart and flesh cry out / for the living God" (vv. 2-3). Here we see that, in a certain sense, the singing assembly is articulating the desire for a true home for the one to be baptized, waiting for God to "look upon the face of [the] anointed" (v. 10). The church, already sheltering the community in a physical presence, now becomes the home by virtue of the community of the blessed, seen and unseen. The neophyte, with cross traced on his or her head, journeys to the homeland as a disciple with the support of the community of faith; along this road there will be the guidance of the teaching church, even as the image of the trinitarian God is about to impress itself on the baptized to be drawn into perfect unity.

Strategy for Preaching

The readings selected for this particular celebration of the rite of baptism are a fresh reminder that this sacrament is an immersion into the Christian mystery of initiation. As the newly baptized has been claimed by the church through its minister, there is a new birth through water and the Spirit, leading the neophyte into the nascent stirrings of Christian discipleship. The rite makes it quite clear that the familial, natural world has been reordered by the supernatural. Sons and daughters are remade, even as they are reborn children of God. So the focus sentence for this homily might be the following: Christian baptism delivers us into the hand of Christ, and so the community gathered are midwives and witnesses to a new order of creation.

The homilist might take the lead from Jesus, of course, and use the natural symbol present in the midst of the congregation: the child. We could use the special relationship that a mother owns exclusively with her children of her flesh as a connection like no other. That bond could be raised in order to point out that even this most unique of relationships in the created order has shifted in the celebration of baptism. The womb of Mother Church, fashioned of water and the Spirit, has been disclosed in the baptismal font.[12]

12. My colleague and coauthor of this volume, Deacon Frank Agnoli, astutely suggests that an apt touchstone for preaching here might be a reference to the inscription on the Lateran Baptistery. For the full inscription in Latin with translation, see, for instance, http://www.josemariaescriva.info/opus_dei/Lateran.pdf. I am grateful to Deacon Agnoli for his other suggestions throughout this section on preaching baptism.

So there follows the logic of what has been said above: baptism takes N._____ to another birth, a discipleship where a new family has been drawn into a relationship for the one who has been baptized. There is a lesson here that Jesus points to in the gospel that serves as an illustration for those already baptized. We trace our origins as a people of faith from this font of blessing, and so Christian baptism remains a gift to reflect upon for a lifetime. As we have been raised in God's family, we now are asked to midwife N. _____ into that same nurturing family. It takes a great deal of courage for a community to commit to raising a child of God, the same kind of courage that the parents of N. _____ have demonstrated by entrusting their beloved child into the arms of the church and its ministers. The discipleship modeled for the newly baptized will come from these parents who know what matters first and foremost. Their own humility has shown us that their primary role as parents is as servants of God and the church. That is sacrificial love that only a parent can know. (Perhaps a brief illustration of heroic love can be given here.)

Therefore this sacrament is not only an encounter with initiation into the Christian mystery of baptism but a celebration of an encounter with Christ and divine hospitality. The church has welcomed a new member into the Body of Christ today who will dine at the table of the Word and the Eucharist and wait in joyful hope for the coming of God's kingdom. There is no loss of a family, but the expansion of a natural relationship into a supernatural one. Love has triumphed here because with humility and gentleness this child has led us to the font of life and shown us who we really are and who loves us most deeply—more than we can possibly imagine. The faithful people of God now rejoice in our common origin, making us children of God.

13. First Peter 2:4-5, 9-10; John 9:1-7

Readings from the Ambo

The language of this portion of the first letter of Peter, which many scholars regard as the heart of the epistle, can be unsettling particularly if the images, symbols, and metaphors deployed in the text are not adequately and imaginatively explored. "You are a chosen race" sounds mightily offensive, given this country's ugly history of the slavery of African Americans, genocide of Native Americans, and increasing racial tensions in our time. Indeed, in the context of a pluralistic society, the "city on a hill," once famously coined by Puritan John Winthrop, continues to haunt and define American exclusiveness and manifest destiny, mistakenly justified by Divine Providence. There is no denying that (Christian) white imperialism against people of color formed the American racial bias and bigotry that is still with us. So using the terms "holy nation," "a chosen race," and "a people set apart" is going to be potentially problematic. Given the persistent problems with racism in our culture, do we want to use language that reinforces separation, ironically in a sacrament of unity and initiation into the mystery of the Trinity? Even if some have heard such expressions before in liturgical language, the diverse assembly at a baptism hearing the Scriptures might have an altogether different take on these expressions than the Sunday assembly.

So what to do? First Peter adopts a number of images in the Hebrew Scriptures to reframe the language of the covenant, now newly established in Christ. A key passage to consider in this regard is Deuteronomy 26:16-19: "[T]oday the LORD has accepted your agreement," Moses tells the people. "[Y]ou will be a people specially his own." This is the language of exclusiveness and Israel understands it, the language of the covenant initiated by God out of love. The opening portion of 1 Peter alludes to Psalm 118:22 and references later in the text a sign of God's power to overcome and thwart human pretensions and edifices of power. "The stone the builders rejected / has become the cornerstone" (v. 7). For the author of 1 Peter, the point is that the cornerstone is living, "chosen and precious in the sight of God." If we come to this living stone and allow ourselves to be "built into a spiritual house," we become this "holy priesthood," which is made holy only through Christ Jesus. So the chosen race is not based on national merit or manifest destiny or twisted notions of genetic superiority, but by *being in relationship with the rejected Christ*. Far from being a *powerful* chosen nation, the Christian community is a *suffering Body* joined to Christ, the cornerstone. Our destiny is manifested not in conquest but in unity with the suffering God as his Holy Body.

The work here is God's alone, who has formed us by a new covenant in Christ into a people of his own and calls us "out of darkness into his wonderful light." The only thing manifest in our destiny is the way that almighty God will lead us by an inscrutable will into the mystery of Divine

Providence. In this regard, we can see an apt connection to John 9:1-7 in which Jesus reveals himself through a sign that he is the Light of the World. As most preachers know, the present gospel should also be seen, as 1 Peter, in the context of a larger whole. Chapter 9 in its entirety not only discloses the Lord's healing and restoration of sight to the man born blind but discloses something darker: the blindness of those who witness this miracle of God's power. It would not be the first time—or the last—that we would find a powerful irony embedded in a narrative in which those who claim to see are, in fact, blind. At the same time, the one who is blind now has new vision and truth. John has set the scene in which a literary drama uncovers a theological meaning: the religious leaders at the time of Jesus failed to see God's glory working in their midst. Paradox upon paradox abounds. In fact, besides Jesus, the only one in this drama who is not utterly baffled is the blind man himself, who comes to the truth of discipleship. This revelation prepares us for chapter 10 in which Jesus discloses himself as the Good Shepherd, protecting the flock from thieves who pretend to be someone else. So the invitation becomes even more pointed as the Shepherd gives new vision to the sheep—the new nation, the new holy people who see the Lord, rejected by (blind) builders, in the fullness of truth.

Connecting the Bible and the Liturgy

Although the language of 1 Peter and its use of politically charged expressions such as "a chosen race" might appear off-putting or even terribly offensive for some, the process of baptism is, in fact, a celebration of belonging to a new reality—the Mystical Body of Christ. For those in the RCIA, this journey includes a rite of election, which already begins to disclose the free choice of those entering into the catechumenate with the intention of becoming fully incorporated into the Catholic Church.

For its part, the rite of baptism could not be more demonstrable when it comes to deploying signs and gestures of election. From the very beginning, parents formally name the child as they accept the responsibility for training the young one in the practice of the faith. The call to be a chosen race or holy nation is really not about race or nationalism at all, of course. Rather, this language ratifies the inclusion and hospitality offered by the Body of Christ, the church. The celebrant addresses the child, as if to underline the new personhood that is at stake in this invitation, and says, "N. _____ the Church of God welcomes you with great joy. In its name, I claim you for Christ, our savior by the sign of the cross."

In my view, there is another moment in the rite that reinforces this opening dialogue. The Prayer of Exorcism and Anointing before Baptism underlines the reality of the child being purchased by Christ to be part of a "holy nation." This is a tactile and symbolic gesture meant to rescue the one to be baptized out of darkness and into light. With this in mind, the rite of exorcism and anointing before baptism functions somewhat like Jesus' cleansing of the temple in John 2:13-22. Now purged of what is not clean, and constructed as the new temple, the child prepares to be rebuilt as an altogether new edifice, with Christ as the cornerstone. As the prayer asks God to cast out the power of Satan and to rescue humanity from the kingdom of darkness and bring us into the kingdom of light, the promise of the covenant is renewed for another structure: "Set him (her) free from original sin, make him (her) temples of your glory, and send your Holy Spirit to dwell with him (her)." Therefore the child becomes a new temple, built with "living stones," even as the Holy Spirit becomes its most welcome guest.

As if to consecrate a holy edifice, the anointing follows "with the oil of salvation in the name of Christ our Savior." After the baptism itself is performed, the anointing with chrism reminds us about the close association that exists between consecrating a church or altar and anointing the newly baptized. The new structure is made holy and becomes a place for the Holy Spirit to live and move. Here again, we see the language of being set apart and being made holy so that God might dwell near. After all, Christ has rebuilt humanity into a living temple of his body, which is indeed set apart. As Preface I for the Sundays in Ordinary Time reminds us, "For through his Paschal Mystery, / he accomplished the marvelous deed, / by which he has freed us from the yoke of sin and death, / summoning us to the glory of being now called / a chosen race, a royal priesthood, / a holy nation, a people for your own possession, / to proclaim everywhere your mighty works, / for you have called us out of darkness / into your own wonderful light." In the end, the Preface more than hints at the reason we are called a people set apart. Far from privilege or superiority, we have been called to proclaim everywhere God's mighty works; that is the call to mission. Set apart: yes; for love, purchased not by violence but by complete divine self-emptying.

Strategy for Preaching

Powerful symbols and metaphors abound in our readings, and, as always, the liturgy proves to be a supportive conversation partner to enable the preacher to expand the biblical witness and draw out the homily with liturgical as well as scriptural language. I will underline what 1 Peter has to say about Christ as the cornerstone in the context of Christian baptism and suggest that a building metaphor provides the homilist with a window to view the sacrament and lay out a blueprint for a kind of architecture of the soul for the hearer. So a focus sentence might simply be: Today Christ has laid the cornerstone for N. _____ that will house the Holy Spirit.

How about using the child as the dominant agent in developing this homily? We know that children are natural builders by an early age and flourish with their colorful blocks, dollhouses, forts, and other toys. Yet the time will come when these things of childhood will be set aside for the sake of a single cornerstone: Christ. Being with the Lord is a relationship that lasts for eternity and begins to be constructed here in this church by the living witnesses of the church.

There follows an explication of God's role in this baptism: God once again has renewed his covenant. We might find some of the language of 1 Peter a little dated and maybe even offensive. Can the preacher begin to negotiate new meaning from this language? From the biblical author's point of view, entering into a new covenant with God is not an exclusive club or some special entitlement separating us from humankind. We are a holy people because we have entered into a personal relationship with God through his Son. Now the Spirit lives in us. So we really are peculiarly God's own children because we have been adopted by God. We know that the rite of baptism invites the parent to freely renounce everything that is not of God in order to lay this cornerstone. For the church's part, the community of love has laid claim to N. _____ for Christ and his kingdom of justice and peace. The structure is being built before our very eyes. Like a holy building, the newly baptized will be anointed and consecrated.

So we celebrate with N. _____ and her (his) family not only today but for the rest of her (his) life. Christ will not leave this new building, his beloved, empty. But the members of the holy church, a holy nation of peace and love, keep the space burning brightly with a light. We will walk with N. _____ on the first floor of the elementary school. Then we will ascend the stairs with him (her) to the second, third, fourth floors and beyond, to adolescence, young adulthood, middle age, and advanced years. All our lives are companioned together with Christ in this community of faith no matter where our feet or God will take us. We are all in a new covenant with the God who loves us so much he gave his life. Blood and water poured out from Christ's side on the cross from which we still drink at the Eucharist and baptism. What a future for N. _____! What a future for us all in the wonderful structure God has built for his people!

14. Psalm 34:2-3, 6-7, 8-9, 14-15, 16-17, 18-19; (with or without) John 6:44-47

Readings from the Ambo

This extraordinarily beautiful psalm rolls so pleasantly off the lips, doesn't it? As a responsory to a biblical reading there are few to match its breadth of wisdom, tapping into gratitude for the Creator and, indeed, all creation. Just from the perspective of images alone, Psalm 34 harvests a superabundance of riches: a singer who cannot cease a song of praise who is radiant with joy; an angel who delivers us from distress; a God who is not distant but can be tasted in his very goodness; a Lord who hears the cry of the poor. In his Prologue to the Rule for monks, St. Benedict turns to this particular psalm often in order to express the call to "the school of the Lord's service," and invites a multitude into the work of God's vineyard. Even the suggested responsorial refrains tap into this treasure of literary and scriptural abundance: "Look to him, that you may be radiant with joy!" or "Taste and see the goodness of the Lord." Does it get any better? No, it doesn't. The psalm is clearly meant to witness to gratitude as one of Israel's thanksgiving hymns. Indeed, in Hebrew each line begins with a sequential letter from the alphabet. In some sense, this text was probably memorized by the community, a group of people, or an individual, with the order of the alphabet serving as some kind of mnemonic device. That tells us that the text was internalized by the community of Israel as a response in gratitude to God.

But I will point out that there is a little snag that catches us in the beginning of the psalm. "I will bless [*'avarakha*; note the *aleph* as it begins the alphabetical structure] the LORD at all times; / his praise shall be ever in my mouth." Really? How many times will a community give thanks? Even during the bad times? When things do not go according to plan? What about me? Yet the psalmist accounts for this very difficult reality by narrating why the community has been propelled into thanksgiving: they have been delivered. Scholars point to the superscription, which alludes to David playing an insane person in 1 Samuel 21:14 and thereby delivered. In a verse not in the selection from Various Texts for Use in the Celebration of Baptism, the author notes, "I sought the LORD, and he answered me, / delivered me from all my fears" (34:5). The psalm goes on to speak not so much about the fate of the author—who is saved from danger—but the works of the Lord. The poem is a celebration of the God who hears the lowly: "When the just cry out, the LORD hears them, / and from all their distress he rescues them." That is why the Lord is blessed at all times. The truth is that misfortunes surround us, even as David faced his own adversaries, but God delivers those who remain faithful.

Jesus' testimony to the crowds in John 6:44-47 is that he will also remain faithful. Having been drawn in by the Father, the one who comes to Christ will find refuge. Even in death, "[t]he LORD is close to the brokenhearted, / and those who are crushed in spirit he saves," because, as Jesus says, "I shall raise him on the last day." The faith that the Lord proclaims as the spine of our relationship with him becomes the source of eternal life. Steadfast fidelity, even in the face of difficulty, can only deepen a relationship with the Lord who has come to raise up the fallen. In the end, Jesus is the faithful witness himself, the Son who has seen the Father and who "has eyes for the just / and ears for their cry." Christ is the Angel of the Lord who "encamps / around those who fear him, and delivers them." He delivers those who believe, even as he himself has been raised up by God. That is the reason we "bless the LORD at all times."

Connecting the Bible and the Liturgy

The psalm is characterized by rejoicing in God's works in the midst of the baptismal liturgy, and so it is a natural link to the rite itself. Indeed, the Christian assembly is positioned as the faithful witness who blesses the Lord at all times, celebrates God's actions in the world, and has been rescued from sin by Christ. The community of faith has already been shaped by the eucharistic liturgy and brought to this baptismal moment of faith, ways that intersect with the psalm being deployed as a responsorial song.

Psalm 34 reminds me of the essential characteristic of the religious person: gratitude. The most emphasized phrase common to virtually all the prefaces for the eucharistic liturgy risks something that we may want to ponder more deeply: "It is truly right and just, our duty and our salvation, / always and everywhere to give you thanks, / Lord, holy Father, almighty and eternal God." We find ourselves, much like the psalmist, in a position where we are blessing the Lord at all times—good or bad. As is well known, the great patristic authors like St. Augustine read some of the psalms as Christ speaking to the Father. As the Body of Christ, we are also speaking a word to the Father. The prefaces in the church's Eucharist acknowledge this reality of gratitude first and then go on to praise God's actions in the world through Christ. And so thanksgiving is *normative* out of recognition of what God has done and continues to do. As the Body of Christ, the church has invited its members to affirm in faith the Father's actions in the world. In so doing, Christ lives and works in us, with the promise of eternal life.

Christ, the intermediary between God and humanity is the guardian, aptly described as the Angel who delivers us from the reign of death. Baptism takes the neophyte into this new world of redemption. In Eucharistic Prayer I (Roman Canon), the celebrant asks God to accept the offerings the congregation has laid before him and asks God to "command that these gifts be borne / by the hands of your holy Angel / to your altar on high / in the sight of your divine majesty, / so that all of us, who through this participation at the altar / receive the most holy Body and Blood of your Son, / may be filled with every grace and heavenly blessing." This portion of the Roman Canon is a wonderful example of Christ the Intercessor who never fails to be faithful, even as he redeems his people. Christ, the Faithful Witness, continues to be close to the brokenhearted and rescues those in distress. So, too, are all of us rescued from the powers of darkness and transferred into the kingdom of justice and peace.

We know that the witness of faith has no small part in the baptismal liturgy. The psalm helps to underline the corporate commitment to the God who never fails to deliver his people; the celebration of the sacrament once again unfolds that divine reality. In fact, the celebrant will test the spirits of the parents and godparents up to the very last moment. In the

Renunciation of Sin and Profession of Faith, he says to them, "If your faith makes you ready to accept this responsibility, renew now the vows of your own baptism. Reject sin; profess your faith in Christ Jesus. This is the faith of the Church. This is the faith in which these children are about to be baptized" (56). The questions follow that explicitly ask the parents and godparents to attest to their own faith publicly. In a certain sense, such a testimony champions the voice behind Psalm 34, the fearless singer who blesses the Lord at all times, even in the midst of "the glamor of evil." Why? "This is the faith of the Church. We are proud to profess it, in Christ Jesus our Lord" (59).

Strategy for Preaching

By my reckoning, the Psalms (and, more generally, the Hebrew Scriptures) deserve higher priority at the Christian ambo. And so Psalm 34 showcases an opportunity to preach through one of the most moving of the psalms of thanksgiving, inviting the congregation to "bless the Lord at all times." When used effectively with a refrain, this religious hymn of gratitude also presents itself as a focal point to *all* those in attendance. Arguably, I suppose, gratitude is the most basic and important virtue from a simply human perspective. If there is a diverse group attending the baptism, Psalm 34 is the "go to" text. If the psalm is used with John 6:44-47, then Jesus' disclosure as the faithful witness who raises up the fallen is a nice complement to what the tradition reckons as David's song of gratitude to the Lord for rescuing him from danger. So the focus sentence here could be: Baptism in the Lord brings us into a song of praise and thanksgiving, as God continues to work wonders through Christ.

When evolving an introduction, I would confront fairly directly the challenge of being asked to "bless the Lord at all times." There are blessings that seem obvious and true when celebrating baptism. But there will be those in the congregation, whether they are people of faith or not, who for one reason or another struggle with a God who is absent or silent in their own lives. So the preacher here simply poses a question as to why we would want to bless the Lord at all times—even in the midst of difficulty and tragedy.

The psalm tells us that in spite of problems that confront us, God is present. The homily could then sketch briefly and illustratively the persona behind the psalm who has felt deliverance. Then, despite our often tremendous difficulties, God remains faithful. Baptism is yet one more sign of God's action in the world, an encounter with Christ who has delivered this day our beloved N. _____ from sin and death. (There could be a short catechesis on the effects of baptism taken from the *Catechism of the Catholic Church*.)

The Christian community sees this labor of the Holy Spirit in the work of Christ not only here but everywhere, especially in the Eucharist, which will sustain N._____ throughout his (her) life. The prefaces at the liturgy remind the baptized assembly that we give thanks "always and everywhere" for Christ's work of redemption. (Example: Christ as the Angel who "encamps" around his beloved to rescue them; the same Angel brings us to God's altar, cf. Eucharistic Prayer I.)

The risen Christ is steadfast in his presence with the Christian community and will be with N. _____, who will be raised up to eternal life. All the more reason to have faith, hope, and love as we gather here. In just a few moments, we will see a testimony to that faith as the parents and godparents, N. and N._____ , profess their own faith in the God who refuses to let go of us. They speak for the church, into which N._____ has now been made a member. They proclaim the saving works of God as they renounce what holds them back from a full vision of God. This is the gratitude of the church, which rejoices today on the day of N._____'s baptism.

Bibliography

Anderson, E. Byron. "Performance, Practice and Meaning in Christian Baptism." *Worship* 69 (1995): 482–505.

Best, Thomas F., ed. *Baptism Today: Understanding, Practice, and Ecumenical Implications.* Collegeville, MN: Liturgical Press, 2008.

Collins, Adela Yarbro. "The Origin of Christian Baptism." *Studia Liturgica* 19 (1989): 28–46.

Covino, Paul F. X. "The Postconciliar Infant Baptism Debate in the American Catholic Church." *Worship* 56 (1982): 240–60.

Cullmann, Oscar. *Baptism in the New Testament.* Translated by J. K. S. Reid. London: SCM Press, 1950.

Ferguson, Everett. *Baptism in the Early Church: History, Theology, and Liturgy in the First Five Centuries.* Grand Rapids, MI: Eerdmans, 2008.

Hamma, Robert M. *Together at Baptism.* Notre Dame, IN: Ave Maria Press, 2012.

Hilkert, Mary Catherine. *Naming Grace: Preaching and the Sacramental Imagination.* New York: Continuum, 1997.

Jensen, Robin M. *Baptismal Imagery in Early Christianity: Ritual, Visual and Theological Dimensions.* Grand Rapids, MI: Baker Academic, 2012.

———. *Living Water: Images, Symbols and Settings of Early Christian Baptism.* Boston: Brill, 2011.

Johnson, Maxwell E. *Images of Baptism.* Forum Essay 6. Chicago: Liturgy Training Publications, 2001.

———. *The Rite of Christian Initiation: Their Evolution and Interpretation.* Collegeville, MN: Liturgical Press, 1999.

———. "Back Home to the Front: Eight Implications of a Baptismal Spirituality." *Worship* 71 (1997): 482–504.

Joncas, Jan Michael. "Preaching from and for the Liturgy: A Practical Guide." In *We Preach Christ Crucified,"* edited by Michael E. Connors, 44–65. Collegeville, MN: Liturgical Press, 2014.

Kavanagh, Aidan. *The Shape of Baptism.* 1978; repr. Collegeville: Liturgical Press, 1992.

Larere, Philippe. *Baptism in Water and Baptism in Spirit: A Biblical, Liturgical and Theological Exposition.* Translated by Patrick Madigan. Collegeville: Liturgical Press, 1998.

Lathrop, Gordon. "Baptism in the New Testament and Its Cultural Setting." In *Worship and Culture in Dialogue,* edited by S. Anita Stauffer, 17–38. Geneva: Lutheran World Federation, 1994.

———. "The Origins and Early Meanings of Christian Baptism: A Proposal." *Worship* 68 (1994): 504–22.

McDonnell, Kilian. *The Baptism of Jesus in the Jordan: The Trinitarian and Cosmic Order of Salvation.* Collegeville, MN: Liturgical Press, 1996.

Miller, Charles E., *Ordained to Preach: A Theology and Practice of Preaching.* New York: Alba House, 1994.

Radcliffe, Timothy. *Take the Plunge: Living Baptism and Confirmation.* London: Bloomsbury, 2012.

Sánchez, Patricia Datchuck. *The Passages We Celebrate: Commentaries on the Scriptural Texts for Baptisms, Weddings and Funerals.* Kansas City, MO: Sheed and Ward, 1994.

Searle, Mark. *Christening: The Making of Christians.* Collegeville, MN: Liturgical Press, 1980.

Spinks, Bryan D. *Early and Medieval Rituals and Theologies of Baptism: From the New Testament to the Council of Trent, Liturgy, Worship and Society.* Burlington, VT: Ashgate, 2006.

———. *Reformation and Modern Rituals and Theologies of Baptism: From Luther to Contemporary Practices, Liturgy, Worship and Society.* Burlington, VT: Ashgate, 2006.

Stasiak, Kurt. *Return to Grace: A Theology for Infant Baptism.* Collegeville, MN: Liturgical Press, 1996.

Turner, Paul. "Preaching the Rites of Initiation." In *To All the World: Preaching and the New Evangelization,* 38–51. Collegeville, MN: Liturgical Press, 2016.

Wallace, James. *Preaching to the Hungers of the Heart.* Collegeville, MN: Liturgical Press, 2002.

Whitaker, E. C., ed. *Documents of the Baptismal Liturgy*, revised ed., Maxell E. Johnson. Collegeville, MN: Liturgical Press, 2003.

Witczak, Michael G. *The Sacrament of Baptism.* Collegeville, MN: Liturgical Press, 2011.

Wood, Susan K. *One Baptism: Ecumenical Dimensions of the Doctrine of Baptism.* Collegeville, MN: Liturgical Press, 2009.

PREACHING WEDDINGS

David Scotchie

A Catholic wedding is an evangelizing event. Many present are likely not Catholic. More than a few of the Catholics present have probably not attended Mass recently. Some are divorced, some are remarried, and some are in imperfect situations.

In the midst of this mixed assembly, a man and woman are joined together to "signify and participate in the mystery of the unity and fruitful love between Christ and the Church" (*The Order of Celebrating Matrimony*, 14).[1] They publicly declare their consent to be faithful to one another, in good times and in bad, in sickness and in health, and to love and honor each other all the days of their lives. The Lord strengthens their consent with a sacred seal. This is good news!

The homily is an integral part of this evangelizing event. *The Order of Celebrating Matrimony* instructs the priest or minister to "expound the mystery of Christian Marriage, the dignity of conjugal love, the grace of the Sacrament, and the responsibilities of married people" (OCM 57, 91). Rather than give the preacher citations from the *Catechism of the Catholic Church*, the OCM gives the preacher a multitude of prayers, Scripture readings, acclamations, and ritual action that expound the mystery of Christian marriage. The rule *lex orandi legem credendi*, meaning that how we pray determines what we believe, is in full force in the liturgy for matrimony. Our understanding of marriage follows from our celebration of the wedding liturgy. This commentary is to guide the preacher to connect the Bible, the liturgy, and the homily so that the importance and dignity of marriage in the mystery of salvation is made known and the Good News is proclaimed.

---

1. *The Order of Celebrating Matrimony*, English Translation According to the Second Typical Edition (Collegeville, MN: Liturgical Press, 2016). All references are to this edition, also referred to as OCM.

Three Sections

This commentary for preaching the wedding liturgy follows the organization of the first three chapters of *The Order of Celebrating Matrimony*. The OCM has four chapters. Chapter 1 is The Order of Celebrating Matrimony within Mass. Chapter 2 is The Order of Celebrating Matrimony without Mass. Chapter 3 is The Order of Celebrating Matrimony between a Catholic and a Catechumen or a Non-Christian. (Chapter 4 is Various Texts to Be Used in the Rite of Marriage and in the Mass for the Celebration of Marriage.)

I have organized the Scripture readings, prayers, and strategies for preaching matrimony into three sections corresponding to the first three chapters of the OCM. Their organization is simply suggestive. With two qualifications that I discuss later, any of the readings and prayers given in the OCM can be in any of the three orders for celebrating matrimony. The sections are to help you match the readings and prayers with the assembly so that they hear the Good News.

Section I of this commentary is for use with chapter 1: The Order of Celebrating Matrimony within Mass. It presumes that both the bride and the groom and a substantial part of the assembly are Catholic. They have familiarity with the Mass and responses. They know when to sit and stand during Mass. They are accustomed to Scripture readings and may even have a favorite Scripture passage. The Catholic tradition is their tradition. Going beyond piety, the first section presumes that they understand what it means to be a disciple. They believe that God loves them. They have put their hope in the death and resurrection of Jesus Christ. They have committed their lives to the Lord. They have taken responsibility for their faith and help others in their faith journey. Complementing the Liturgy of the Eucharist, section I favors readings and prayers with themes of covenant, unity, and mission.

Section II of this commentary is for use with chapter 2: The Order of Celebrating Matrimony without Mass. Following the OCM, it presumes that either the bride or the groom is Catholic and that the other is a baptized non-Catholic Christian. Convalidation of a civil marriage often fits best in this second section. The readings and prayers suggested for this second section presume that many of the non-Catholic Christians present are churched. This assembly not only knows the faith; it lives the faith. Having had a conversion, bringing them to a living relationship with the risen Christ, they consider themselves to be disciples of Jesus Christ. The selected readings and prayers emphasize the Liturgy of the Word and the themes of discipleship, mission, and revelation in a marriage.

Section III of this commentary is for use with chapter 3: The Order of Celebrating Matrimony between a Catholic and a Catechumen or a Non-Christian. In this case, the bride or groom is Catholic while the other is Jewish, Muslim, Hindu, or otherwise unbaptized. At least as likely in this age, the non-Catholic bride or groom might be a "None," baptized but identifying with no religion and probably unfamiliar with Christian Scripture and ritual. For the celebration of matrimony where mature Christian faith is not certain, we favor readings and prayers with themes of unity, fidelity, and fruitfulness.

While some of the comments are specific to a section, many of the comments within each section often have general importance to the wedding liturgy. For example, the comments on the Nuptial Blessing in section II apply to the use of the Nuptial Blessing in section I and section III. The comments on the Questions and the Consent in the Celebration of Matrimony in section III are valid in sections I and II. The option to omit the blessing and giving of rings in the ceremony with a non-Christian is part of a general commentary on the rings in section I. As the readings and prayers given in each section may be used in any of the three orders for celebrating matrimony, many comments within a section pertain to all three orders for celebrating matrimony.

Listening to the Listener

Is the homily directed to the bride and groom or to the assembly? The Catholic answer is, both! Realistically, though, the bride and groom, overwhelmed by activity and preparation, are likely not at their most attentive. In general, the assembly is the main target. A sound strategy is to preach through the bride and groom and aim the wedding homily toward the assembly. This strategy raises another question. What kind of assembly is present?

Before the preacher can step into the ambo, he needs to know what kind of assembly will be listening to the preaching. Will the assembly be mainly Catholic or Protestant or non-Christian? Will their faith be reasonably mature, such as at a convalidation, or still growing in maturity, such as with a wedding of recent college graduates? Will the assembly be mainly nonbelieving Nones who were not raised in any faith tradition, or will the assembly be lifelong cultural Catholics?

I suggest that you sit down with the bride and groom to find out about their faith. They are not necessarily representative of their invited guests, but they are one important way to get to know the assembly. Here are some questions for the bride and groom that have helped me to listen to the listener:

- How did you meet? Listen for joy.
- How did you get engaged? Listen for commitment.
- Can you name some blessings coming from all of this? Listen for God.
- Why get married in the Catholic Church? Listen for belonging to the church.
- How have you dealt with suffering? Listen for the paschal mystery.
- What do you want your children to know about Jesus? Listen for discipleship.

A conversation with the couple will help you to know the couple and their story. A personal story from your conversation with the couple can become part of the homily and establish common ground with the assembly. It gains their trust, for "they don't care how much you know until they know how much you care." Time spent with the couple gives you a sense of their personal piety, their familiarity with Catholic liturgy, and their practice of the Christian life. Their responses help you to understand the assembly and how best to preach the Good News to them. Having a better understanding of the couple and their guests, and with this commentary as a guide, you can suggest appropriate Scripture readings and prayers for the wedding liturgy.[2]

Another opportunity to listen to the listener is the wedding rehearsal. The evangelizing preacher welcomes the wedding party and makes them feel at home. He may ask everyone to introduce themselves and tell how they first met the couple (good homily material!). The collect for the wed-

2. A marriage preparation resource for the couple is the website "For Your Marriage" (http://www.foryourmarriage.org/). It is an initiative of the United States Conference of Catholic Bishops. Engaged couples can find tips for planning a Catholic wedding and the many options in the liturgy. The website offers church documents on marriage and teachings on divorce, annulments, cohabitation, Natural Family Planning, between man and woman, and interfaith marriages. It has resources for parenting, family, and Catholic marriage.

ding liturgy can serve as an opening prayer for the wedding rehearsal. After each reader practices their Scripture reading from the ambo, the preacher may lead the wedding party to reflect on the Scripture. As Breaking Open the Word leads catechumens into faith, some questions for the assembly and comments on the Scripture can facilitate a deeper understanding of the sacrament of matrimony. The communal reflection on Scripture might evoke homily material. It might give you a sense of the faith of the assembly attending the ceremony. The wedding rehearsal can conclude with practicing where to sit, stand, and kneel. Your direction of the guests gains their confidence in you and assures them of the care of the church for everyone in the wedding liturgy.

Putting It All Together

Each essay has three parts: "Readings from the Ambo," "Connecting the Bible and the Liturgy," and "Strategy for Preaching."

The first part of each essay is "Readings from the Ambo." The anchor for each essay is one of the ten gospel texts given by *The Order of Celebrating Matrimony*. I offer a brief commentary on the gospel text from the perspective of the theology of marriage. Choosing from the nine Old Testament options, fourteen New Testament options, and seven responsorial psalm options, I give a short commentary on several Scripture readings that might best complement the gospel's imagery and theology. At times, one of the four gospel acclamations serves, as in the Lectionary in general, to orient the listener toward the gospel reading in a certain way.

The second part of each essay is "Connecting the Bible and the Liturgy." Having looked at Scripture, we turn to the prayers and rituals available. There are options for the collect, the Blessing and Giving of Rings, the Nuptial Blessing, and the blessing at the Conclusion of the Celebration. For matrimony within Mass, there are options for the prayer over the offering, the preface, the eucharistic prayer, and the prayer after Communion. As with the readings, I suggest which options in particular correlate with the theology and imagery of the Scripture readings.[3]

3. While it is beyond the scope of this commentary, music can play a powerful part in the preaching. The wedding music—antiphons, hymns, traditional music, the Gloria, psalms, responsories, acclamations, and dialogue—is an integral element of the celebration of matrimony, deserving a separate commentary.

As actions speak louder than words, ritual action is a vital element to consider. The American edition of *The Order of Celebrating Matrimony* introduces the customs of the *arras*, the *lazo*, and the veil. The preacher has a cornucopia of ritual actions that may strengthen the preaching: the procession, the Questions and the Consent, the Blessing and Giving of Rings, and the custom such as the kiss.[4] The church building, the crucifix, the altar, art such as stained-glass windows, and the assembled community of faith itself speak in their own way during the celebration of matrimony. As with the ritual prayers, we consider ritual action that may correlate with the Scriptures.

The third and final part of each essay is "Strategy for Preaching." So that the homily proclaims the mystery of faith to the assembly, I offer direction to the preacher based on the suggested Scripture readings, prayers, and ritual action. Each strategy depends on a focus statement and a function statement. Let me say a word about each.

The focus statement is the message, central idea, bottom line, insight, or principle that holds the homily together. It is the meat and potatoes that the assembly hungers for. Simplicity is essential, such as "God has a plan for marriage," or "Submit to be free." As the homily preparation is a discovery process, the draft focus statement is a work in progress. Preparation discovers what the texts, prayers, and rites say and do not say. Equally important, preparation discovers new things about us preachers: what we did not expect the texts, prayers, and rites to say and what we wish they would say. By definition, the focus statement says one thing. A homily that says two things is two homilies. The challenge is often finding not one idea but setting aside the other three ideas for another day.

If the focus statement is the one thing that the preacher wants the assembly to know, the function statement is what the preacher wants the assembly to do about it. The function statement is the desired effect of the message, such as "that the assembly aspire toward God's plan for marriage." The function is what this particular homily is trying to accomplish. It is the destination where the homily takes them. Answering the questions "so what?" and "now what?," the function statement gives the listener direction.

---

4. The kiss is in fact not part of the ritual. It is a custom. Instead of a kiss at the end of the liturgy, *The Order of Celebrating Matrimony* envisions an acclamation after the Consent. See the essay on OCM 186, John 15:12-16.

Changes in *The Order of Celebrating Matrimony*

The 2016 *Order of Celebrating Matrimony* second edition in English has a number of changes from the 1969 first edition. The title has changed from the *Rite of Marriage* to *The Order of Celebrating Matrimony*. The penitential rite is out. The Gloria is in (for matrimony within Mass). The OCM appendices include the Order of Blessing an Engaged Couple and the Order of Blessing of a Married Couple on the Anniversary of Marriage. For our purposes, I would like to point out two changes.[5]

The first change affecting the Scripture readings is that a wedding during Mass depends on the liturgical calendar. The ritual Mass for celebrating marriage may not take place during the Paschal Triduum; the Nativity of the Lord; the Epiphany; the Ascension; Pentecost; Sundays of Advent, Lent, and Easter; and solemnities. When a wedding cannot take place on another day, the pastoral choice may be a wedding without Mass, using any of the readings and prayers from the OCM. Another option, such as for a Saturday evening wedding Mass during Advent or Easter, is to use the Mass of the day with its own readings and presidential prayers and to include the Nuptial Blessing (OCM 34).[6]

The second change affecting the Scripture readings is that at least one reading explicitly speaking of marriage must be included in the Liturgy of the Word. This is the case whether the celebration of matrimony is within Mass, without Mass, or between a Catholic and a catechumen or a non-Christian. In chapter 4 of the OCM, which lists the various texts, these readings are marked with an asterisk. Seven of the nine Old Testament options, two of the fourteen New Testament options, one of the seven psalms, and two of the ten gospels are marked with an asterisk. This commentary includes the asterisk with the appropriate readings and lists the Scripture readings and their asterisks in appendix I.

---

5. A pastoral guide such as the book *One Love* by Paul Turner can walk you through the many details and changes in the 2016 second edition.

6. Marriage is not forbidden during Lent. "If a Marriage is celebrated on a day having a penitential character, especially during Lent, the pastor is to counsel the spouses to take into account the special nature of that day" (OCM 32). As a practical matter, marriage during Lent is like Christmas in July. Lenten weddings are celebrated most often for the convalidation of the marriages of those entering the church during the Easter season.

Pope Francis wrote, "Love always gives life."[7] The Catholic wedding gives life in its proclamation of the life-giving love between Christ and the church. Word and sacrament, Scripture and prayer, homily and ritual action, come together to proclaim the good news of Jesus Christ. Through the celebration of matrimony, the bride and groom are no longer two but one, and the Good News is made known.

Section I: Preaching Matrimony within Mass

Section I accompanies chapter 1: The Order of Celebrating Matrimony within Mass in *The Order of Celebrating Matrimony*. It presumes that both the bride and the groom and a substantial part of the assembly are Catholic. They make the sign of the cross and respond, "And with your spirit." Some Scripture readings are familiar to them, and they may have a favorite Scripture verse or story. The Catholic tradition is their faith tradition.

Faith is more than pious practice. Beyond piety, the first section presumes that the couple and the assembly have faith. They believe that God exists and that he loves them. They have encountered Jesus Christ and trust in him. They believe that Jesus suffered, died, and rose from the dead, and that in the end they will share his victory in heaven. Having committed their lives to the Lord, they believe that all aspects of their lives, including sexuality and family life, live out the mission to love as Jesus taught and lived.[8]

The faith of many adult Catholics, beginning with the bride and groom, cannot be assumed to be a mature faith. More than one Catholic couple has had a nuptial Mass simply because one of the mothers insisted upon it. But for the purpose of this commentary, we are assuming that the celebration of matrimony within Mass means they are "churched" and show evidence of a living, mature faith.

7. Francis, *Amoris Laetitia* (Post-Synodal Apostolic Exhortation, *On Love in the Family*, March 19, 2016), 165.

8. For an inspiring profession of faith in the context of the family, see the Summary Statement from the World Meeting of Families, *Love Is Our Mission: The Family Fully Alive*, a preparatory catechesis for the World Meeting of Families (Philadelphia: World Meeting of Families, 2014), 6–7.

As this section is for the nuptial Mass, the readings and prayers chosen for this first section reflect themes from the Liturgy of the Eucharist. The teaching on divorce in Matthew (OCM *181) highlights the blessing of the unity and indissolubility of marriage. Marriage is not a purely human institution but part of God's plan written into the nature of man and woman created by God. The wedding at Cana (OCM *184), the first of Jesus' signs, points to him as the Bridegroom and the church as the bride. It signifies the messianic age that Jesus brings. In the gospel from John 17, the High Priest's prayer, Jesus prays "that they all be one," consistent with communion in the Mass (OCM 187). For the celebration of matrimony within Mass, we favor readings and prayers with themes of covenant, unity, and mission.

OCM *181. Matthew 19:3-6

"What God has united, man must not separate."

Readings from the Ambo

The Order of Celebrating Matrimony within Mass provides a set of readings for the Liturgy of the Word (OCM 56). While the preacher has a wide selection of Scripture to mix and match, the *Order of Celebrating Matrimony* editors selected a reading from the Old Testament, a psalm, a reading from the New Testament, and a gospel that particularly express the importance and dignity of marriage. Let us look at these readings in the sequence that the listener will hear them.

The first reading provided by the OCM is from the first chapter of Genesis (OCM *144). This text is part of the first reading that begins the Liturgy of the Word in the Easter Vigil. The first of the two creation stories, it differs from the creation story in the second chapter of Genesis in that it tells us that God created humanity in his image, "male and female he created them." God who is love created humanity out of love. The mutual love of man and woman is an image of the abiding and supreme love of the Creator for humanity. This mutual love is meant to be a fertile and fruitful continuation of the work of creation. Additionally, the first creation story suggests a liturgical procession. In the beginning when all was chaos and darkness, God created light and saw that it was good. Merely uttering a word, he then created the sky, earth, and sea. Next came trees and plants, the sun and the moon, birds in the air and fish in the waters, and the animals tame, wild, and crawling. Last of all, he created man and woman. The sequence of creation, like a liturgical procession, tells us that the creation of male and female in the image of God is the crown of creation. God looked at all he made and found it very good.

The psalm provided by the OCM is Psalm 128 (OCM *171). It is the only psalm with an asterisk, which signifies that it explicitly speaks of marriage. It echoes the command from the Genesis reading "fill the earth and subdue it" with the phrase "By the labor of your hands you shall eat." Passing over the optional refrain, "See how the Lord blesses those who fear him," the refrain given is "Blessed are those who fear the Lord." Our modern ear, associating fear of someone with domination, threat, and violence, has trouble with the ancient phrase "fear of the Lord." To our ancestors in faith, however, fear of the Lord meant reverence. Psalm 128 tells us that those who fear the Lord (or better, revere the Lord) and walk in his ways will be blessed with prosperity, a wife like a fruitful vine, and abundant children like shoots of the olive tree. The final verse of this short psalm of ascent offers a lyrical blessing, "May you see your children's children."[9]

The second reading provided by the OCM is the Letter of St. Paul to the Ephesians (OCM *159). That the modern listener perhaps hears better the connection with the Genesis reading, it skips over the full pericope in Ephesians chapter 5 that notoriously exhorts, "Wives should be subordinate to their husbands as to the Lord." Instead, the short form of the reading instructs husbands to "love your wives, / even as Christ loved the Church." The bond of man and woman from the beginning of creation becomes something more when both spouses are baptized into Christ's death and resurrection. The Christian union of male and female, made in the image of God who is communion, symbolizes and lives out the spousal love of Christ and the church. Loyalty and devotion in Christian marriage reflects Christ who loved the church and gave himself for her sanctification.

Interestingly, the gospel acclamation provided by the OCM is not one of the four options in the OCM, chapter 4, or in the Lectionary. The acclamation "May the Lord bless you from Zion, he who made both heaven

---

9. Pope Francis begins his post-synodal apostolic exhortation *On Love in the Family* with the first chapter almost entirely dedicated to his reflection on Psalm 128 (see *Amoris Laetitia*, 8–26).

and earth" (Ps 134:3) recalls the creation story from the first reading and the blessings of Psalm 128. In general, the gospel acclamation is more than travel music from the presider's chair to the ambo. It is a lens to look at the gospel reading. The choice of this particular acclamation cues the listener to expect the gospel reading to be about how God the Creator blesses us.

The gospel reading provided by the OCM to complete the set of Scripture readings is Jesus' response to a question about divorce (OCM *181). He references the second creation story in Genesis where "the two shall become one flesh," joined together by God. The unbreakable union of two lives recalls the plan of the Creator "from the beginning." The choice of this gospel reading in light of the gospel acclamation highlights the blessing of the unity and indissolubility of marriage. Marriage is not a purely human institution. It is part of God's plan written into the nature of man and woman created by God. Through marriage, God blesses us.

Connecting the Bible and the Liturgy

Through these Scripture readings, from the unfolding of creation within Genesis to the deepening reflection on marriage in subsequent readings, we see movement. The scriptural understanding of marriage is not static any more than the big bang is static. There is movement from seeing marriage as a natural bond to seeing marriage as a reflection of Christ's union with his church. Liturgically, the entrance procession captures this movement. Like the creation story, the entrance procession of a wedding dramatically sets in motion the fruits of months of planning.

The OCM offers two forms of the entrance in the introductory rites. In the First Form envisioned (OCM 45–47), the priest warmly welcomes the bridal party at the door of the church to help them transition from the secular world to the sacred. The liturgical ministers process to the altar as for a normal Sunday Mass. The bride and groom can enter last and together as they are the principal ministers of marriage and confer the sacrament on each other.[10] The Second Form (OCM 48–50) does not

---

10. The custom where the father walks the bride down the aisle and gives her away to the groom is in contrast to the reality that the bride is not property to be handed over. The bride, not the father, gives her free consent to the marriage. Consider the reaction if the mother walked the groom down the aisle and handed him over to the bride.

mention a procession. The priest simply greets the couple warmly when they arrive at their place. No explanation how they arrive is given.

In planning the liturgy with these readings provided by the OCM as a set, an inspiring conversation may encourage the couple to set aside tradition to embrace Tradition. Their side-by-side entrance in a single procession would cue the assembly that something different is happening. The First Form of the entrance procession sets the stage to go beyond the social custom of marriage and instead recall God's plan for marriage and its place as the crown in the order of creation. Finally, the entrance procession for the nuptial Mass following the norm of the entrance procession for Sunday Mass puts the marriage in its ecclesial context. It announces that the couple is not marrying in isolation from the church community but is marrying "in the church" literally and liturgically.

The Roman Missal offers three sets of Mass formularies (A, B, and C) for the celebration of marriage found in the ritual Masses. The rubric in the Roman Missal makes clear that the prayers and Nuptial Blessing in one set of Mass formularies may be exchanged with other prayers. Formulary A, complementing Matthew 19:3-6, emphasizes the indissolubility of marriage with phrases such as "a bond of inseparable love" (Collect OCM 189), "a sweet yoke of harmony," and "an unbreakable bond of peace" (Preface OCM 199). Formulary B, complementing Ephesians 5, has phrases such as "foreshadow the Sacrament of Christ and his Church" (Collect OCM 188) and "a sign of Christ's loving gift of grace" (Preface OCM 200). The Nuptial Blessing in Formulary B (OCM 207) in particular echoes Genesis 1 with phrases such as "formed man in your own image, male and female you created them" and praying that God the Father "graciously crown with your blessings your daughter." Either Formulary A or B in the Roman Missal fits well with the given readings, and additional exchanges in the prayers can even more adjust the fit.[11]

The final liturgical element for celebrating matrimony within Mass is the blessing at the Conclusion of the Celebration. At the conclusion of the Mass, the priest or deacon greets the people, "The Lord be with you," to which they respond, "And with your spirit." As in the Roman Missal, the

---

11. Appendix II of this commentary details the prayers selected in the Roman Missal for the Formularies A, B, and C for the celebration of marriage.

priest or deacon instructs, "Bow down for the blessing," before extending his hands over the bride and bridegroom to give them the threefold solemn blessing.[12]

The solemn blessing is a triple blessing of the couple followed by a blessing of all who are gathered. Each blessing is slightly different. OCM 213, "May you be witnesses in the world to God's charity, so that the afflicted and needy who have known your kindness may one day receive you thankfully into the eternal dwelling of God," makes explicit the missionary meaning of marriage. OCM 214 is trinitarian, with a blessing each from God the all-powerful Father, the Only Begotten Son of God, and the Holy Spirit of God. Interestingly, OCM 215 is a triple blessing from the Lord Jesus. Although a music setting is not given, chanting the final blessing would help the assembly to respond "Amen" to each of the three blessings.

Strategy for Preaching

Scriptural Texts: *Genesis 1:26-28, 31a; *Psalm 128; *Ephesians 5:2a, 25-32; *Matthew 19:3-6[13]

Liturgical Texts: Collect OCM 189; Preface OCM 200; Nuptial Blessing OCM 205; Solemn Blessing OCM 213

The Gospel of Matthew, chapter 19, has strong words about divorce. Considering that some in the assembly may be divorced, this can appear awkward. But instead of explaining away Jesus' teaching or conversely indulging in stern words, the homily can help all present to look beyond their struggles and inspire them to seek what God has intended from the beginning of creation.

---

12. The solemn blessing is obligatory in the celebration of matrimony within Mass (OCM 77). When Mass is not celebrated and Holy Communion is not distributed, the final blessing of the people immediately follows after the Nuptial Blessing of the bride and bridegroom. The minister blesses the people using the simple form, saying, "May almighty God bless all of you, who are gathered here, the Father, and the Son, and the Holy Spirit," to which the people reply, "Amen" (OCM 116, 141). When Holy Communion is distributed without Mass, the rite concludes with either the solemn form or the simple form of blessing (OCM 116).

13. Note that at least one reading designated with an asterisk (*) must be used in the wedding liturgy.

After the entrance procession and before the Communion procession, there is the preparation of the gifts.[14] Coming after the bride and groom have given their consent and rings, the procession of the bread and wine to the altar seems like an anticlimactic lull in the action. In actuality, the procession at the preparation of the gifts is the hinge between the entrance procession and the Communion procession. The sequence of the three processions can provide three moves in a homily whose focus statement can be "God has a plan" and whose function is to encourage the assembly to aspire to God's plan for marriage.

The preacher can first draw the connection between God creating heaven and earth and the couple planning the wedding day. In other words, the "creation" of the wedding day is like the creation of heaven and earth and all that fills them. Made in the image and likeness of God, the bride and possibly the groom have spent months "creating" this day: planning the events, inviting guests, and dealing with surprises. From nothing they have created something, and they see that it is good. What they have done is to live out their nature, made in the image and likeness of God, to create.

As the wedding is for a day and marriage is for a lifetime, creation similarly set all things in motion. It was only the beginning of God's plan. God is the Creator with a capital C. We who are made in his image are creators with a small c. As such, we have a role in God's plan. The preparation of the gifts begins with the procession of bread and wine. Unlike the entrance procession of the bride and groom, it does not stop at the foot of the altar. It goes all the way forward. The bread and wine are placed on the altar of the Lord. The priest prays, "Blessed are you, Lord God of all creation, / for through your goodness we have received / the bread we offer you: / fruit of the earth and work of human hands, / it will become for us the bread of life." In other words, God the Creator gave us grains of wheat that we grow, harvest, mill, and bake to make bread. Our hands change hard grain into delicious bread that feeds our bodies. God takes the bread we offer him on his altar and, through the power of the Holy Spirit, changes the bread into the Body of Christ. It becomes the Bread of Life which feeds our souls. We are cocreators with God. When we offer him what we have received from him, he wonderfully transforms it and us.

---

14. The OCM specifies that the bride and bridegroom, if appropriate, may bring the bread and wine to the altar (OCM 70).

This explanation of the preparation of the gifts can serve as an image of marriage. The natural bond of a man and woman, who are made in the image of God and declared very good, becomes in the hands of God a sacrament. It is not only very good. It is holy. It reveals Christ's union with his church. Christ's sacrifice that we celebrate at Mass gives grace to the bride and groom so that they love each other, renounce themselves, and take up their crosses daily. Their marriage gives witness to the covenant between Christ and his church.

The homily makes the link to Communion when it concludes with the third procession, the Communion procession. Processing to the altar at Communion, the bride and groom and all the faithful receive the Body and Blood of Christ. They share in the union that Christ has made with his church. This preaching strategy moves an assembly broken by divorce and limited in its dreams to embrace God's dream that all might one day process to the altar and renew their communion with Christ.

OCM *184. John 2:1-11

"Jesus did this as the beginning of his signs at Cana in Galilee."

Readings from the Ambo

"There was a wedding in Cana in Galilee . . ." So begins the familiar story. The wine runs out (one commentator speculated that the presence of twelve fishermen might have been a contributing factor), Jesus provides "good wine" from six stone water jars, and his disciples begin to believe in him (OCM *184). The final verse punches the point highlighted in the *Order of Celebrating Matrimony* heading, that "Jesus did this as the beginning of his signs in Cana in Galilee and so revealed his glory" (John 2:11). In short, the story reveals that Jesus is the Messiah.

Earlier in the story, the presence of only six stone water jars hints at Jesus' true identity. The number six was a sign that something was missing. Seven is a number that means "complete." For example, a complete week has seven days. The seven days of the week recall the seven days of creation when God created the heavens and the earth in six days and rested on the seventh. The fact that there were only six stone water jars meant that one jar was missing. Where was the seventh? Another clue to understanding the story is its placement in the Sunday Lectionary, Year

C. In the Sunday Lectionary, the wedding in Cana follows two Sundays of theophanies, the Epiphany of the Lord and the Baptism of the Lord. In the Scripture and in the liturgy, therefore, the wedding in Cana is not only about Jesus blessing marriages. It is a theophany. In sign language, through actions louder than words, the sign of the water-become-wine pointed to Jesus himself. He had come to transform not just water into wine. He had come to transform sinners into believers. He had come to usher in the messianic age and transform the world. The story of the wedding in Cana reveals the restoration of the marital covenant between God and his people in Jesus Christ.

The Old Testament selection from the prophet Jeremiah (OCM 152) sets up the expectation of the restoration of the covenant between God and his people. "The days are coming, says the LORD, / when I will make a new covenant with the house of Israel / and the house of Judah." Unlike the covenant made between the Lord and his people at Mt. Sinai and written on stone tablets, the Lord will write this covenant upon their hearts. No longer will they need to teach how to know the Lord. They shall know the Lord. The sign of the promised covenant is not a rainbow in the sky signaling the end of the Great Flood. It is not a circumcision that changes the body as in the covenant with Abraham. It is not even a change in behavior required by the law given to Moses. The sign of the new covenant is the memorial of the death and resurrection of Jesus Christ celebrated and renewed in the Mass. In the words of St. Paul, the sign is the circumcision of the heart that changes one's heart (Rom 2:25-29). The people do not just know about the Lord. They know the Lord. Jeremiah ends with the stirring divine assertion that has sounded through the ages, "I will be their God, and they shall be my people" (Jer 31:31-32a, 33-34a).

For a responsorial psalm fitting to the covenant anticipated in Jeremiah, Psalm 34 invites us with the refrain, "Taste and see the goodness of the Lord" (OCM 168). The covenant with the Lord is not just an idea that is nice to think about. It is a reality that we can taste and see, touch and behold, in our own experience. The psalmist blesses the Lord and praises him. His soul boasts in the Lord, and the humble are gladdened. We are given an invitation, "Glorify the LORD with me; / together let us praise his name." The call is repeated, "Look toward him and be radiant; / let your faces not be abashed." The psalmist encourages us with his own experience that the Lord has set him free from all his terrors. The Lord heard his call and rescued him from all his distress (Ps 34:2-3, 4-5, 6-7,

8-9). The experiences of the Lord's goodness that we can taste and see are signs of the covenant he has made with us. Similarly, the marriage covenant is where we can taste and see the goodness of the Lord.

The New Testament selection from the book of Revelation (OCM 166) brings out the marital meaning of the covenant implicit in Jeremiah and John. The visionary heard the multitude in heaven praising God, "Alleluia! / Salvation, glory, and might belong to our God." Again, "Praise our God, all you his servants, / and you who revere him, small and great." And finally, an invitation to rejoice and be glad and give him glory, "For the wedding day of the Lamb has come." Revelation echoes Hosea, Isaiah, and Ezekiel who described the covenant as a marriage. "For as a young man marries a virgin, your Builder shall marry you; and as a bridegroom rejoices in his bride so shall your God rejoice in you" (Isa 62:5). The Lord God is the Bridegroom who rejoices in his people. The church is the bride, dressed in bright, clean garments representing the righteous deeds of the holy ones. It is no coincidence that the Revelation text is the New Testament canticle in the Liturgy of the Hours for Sunday Evening Prayer. Concluding each Sunday, it underscores that the Mass is the wedding feast of the Lamb. The selection from Revelation culminates with the angel instructing John in his vision to write, "Blessed are those who have been called to the wedding feast of the Lamb" (Rev 19:1, 5-9a).

Connecting the Bible and the Liturgy

One moment where these Scripture readings and the liturgy connect is Holy Communion during the nuptial Mass. We heard in the reading from the book of Revelation, "Blessed are those who have been called to the wedding feast of the Lamb." It reappears almost word for word as the priest lifts up the Host and chalice just before Communion and says, "Blessed are those called to the supper of the Lamb." The words connect covenant with Communion.

The US bishops wrote in 2009 an inspiring and instructive pastoral letter, "Marriage: Love and Life in the Divine Plan." In their conclusion, they aim marriage toward eternal life. The love of spouses finds its completion in the end of time when the entire church is assumed into the glory of the risen Christ. The church itself fully receives the self-giving love of her spouse—the Lord Jesus Christ. "This is the glorious wedding supper of the Lamb, to which the Spirit and the Bride say—Come! (Rev 19:9;

22:17). Just as Christ once proclaimed the greatness of marriage by his presence at the wedding feast in Cana, so now, at the heavenly wedding banquet, marriage and all the blessings of the Holy Spirit, given to us by the Father through Christ, his Son, will find their ultimate consummation because we will be in perfect union with God." Christian marriage, like the communion shared at the supper of the Lamb, foreshadows our perfect union with God. Marriage is a sign and instrument of the communion offered us by God in Christ. It is a sacrament.

An important sign in the celebration of matrimony is the Blessing and Giving of Rings (OCM 66–67A). When the couple gives their consent and the minister receives it, they become husband and wife. They next give rings to one another. The rings are a physical sign to accompany the words of marriage.

The priest or deacon blesses the rings "as a sign of love and fidelity." The OCM offers two other formulas for the blessing of rings. One adds "so that those who wear them / may remain entirely faithful to each other, / abide in peace and in your will, / and live always in mutual charity" (OCM 194). In the other prayer for the blessing of rings, the priest or deacon blesses the couple instead of the rings, saying, "Bless and sanctify your servants / in their love, O Lord, / and let these rings, a sign of their faithfulness, / remind them of their love for one another" (OCM 195). The presider has the option to sprinkle the rings with holy water before giving them to the couple.

The husband places his wife's ring on her ring finger and may say, "N., receive this ring / as a sign of my love and fidelity. / In the name of the Father, and of the Son, / and of the Holy Spirit."[15] The first edition of the OCM reads, "Take this ring." The verb "receive" in the second edition of the OCM instead captures the giving of the ring from one spouse to the other, who "receives" the ring like a gift rather than "takes" it. The wife says and does likewise with her husband's ring. A hymn or canticle of praise may be sung by the whole community to underscore the giving of rings (OCM 68).[16]

15. The husband and wife may recite the ring formula. It is not required. The rubric instructs, "The husband places his wife's ring on her ring finger, saying, as the circumstances so suggest . . ." (OCM 67A).

16. In the ceremony with a non-Christian, the trinitarian formula, "In the name of the Father, and of the Son, and of the Holy Spirit," may be omitted (OCM 132). Going further, if circumstances such as cultural reasons so suggest, the Blessing and Giving of Rings may be omitted (OCM 131).

According to Paul Turner, Clement in the first century and Tertullian in the third century mention the engagement ring. A ring ceremony took place at the ninth-century wedding of the daughter of Charles the Bald to Ethelwulf, king of East Anglia. The ring on the fourth finger, also known as the ring finger, is from the belief that a vein in that finger carries the blood to the heart. With this long history, the rings worn by the husband and wife have become a widespread sign of marriage.[17]

Another sign of unity in the nuptial Mass is the sign of peace. Immediately following the Nuptial Blessing in the wedding Mass, the presider says, "The peace of the Lord be with you always." The bride and bridegroom and all present offer one another a sign that expresses peace and charity (OCM 75). If in keeping with local custom, that sign may be the kiss of peace.[18] It is important to note that the sign of peace is placed before Holy Communion instead of after the couple's Consent, meaning that the sign of peace is not a celebration of matrimony. The sign of peace is a preparation for Holy Communion.[19]

Strategy for Preaching

*Scriptural Texts: Jeremiah 31:31-32a, 33-34a; Psalm 34; Revelation 19:1, 5-9a; *John 2:1-11*

Liturgical Texts: Collect OCM 188; Preface OCM 201; Nuptial Blessing OCM 207; Solemn Blessing OCM 214

As you reflect on the Scripture and the wedding liturgy, consider to whom you are speaking. In a nuptial Mass, you might well assume that the assembly is mostly Catholic and mostly churched. They would have some familiarity with the ideas, if not the words, of covenant, sacrament, and sign. Next you consider what you want to say to them, the one thing that you want them to know that flows from the Scripture and liturgy.

---

17. Paul Turner, *Inseparable Love: A Commentary on* The Order of Celebrating Matrimony *in the Catholic Church* (Collegeville, MN: Liturgical Press, 2017), 102–11.

18. Some couples give flowers to their parents. The instruction from OCM 29 allows for appropriate local customs.

19. The sign of peace is part of the wedding without Mass only if Holy Communion is distributed. In the wedding ceremony with a catechumen or a non-Christian, as there is no Holy Communion, there is no sign of peace.

The message preached from the wedding in Cana and the nuptial Mass might be, "Marriage points to Christ and his church." The formation of the message statement might benefit from imagining a title or a short phrase posted on the church roadside sign to capture interest of those driving by. A roadside title for this message might be the pun "Sign Language Spoken Here." With these decisions made, the homily is ready to take shape. This homily sketch has four moves. Starting with personal experience about the sign language of marriage, it looks next at the sign language of married love through the lens of Scripture. The third move reveals the "Aha!" The fourth move answers the question "So what?" Finally, the conclusion directs the assembly to look in a different light at the marriage and the Mass.

A good place to begin a homily is with a relevant personal experience. For example, while visiting families to bless their homes, I like to ask the kids, "How do you know that your mom and dad love each other?" "They kiss." The kids squirm. "They hold hands." I prod, "Do they have special names for each other?" The children look at each other and then at their parents. "Mom calls him 'Sweetie.' Dad calls her 'Darling.'" The children tell me that their parents get a babysitter and go on date nights. They see their parents cuddle on the couch. Sometimes they even tell me that their parents pray together. Their mom always wears her fancy diamond ring and their dad always wears his simple gold band (except when he is washing dishes). What the children are telling me is that marriage has its own sign language. They see their parents say without words that they love and honor each other, and the children notice. Relating my personal experience from these home visits, besides establishing the preacher as sincere and trustworthy, orients the assembly to expect the homily to be about how we know that a couple loves each other.

The homily builds on experiences that kids might not see. When a husband changes the diapers of his wife suffering from Alzheimer's disease, his care recalls his wedding promise to be faithful in sickness and in health. When a married couple makes the decision to pass on a promotion at work so that they have more time with the family, they put into action the wedding promise to accept children lovingly from God and raise them in the faith. Their actions speak louder than words. What is the most loving sign language of marriage? When couples tell me that their wedding anniversary is coming and they would like to renew their wedding promises, my first thought is, "Get a room!" Giving themselves entirely to each other in conjugal union is the sign language of marriage. It renews their consent given on their wedding day, "I promise to be faithful to you all the days of my life." Holy matrimony speaks with sign language. Beyond a ring on the finger, the actions of a man and woman say loud and clear, "We're married!" for people to see.

Having considered several examples of the sign language of married love, the second move in the homily looks at the sign language of married love through the lens of Scripture. Referring to the story of the wedding in Cana, your first statement builds a bit of suspense when you assert that the six stone water jars were a sign that something was missing. Recall that when the wine had run short, the mother of Jesus told the servers, "Do whatever he tells you." Jesus took charge and told the servers, "Fill the jars with water." The story tells us that there were six water jars at the wedding for the Jewish ceremonial washings, each holding twenty to thirty gallons. The number six was a sign that something was missing. Seven is a number that means "complete." The walls of Jericho came tumbling down after Joshua commanded seven priests with seven trumpets to march around Jericho seven times. Not six times. Seven. Jesus said to his disciples, "Forgive not seven times but seventy-seven times." Six times or even sixty-six times was not enough. In the Acts of Apostles, the apostles appointed several men to serve the people. Guess how many they chose? Seven. Those seven men were the first deacons. The book of Revelation was written to the churches in Asia Minor. Any idea how many churches there were? Seven. When Jesus was crucified at about the sixth hour (around noon, see Luke 23:44), this was not a time check. It meant that something more was to come. There certainly was—the resurrection of Jesus from the dead—but that's another story. After naming a number of examples of sixes and sevens in Scripture, you repeat that the number six means that something is missing. Six gives us a heads up to look forward to more to come. The fact that there were only six stone water jars meant that something was missing. Where was the seventh jar? The question builds suspense. (Who could have imagined that Scripture was exciting?)

The third move makes the connection between the sign language of marriage in the first move and the sign language of the six stone water jars in the second move. It relieves the suspense with an "Aha!" as you remind the listeners that the story of the wedding in Cana ends with the punchline, "Jesus did this as the beginning of his signs in Cana in Galilee." In other words, the water-become-wine was not a party trick. It was not merely a miracle. It was a sign. In sign language, through actions louder than words, the sign of the water-become-wine pointed to Jesus himself. He had come to transform not just water into wine. He had come to transform sinners into believers, darkness into light, and the cross into the resurrection. He had come to transform the world. Like the good wine served after the inferior wine, Jesus Christ is the good wine. He is the missing seventh jar that completes the six stone water jars. He is the long-awaited Savior who, like good wine, brings joy to the world.

The fourth move answers the question "So what?" It might be of interest that both marriage and the six stone jars speak in sign language. The discussion about the numbers six and seven was novel. The listeners, however, want more than information. They are thirsting for inspiration. And inspiration takes place when you help them imagine what happens when Jesus and marriage connect. The key here is the wine. Wine, after all, means joy. When someone invites you to a party, you do not say, "Great, I'll bring the water!" No. If you want to be invited to the next party, you bring a bottle of wine. Wine makes a gathering into a party. Wine and a champagne toast make a wedding reception into a wedding celebration. Hilaire Belloc connected the Catholic faith with wine and joy when he penned, "Wherever the Catholic sun doth shine, There's always laughter and good red wine." Yes, we need bread to survive. But we need wine to thrive. Wine makes life worth living. On another occasion, Jesus compared himself to a grapevine. A grapevine grows grapes that become wine. He tells his disciples to remain in him and bear fruit. In other words, remain in him to become joy-giving wine. "I have told you this so that my joy may be in you and your joy may be complete" (John 15:11). Each of those six stone water jars held twenty or thirty gallons of water-become-wine. Imagine 150 gallons of fine red wine! Jesus, the long-awaited Savior, came to bring joy to the world. This is the inspiration we long to hear.

A good conclusion does not summarize what you just said any more than the final verse of the wedding in Cana summarizes the story. Instead, the conclusion directs the assembly to look in a different light at what takes place next. Namely, in a few minutes, we bring bread and wine to the altar. Through the Holy Spirit, the bread and wine become the bread of life and the cup of salvation, the Body and Blood of Christ. They are our communion with Christ so that we remain in him and he in us. But first, we invoke the same Holy Spirit upon N. and N. They declare their consent before God and his church to enter into the covenant of holy matrimony. In the sacrament of matrimony, they are transformed. They are no longer just N. and N. They become a sign. Their married life forever points to Jesus Christ, who loves us as a young man loves his beloved and as a husband loves his wife. Through the marriage of N. and N., may the joy of Christ be theirs in abundance. Through their marriage, may the joy of Christ overflow into the world.

OCM 187. John 17:20-26 (or Short Form 17:20-23)

"That they may be brought to perfection as one."

Readings from the Ambo

At the Last Supper in the Gospel of John, Jesus gives his farewell discourse. Jesus tells the disciples about the coming of the Holy Spirit, the Advocate. He tells them that he is the vine and they are the branches. He concludes the farewell discourse with a prayer to his Father. He raises his eyes to heaven and says, "Father, the hour has come. Give glory to your son, so that your son may glorify you" (John 17:1). His prayer, known as the High Priestly Prayer, reveals the intimacy between Jesus and his Father, an intimacy that Jesus prays that his followers share. Mainly a prayer of intercession as opposed to a prayer of praise or a prayer of thanksgiving, Jesus prays for glory (17:1-8), Jesus prays for his disciples (17:9-19), and Jesus prays for those who believe in him through his disciples' word (17:20-26).[20]

This third part of the High Priestly Prayer, John 17:20-26, is the gospel selection given at OCM 187.[21] Jesus prays that they may all be one as he and the Father are one. The unity of his believers with one another and with the Father and Son, however, is not only for their own sake. After praying "that

20. Brendan Byrne, *Life Abounding: A Reading of John's Gospel* (Collegeville, MN: Liturgical Press, 2014), 280–81.
21. The short form of the gospel text in the OCM, John 17:20-23, zeroes in on Jesus' prayer for the unity of his followers. It omits verses 24-26 where Jesus adds that he knows the Father and has made known the Father's name but that the world does not know him.

they may be brought to perfection as one," he adds, "that the world may know that you sent me, / and that you loved them even as you loved me." In other words, the unity of the community of believers gives witness to the world and draws others to conversion. In the context of the wedding liturgy, the "two become one" is missionary. It is not only about the couple. The "two become one" is for others. The unitive love of marriage reveals the unifying love of God "who so loved the world that he gave his only Son" (John 3:16). Jesus' prayer leads to action. After his High Priestly Prayer, Jesus goes out with his disciples across the Kidron Valley to the garden to enter into his glory.

From the Old Testament offerings, the second selection from the book of Tobit is also a prayer (OCM *148). The book of Tobit is a combination of Arabian Nights romance, Jewish piety, and moral teaching. The tale begins with the God-fearing and virtuous Tobit in exile in Assyria. He tells the reader how as an act of mercy he buried a kinsman who had been murdered (probably strangled by the authorities and left in public as further humiliation). Unclean from touching the dead, Tobit slept outside. Proving that no good deed went unpunished, sparrows perched on the wall above him, and their warm droppings settled in his eyes and brought about blindness. Tobit, blind and no longer able to work, fell into poverty. After a falling out with his wife, Tobit was at the end of his rope. He prayed for death. Meanwhile, his distant relative Sarah had been given in marriage seven times to seven husbands. But the wicked demon Asmodeus kept killing off her husbands on their wedding night. Everyone knew she was cursed, and even Sarah's maid mocked her. Like Tobit, Sarah prayed for death. God heard the prayers of Tobit and Sarah. When Tobit commissioned his son Tobiah to collect a deposit of money in the town where Sarah lived, the angel Raphael went with Tobiah to guide his journey and arrange his marriage with Sarah and deal with her jealous demon.

The Order of Celebrating Matrimony offers two selections from the book of Tobit. The first selection is the scene where Raguel, the father of the hapless Sarah, welcomed Tobiah and gladly gave him the hand of Sarah along with a frank word of warning about the fate of the seven previous suitors (OCM *147). The second selection offered by the OCM picks up the story where, after their marriage ceremony, the couple was left alone in the cursed wedding chamber. Tobiah rose from bed and said, "Sister, get up. Let us pray and beg our Lord / to have mercy on us and to grant us deliverance." He began the prayer with praise. "Blessed are you, O God of our fathers; / praised be your name forever and ever." Only after blessing the Lord for making Adam and Eve and through them the human race, Tobiah asked the Lord to send down his mercy that he and Sarah may grow old together (OCM *148). Then they went to bed. Meanwhile, Raguel, the father of the bride, dug a grave. Fully expecting an eighth dead son-in-law, he sent a maid to check whether Tobiah was dead yet. The maid returned to Raguel and reported that both were asleep and very much alive. The curse had been broken. No doubt thrilled that he had paid for his final wedding, Raguel threw a fourteen-day wedding feast. Tobiah went on to collect the money, and his father Tobit was healed of his blindness. Tobit concluded the tale with a song of joyful praise, "Blessed be God who lives forever, / because his kingship lasts for all ages" (Tob 13:1-18).[22]

Two responsorial psalms go well with Tobiah's wedding night prayer of praise and protection. The responsorial verse of Psalm 145 invites us to exclaim, "How good is the Lord to all." The first stanza extols the Lord who is kind, full of compassion, slow to anger, and abounding in mercy. The second stanza addresses the Lord directly and gives thanks, for "you give them their food in due season." The third stanza echoes the first stanza, proclaiming that the Lord is righteous and holy and close to all who call upon him (OCM 172). Another fitting responsorial psalm is Psalm 148. A psalm of praise, Psalm 148 exhorts the angels and all his hosts to praise the Lord, as well as the sun and moon, shining stars, mountains and hills, fruit trees and cedars, and creeping things and birds on the wing. In short, all of creation is to give praise to the Lord. The psalm exhorts the people—kings of the earth, princes, judges, young men and maidens, old and young together—to do the same as creation and give praise to the Lord. The response says it all, "Let all praise the name of the Lord." These two psalms reverberate with the praise that Tobiah and Sarah lifted up on their wedding night. With all of creation, the church must give praise to the Lord.

Connecting the Bible and the Liturgy

Like Tobiah and Sarah on their wedding night, the first action of the newly married husband and wife is prayer. Having given their consent

---

22. The story of Tobiah and Sarah has a fairy-tale ending. Yet the story has a twist that few fairy tales have: Tobiah and Sarah prayed together on their wedding night. Only after they gave praise to God did they pray for themselves. And they lived happily ever after!

and exchanged rings, they join the assembly in the Universal Prayer, also known as the prayer of the faithful (OCM 69). Before their wedding reception and honeymoon, the freshly married couple prays with the assembly for the church and for the world.

Interceding for others follows from our participation in the mystery of Jesus Christ. We have seen how Jesus the High Priest prayed for the unity of those who believe in him (John 17). All who have received the sacrament of baptism share in Christ's priestly identity. The book of Revelation says that Christ "has made us into a kingdom, priests for his God and Father" (Rev 1:6). The baptized, including married couples, have the responsibility and authority to pray for others. The first letter of Peter, recalling the promise that God made to the Israelites on Mount Sinai, tells us that "you are 'a chosen race, a royal priesthood, a holy nation, a people of his own, so that you may announce the praises' of him who called you out of darkness into his wonderful light" (2:9). Mingling politics and religion, the mixed metaphor "a royal priesthood" describes who we are before God. We are mediators before God on behalf of those in darkness that they too may be called into his wonderful light.

The liturgy provides for the Body of Christ to exercise its priestly ministry of intercession. The *General Instruction to the Roman Missal* instructs that "in the Universal Prayer or Prayer of the Faithful, the people respond in some sense to the Word of God which they have received in faith and, exercising the office of their baptismal Priesthood, offer prayers to God for the salvation of all."[23] In other words, the assembly moves from communal listening to communal prayer.[24] Having heard the word of God and its promise of salvation, the assembly speaks up. It asks the Lord to make his kingdom come here and now for the church, public authorities, the burdened, and the local community. Another intercessory moment in the liturgy is in the eucharistic prayer, when the assembly intercedes that the church and all its members, living and dead, become one Body, one spirit in Christ. The nuptial Mass, as every Mass, is itself a prayer of praise lifted up by the priestly people.

The Universal Prayer takes place in a slightly different place when the Creed is required. On the first four parts listed in the Table of Liturgical

---

23. *The Roman Missal, Third Edition* (2011), 69.

24. See Stephen S. Wilbricht, *Rehearsing God's Just Kingdom: The Eucharistic Vision of Mark Searle* (Collegeville, MN: Liturgical Press, 2013), 115.

Days, the Mass of the day with its own readings is used instead of the nuptial readings and prayers (OCM 34). For example, solemnities of the Lord and of the Blessed Virgin Mary take precedence over a nuptial Mass. In such an event, you would celebrate the rite of matrimony within the Mass of the solemnity and include the Nuptial Blessing. Additionally, matrimony within Mass, if it takes place on Saturday evening during Christmas or Ordinary Time, uses the Mass of the Sunday and requires the Creed.[25] When the Mass requires the Creed, the Universal Prayer takes place before the Creed. Normally, the Creed comes before the Universal Prayer. But as the Universal Prayer is part of the rite of matrimony, it displaces the Creed (OCM 69).

The first appendix of *The Order of Celebrating Matrimony* gives two examples of the Universal Prayer (see OCM 216 and 217). In the first example, the presider invites the assembly to commend the couple to the Lord. The minister announces intentions that the Lord bless their covenant, grant perfect and fruitful love, help the burdened, and renew the grace of the sacrament in all married persons present. The assembly responds, "Lord, we ask you, hear our prayer," or with a similar response. The second set of sample petitions prays for the bride and groom, their relatives and friends, those preparing to enter marriage, families, the departed, and unity among Christians. "At the very end, the Priest, with hands extended, concludes the petitions with a prayer."[26]

Strategy for Preaching

Scriptural Texts: *Tobit 8:4b-8; Psalm 145; Romans 8:31b-35, 37-39; John 17:20-26

Liturgical Texts: Collect OCM 192; Preface OCM 199; Nuptial Blessing OCM 205; Solemn Blessing OCM 215

Jesus prayed for his followers before he entered his glory. Tobiah and Sarah on their wedding night offered up a prayer of praise and protection.

---

25. To be able to use the nuptial readings and prayers for a Saturday evening wedding, one option is to celebrate the wedding without Mass. The obligation to attend Sunday Mass still holds. Another option is to move the wedding within Mass to an earlier time on Saturday.

26. Roman Missal, 138. In a departure from the norm, the prayer concluding the second set of petitions is addressed to the Lord Jesus instead of to God the Father.

Empowered by the same Spirit, the bride and bridegroom follow their example. Once the couple is married, the first act is to intercede for others through the Universal Prayer and, if the ceremony is within a nuptial Mass, give praise to God through the eucharistic prayer. A strategy to preach the importance that marriage praise God and intercede for others can follow the narrative of the book of Tobit. Recall that Sarah's plans were crushed seven times by a jealous demon. Tobiah, determined to marry her anyway, prayed with Sarah on their wedding night, and they lived happily ever after. Intermingling human experience, the homily can follow the Tobit narrative in several moves. In the first move, we make our plans but life does not always agree. In the second and third moves, love makes us do "foolish" things anyway, such as praise God on a wedding night. In the fourth move and the conclusion, we see the fruits of such foolishness and receive reason to praise God all the more.

The introduction to such a homily can begin with a teaser. The Scripture reading from the book of Tobit tells us the story of Tobiah and Sarah. On their wedding night in their wedding chamber, they did something special, but it is not what you might first think. I'll get to that in a minute.

The first move introduces the beautiful and sensible, yet ill-fated, Sarah. Highly sought after, she had been given in marriage seven times to seven suitors. On each of the seven wedding nights, however, an evil jealous demon had slain her new husband. In despair, Sarah prayed to God to take her life. The homily turns to our own experience. Like the beautiful and sensible Sarah, we make our plans but life does not always agree. You plan your wedding for months. You have choreographed the special day. Every last detail has been written down in a list and accounted for. Yet something happens: wilted corsages, broken shoe strap, lost limo driver, upset relatives. The plan to have a perfect wedding gets poked, foreshadowing the surprises in marriage waiting in ambush. We who have lived more than a few years have made a fragile peace with those surprises, such as a tough prognosis, an atypical child, an addiction, or a dead-end job. We can relate to the beautiful and sensible Sarah. She had plans of getting married and living happily ever after. Only, no matter that she tried seven times, that's not what happened. No wonder Sarah begged God to take her life.

The next move introduces Tobiah, the eighth suitor for Sarah's hand. Despite Sarah's previous seven slain suitors, Tobiah was determined to marry the beautiful and sensible Sarah, for he was in love with her and yearned deeply for her. Love made Tobiah do foolish things. Again, the homily turns us to our own experience where love made us do things foolish in the sight of the world. As you wait at the wedding reception for the wedding party to show up from taking pictures at the church, ask other couples this question, "How did you get engaged?" You might hear how a grown man went down on one knee on a sandy beach, popping out a ring from a seashell to the delight and applause of passing beachcombers. You might hear how a man drove overnight to ask the father for the hand of his beloved daughter. One man took his longtime girlfriend to the theater. Although they both enjoyed a good show, she was feeling ill after a hard day at work. To her added annoyance, he told her that they should get there early in order to settle in or some other lame reason (their tickets were assigned seating). She was too tired to fight him and went along. Arriving well before the other patrons, he dragged her upstairs to the bar. She wanted only to sit down and rest her eyes. A drink was the last thing she wanted. Once in the bar, all things became clear. Her boyfriend went down on one knee. A photographer appeared. The bartender popped a bottle of champagne. "Will you marry me?" Her kneeling suitor looked up. "Yes!" She came back to life. It was the best evening ever. Love makes us do things that go beyond sense. For love of us, Christ died for us on the cross while we were still sinners. Talk about foolish. Talk about love! Tobiah was no different. He foolishly ignored the warning from Sarah's father, Raguel, that he would likely join seven other good men now cooling in the earth. Raguel, having done his best to warn Tobiah, shrugged his shoulders. He ordered his servants to slay a ram for wedding feast number eight, a last meal for Tobiah before the cursed wedding night.

The third move is the twist. Love made Tobiah do a foolish thing, but he was no fool. On their wedding night, Tobiah took no chances. As soon as the door of the wedding chamber was shut and they were alone, he said to Sarah, "Sister, get up. Let us pray and beg our Lord to have mercy on us and to grant us deliverance." They scrambled out of bed and hit the floor with their knees. Praying in their wedding chamber? That's an unexpected surprise, something you usually do not see the wedding coordinator check off the clipboard. There's more. Usually people pray that God help them with their plans. They ask God to take care of them in times of trouble and show them mercy. They may ask the Lord to let them live a long and happy life. Tobiah and Sarah prayed for all of these things. But the first thing they did was to praise God. Together they knelt and prayed aloud, "Blessed are you, O God of our fathers; praised be your name forever and ever." They praised God who made Adam and Eve husband and wife and from them brought forth the human race. They blessed the Lord for the gift of marriage and its promise of mutual support based on friendship and love. They thanked God for creating a partner so that they would not be alone. Only after Tobiah and Sarah had given thanks and praise to God did they ask for his mercy on them that they might live not only through the night but live together to a happy old age. Then and only then, they went to bed.

The next move briefly helps us to see what happens when we follow the example of Tobiah and Sarah. It helps us to imagine the fruit of a married couple praying together in praise of God. With Tobiah and Sarah now in bed, Sarah's father, Raguel, meanwhile planned for the worst. He went ahead with his terrible chore and dug a grave in his backyard. When the hour was late, Raguel sent a maid to check whether Tobiah was dead yet. The maid returned to Raguel and reported that both were asleep and very much alive. The curse had been broken! Ecstatic that he had hosted and financed the final wedding for his daughter, Raguel threw a fourteen-day wedding feast. As with any noble love story, Sarah and Tobiah lived happily ever after. This conclusion of the narrative does not conclude the homily. But it does invite the listener to want the same happily-ever-after ending.

The conclusion of the homily leads us to praise God with Tobiah and Sarah. It can echo the opening address in the liturgy where the minister says, "May the Lord hear you on this your joyful day. / May he send you help from heaven and protect you. / May he grant you your hearts' desire / and fulfill every one of your prayers" (OCM 53). Gathered in this church, we begin the marriage of N. and N. with more than prayer. We do more than ask that God seal their love and sanctify their new life together. We gather first of all to join with Sarah and Tobiah and N. and N. in praise to God, who made Adam and Eve husband and wife, who brought forth the human race, and who gives us the gift of marriage as a witness to his undying love for us. Through the marriage of N. and N., may the Lord give us many more reasons to praise him.

Section II: Preaching Matrimony without Mass

Section II of this commentary accompanies chapter 2: The Order of Celebrating Matrimony without Mass. The rite for celebrating matrimony without Mass should be used if a marriage takes place between a Catholic and a baptized non-Catholic (OCM 36).[27]

From the preacher's perspective, it is safe to assume that a significant number of the wedding guests are most likely not Catholic. They need prompting when to sit and stand. The Catholic tradition of full, conscious, and active participation in the sacred liturgy may not be their tradition. On the other hand, the readings and prayers suggested for the celebration of matrimony without Mass presume that many of the non-Catholic Christians present are churched. Familiar with Scripture, the assembly likely has a living relationship with the risen Christ and seeks to live as the Body of Christ.

Given these presumptions, the selected readings and prayers emphasize the Liturgy of the Word. *The Order of Celebrating Matrimony* gives three gospel selections from the Sermon on the Mount. The seated Jesus taught his disciples, and the crowd overheard him. Beginning the Sermon on the Mount, the Beatitudes (OCM 178) envisions the Christian life and promises the bridal party, "Rejoice and be glad, for your reward will be great in heaven." In the second gospel selection from the Sermon on the Mount, Jesus includes the bridal party in his mission, saying, "You are the light of the world." Like the gospel, the second essay exhorts them to let their light shine so that others come to glorify their heavenly Father (OCM 179). The third essay begins with the gospel's conclusion to the Sermon on the Mount. As the wise man built his house on rock, Jesus' disciples are those who listen to his words and act on them (OCM 180). The third essay talks about convalidation and bringing a marriage into the church. Discipleship, mission, and revelation in the readings and prayers are themes that help a mainly non-Catholic Christian assembly discover discipleship, mission, and revelation in matrimony.

---

27. The rite for celebrating matrimony within Mass may be used, but the norms for eucharistic Communion apply to the non-Catholics present including a non-Catholic bride or groom.

OCM 178. Matthew 5:1-12a

"Rejoice and be glad, for your reward will be great in heaven."

Readings from the Ambo

The Beatitudes (OCM 178) begins the Sermon on the Mount. Before Jesus teaches his disciples that they are not to retaliate, hate, curse, take oaths, brag, preen, judge, worry, or backbite, he lists nine blessings or beatitudes.

It is an odd way to begin a sermon. A strong sermon should begin with a story or an image. The Sermon on the Mount contrarily begins with a list of nine blessings. A list is a weak rhetorical device. No one remembers a list. We write down our shopping list in order to remember it. Why begin the Sermon on the Mount with a list?

The litany of blessings at the beginning of the Sermon on the Mount sets the tone for the remainder of the sermon. It cues us that the teachings of the sermon such as "love your enemies" are about blessing. The Sermon on the Mount without the Beatitudes would be Jesus' version of Deuteronomy, a series of commands that the community of believers must do. Instead, the Beatitudes gives us a frame. The behaviors of the Christian life spelled out in the sermon are not so much about following a new ethic. They are our response to being blessed.

"Blessed are those who . . ." tells us who is favored, honored, and esteemed by God. The poor in spirit who have lost hope, the ones who mourn and have no cause for joy, those meek and oppressed, and those starved for justice will be blessed when God's will is done. Those who do God's will and let the kingdom come insofar that they are merciful, clean of heart, peacemaking, and willing to suffer for the sake of what is right are in turn a blessing. Those who know that they are blessed and those who seek to be a blessing to others are called disciples.

The Order of Celebrating Matrimony offers Scripture selections that show how marriage can be a blessing to others. The selection of Sirach 26:1-4, 13-16 from the Old Testament declares, "Blessed [be] the husband of a good wife" (OCM *151). He is twice-lengthened in his days. She brings joy and peace, contentment and a smile. She adds grace upon grace. Like the rising sun, the virtuous wife is the radiance of her home. The good wife is a blessing to her husband and to her home.

The reading from the letter to the Hebrews (OCM 162) looks at how the Christian life can be a blessing for others. Once the honeymoon is over, "Do not neglect hospitality, / for through it some have unknowingly entertained angels." The exhortation recalls Abraham and Sarah, married but childless, who welcomed three mysterious travelers under the shade of a tree. The travelers' visit led to the birth of Isaac and, through him, the Hebrew people. The letter to the Hebrews continues, "Be mindful of prisoners as if sharing their imprisonment, / and of the ill-treated as of yourselves, / for you also are in the body." The Christian life looks beyond the white picket fence and toward the welfare of the prisoners and abused. "Let marriage be honored among all / and the marriage bed be kept undefiled" holds up the fidelity promised in marriage. "Let your life be free from love of money / but be content with what you have, / for he has said, *I will never forsake you or abandon you*" charges the listener to put their money where their mouth is and trust in the Lord. In sum, Christian marriage can be a blessing not only for a husband and wife but for travelers, prisoners, the ill-treated, the promiscuous, and the greedy. The Christian marriage and family is a place of mercy, safety, friendship, and support. It is a blessing for society.

Connecting the Bible and the Liturgy

Blessings for the couple and their marriage are not only in Scripture. Blessings are part of the wedding liturgy. The main blessing in the wedding liturgy for the newly married couple is the Nuptial Blessing.

The Nuptial Blessing prays that the Lord pour out his grace on the newly married couple. Praising God for the creation of man and woman and for the gift of matrimony, it asks that they may always be bound together by love for one another. That the couple be a blessing for their children and beyond, it prays that they "may bear true witness to Christ before all" (OCM 205B) and again "bear witness to you in the world" (OCM 209).

The first version of the Nuptial Blessing (text without music, OCM 74, 105; text with music, OCM 205B) is based on an ancient version from the *Verona Sacramentary*. The last two versions (OCM 206 and OCM 208) are recent compositions. After the Second Vatican Council, two changes have been made to the Nuptial Blessing.

First, instead of a blessing only for the bride, we pray for the groom as well. We pray that the bride adorn her home with warmth and welcoming graciousness. We pray that the groom may be a worthy, good, and faithful husband. We pray that the couple together share God's love and are a sign of his presence. In the Nuptial Blessing, both bride and groom are blessed.

Second, an epiclesis was added to the Nuptial Blessing. In the eucharistic prayer, the priest invokes the Holy Spirit that the bread and wine become the Body and Blood of Christ. In the rite of baptism, the priest or deacon prays over the baptism font that the water become the life-giving waters of baptism. In the same way, the priest or deacon extends his hands over the bride and groom for the Nuptial Blessing. Invoking the Holy Spirit, we pray that the Lord send down on the newly married couple the grace of the Holy Spirit. We pray that God stretch out his hand and pour into their hearts the power of the Holy Spirit and set their hearts aflame.

The OCM offers musical chant settings of all three Nuptial Blessings, emphasizing the reverence and beauty to be accorded to the Nuptial Blessing. The Nuptial Blessing within Mass follows the Lord's Prayer and replaces the embolism "Deliver us" (OCM 72). If the wedding is without Mass, the Nuptial Blessing follows the Lord's Prayer. The rubrics instruct that the Nuptial Blessing is never omitted.[28]

The OCM has added in its appendices the Order of Blessing an Engaged Couple and the Order of Blessing a Married Couple within Mass on the Anniversary of Marriage. The orders are more recent translations of the Orders of Blessing found in the 1989 *Book of Blessings*.[29] Placing these two blessings in the OCM underscores the importance of blessing and marriage. A blessing is not solely for the wedding day. Blessing is for the engaged couple and for the long-married couple. Blessing is part of the celebration of married life in all its stages.

---

28. The exception may be in the celebration of matrimony between a Catholic and a catechumen or a non-Christian. If, because of circumstances, the Nuptial Blessing is omitted, the minister prays over the bride and bridegroom, "Be attentive to our prayers, O Lord, / and in your kindness uphold / what you have established for the increase of the human race, / so that the union you have created / may be kept safe by your assistance. / Through Christ our Lord. / Amen" (OCM 140). The prayer is identical to the Collect OCM 192 except for the use of the simple conclusion.

29. The general introduction to the *Book of Blessings* has a beautiful discussion of blessings in the history of salvation and in the life of the church.

The Order of Blessing an Engaged Couple can be used when couples come together for marriage preparation. When the blessing of an engaged couple is celebrated within the two families, one of the parents may preside at the rite of blessing. A priest or deacon may also preside as long as everyone knows that the rite is not a celebration of marriage. It is never to be combined with the celebration of Mass (OCM 219–221).

The Order of Blessing a Married Couple within Mass on the Anniversary of Marriage encourages the anniversary celebration to be part of the community gathered for liturgy. The OCM offers a beautiful alternative to the repetition of the exchange and consent from their wedding, which is given only once and forever. Instead of the husband and wife repeating, "I take you . . . ," from the original celebration of matrimony, the husband and wife separately say, "Blessed are you, Lord, / for by your goodness I took N. as my wife/husband." Then with one voice they bless the Lord for standing lovingly by their side in good times and in bad. They ask the Lord to help them remain faithful and be witnesses to his covenant with humankind (OCM 242).

Strategy for Preaching

*Scriptural Texts: *Sirach 26:1-4, 13-16; Psalm 148; Hebrews 13:1-4a, 5-6b; Matthew 5:1-12a*

Liturgical Texts: Collect OCM 193; Blessing of Rings OCM 195; Nuptial Blessing OCM 207

Inspired by the Beatitudes, the homily can inspire blessing. A focus statement might be "a blessed marriage blesses." The intention is to move the assemblies' expectation about marriage from a self-centered "happily ever after" to the desire for their marriage to be a blessing for others. One way to make this shift is to start with the culture, offer an "Aha!" faith insight, and sketch how we can live as a blessing.

To begin, the homily can engage the cultural understanding of marriage. Mimicking the list of Beatitudes, it can offer a list of cultural ideas of a happy marriage. "Happy are those who . . . find their soul mate, hold good jobs, have two well-behaved kids in sports and dance, live in a nice neighborhood, and enjoy good health." While there is nothing wrong with this picture of a marriage, something is missing. Like a selfie photo, it does not include others.

The "Aha!" faith insight turns on the word "blessing." The translation "Happy are those who . . . " misses the mark. "Happy" mainly means an emotional state. It suggests that feeling good is the ultimate good. In contrast, our faith sees that there is more to life than avoiding suffering and feeling good. The good life is the blessed life.

Disciples are those who know that they are blessed in good times and in bad, in sickness and in health. They see that all is a gift from God. Suffering—grief, poverty, illness, oppression, persecution—is part of life. Surrendering ourselves into the hands of God, our suffering can be a blessing. Our trust is in God who brought forth from the cross the greatest blessing, our salvation.

Disciples not only know that they are blessed. No matter the cost to themselves, they seek to be a blessing to others. At this point, the assembly needs a story or image to see how a marriage might be a blessing to others.

One example is the custom of the giving of the *arras* (coins). After the Blessing and Giving of Rings, if the occasion so suggests, the minister blesses the coins. According to one tradition, twelve coins, one for each month, symbolize care for the household. The thirteenth coin symbolizes care for others, showing that the love of the couple necessarily moves outward in charity. The husband hands the *arras* to his wife, saying, "N., receive these *arras* as a pledge of God's blessing / and a sign of the good gifts we will share." The wife returns the *arras* to the husband with the same words (OCM 67B).

Another example might be the Hispanic custom of *Bendición*. Spanish cultures have a beautiful custom. A child comes before his mother or father and says, "Bendición." The parent places his hand on the child's head or traces the sign of the cross on the child's forehead, and says, "Que Dios te bendiga." *May God bless you.*

Before going to school, children ask their parents, "Bendición." The parents bless them, "Que Dios te bendiga," that they are protected and prepared for their studies. Before going out with friends, teenagers ask their parents, "Bendición." The parents bless them, "Que Dios te bendiga," that they are safe on the roads (and return before curfew). At bedtime, parents make the sign of the cross on the forehead of the child and say, "Que Dios te bendiga."

Aunts and uncles bless nephews and nieces, grandparents bless grandchildren, and godparents bless godchildren. Above all, parents bless children. Parents would not let their children go to school without shoes. Nor would they let their children out the door without a hug and kiss.

In the same way, parents are responsible for their children's spiritual well-being. Why would we send our children into the world without a blessing? We cannot always be with our children to protect them. We might worry about "stranger danger" or fear that a child will be bullied. What happens during snack time if she chokes on a peanut? The good news is that we do not have to be with our children all of the time. When we give our blessing to our children, we receive peace of mind. We trust, and the children learn, that the Lord is with them.

To include those not familiar with this custom, the preacher can note that giving a blessing is not just a custom from Spanish cultures. Giving a blessing is from Scripture. The Lord said to Moses: "Speak to Aaron and his sons and tell them: This is how you shall bless the Israelites. Say to them: / The Lord bless you and keep you! / The Lord let his face shine upon you, and be gracious to you! / The Lord look upon you kindly and give you peace! / So shall they invoke my name upon the Israelites, and I will bless them" (Num 6:22-27).

We do not have to be Moses or a Catholic priest to invoke a blessing. In virtue of baptism and confirmation, we have the ability to bless. We have the authority and responsibility to invoke the name of the Lord on behalf of others.

Bringing the homily home to the wedding, you can point to N. and N. Through their marriage to each other, they become a blessing. First, they are a blessing to each other. Next, they are a blessing to their children. They may, as Scripture suggests, be a blessing for travelers, prisoners, and the ill-treated. They may be a blessing to friends who struggle in their own marriage. The source of their blessing is God our Father. In the marriage of N. and N., he blesses them. The two become one. Through them, he blesses us. In their faithfulness to one another as long as they live, we are blessed.

OCM 179. Matthew 5:13-16

"You are the light of the world."

Readings from the Ambo

The Sermon on the Mount is the first of five discourses in the Gospel of Matthew. Jesus, seeing the crowds, went up the mountain and sat down to teach his disciples gathered around him. The sermon is addressed to his disciples. The crowd simply overhears. After the preamble of the nine Beatitudes, beginning with "Blessed are the poor in spirit, / for theirs is the Kingdom of heaven," Jesus tells the disciples that they are the salt of the earth and the light of the world.

One way to reflect on the Sermon on the Mount is to pick some particular teaching, such as "do not lust," and shine it like a flashlight into our conscience to see how we are doing. One may ask, "Have I looked at someone with lust in my heart? What do I need to do to turn from this sin?" This short passage on salt and light, however, gives us the clue that the remainder of the sermon is not an examination of conscience. Categorically stating, "You are the salt of the earth" and "You are the light of the world," the Sermon on the Mount becomes not so much a checklist for the moral life as a call to witness. The actions of disciples are to shine so that others take notice. A community that refuses to retaliate, hate, curse, take oaths, brag, preen, worry, or backbite, and instead loves its enemies is bound to draw attention. Like a light, the Christian life shines before others. It attracts attention as a light attracts the eye.

Reading the text quickly, one might draw the conclusion that good deeds shining before others glorify the heavenly Father. The text actually reads, "that *they* [who see your good deeds] . . . glorify your heavenly Father" (emphasis added). The point of the entire sermon is that, drawn by the way of life of the disciples, nonbelievers become disciples themselves! Their lives change to become radiant with light and so "glorify your heavenly Father." The Sermon on the Mount is less a moral compass for believers as a way to witness to nonbelievers.

When it appears on the Fifth Sunday of Ordinary Time in Year A, Matthew 5:13-16 is preceded by Isaiah 58:7-10, which stipulates behaviors such as "clothe the naked when you see them, / and do not turn your back on your own. / Then your light shall break forth like the dawn." In the same vein, readings that instruct in ways that are distinctive to Christian marriage may well accompany Matthew 5:13-16.

From the Old Testament selections given in *The Order of Celebrating Matrimony*, two readings bring out the distinctive character of Christian marriage. Genesis 2:18-24 (OCM *145), where the two become one body, makes clear that Christian marriage is a lifelong commitment. Tobit 8:4b-8 (OCM *148) shows that, as Tobiah and Sarah prayed on their wedding night for mercy and deliverance, spousal prayer is part of Christian marriage.

From the New Testament selections, Romans 12:1-2, 9-18 (OCM 154) is a litany of instructions not to conform to this age, but instead "to offer your bodies as a living sacrifice, / holy and pleasing to God." One can find the discipleship spirit of the Sermon on the Mount in Ephesians 5:2a, 21-33 (OCM *159); Philippians 4:4-9 (OCM 160); Colossians 3:12-17 (OCM 161); Hebrews 13:1-4a, 5-6b (OCM 162); and 1 Peter 3:1-9 (OCM 163). In the context of the celebration of matrimony, these readings instruct the bride and groom how to let their light shine through their married life.

Appropriate psalm refrains are Psalm 112 (OCM 170), "Blessed the man who greatly delights in the Lord's commands," and Psalm 128 (OCM *171), "Blessed are those who fear the Lord." The two psalm refrains promise blessings upon the disciples who revere the Lord and follow his teachings.

Connecting the Bible and the Liturgy

Several of the prayer options pick up the idea that marriage is a shining light to help others see Christ. From among the six possible collects, OCM 189 prays that "these your servants . . . may become, by your grace, witnesses to charity itself." The prayer names the couple as servants of God, which is consistent with the role of a disciple, and it introduces the theme of witness. Salt of the earth and light of the world by the grace of God, Christian marriage gives witness to the love of Christ for his church.

The first of the three Nuptial Blessings (text without music, OCM 74, 105; text with music, OCM 205B) similarly implores the Lord that "these your servants / hold fast to the faith and keep your commandments." In keeping the commandments of the Lord, "may they bear true witness to Christ before all," calling to mind the gospel command that disciples let their light shine before others that they may see the good deeds of the disciples and they themselves come to glorify their heavenly Father. The Nuptial Blessing concludes with the hope held by those who revere the Lord and delight in his commands (see Psalm 112 and Psalm 128) that "they may come to the life of the blessed / in the Kingdom of Heaven." The Blessings at the End of the Celebration

(OCM 213) share in the theme of witness when stating, "May you be witnesses in the world to God's charity."[30]

The liturgy itself offers possibilities to connect the Scripture with ritual action in order to highlight the witness of Christian marriage. The first witness is the ceremony itself. Rather than a self-scripted affair held in the ballroom of a hotel as a prelude to a large wedding reception dinner and dance, the ceremony in the church building signals that the life of the married couple is to be within the church. Their marriage is their way to live out the call to discipleship. Before their marriage, they were disciples. Once married, they continue to live as disciples. The marriage ceremony in the church building, whether within Mass or not, gives witness to all gathered.

Before the wedding ceremony as part of preparation, the presider can encourage the bride or groom to receive the sacrament of penance, if necessary (OCM 18). The Catholic bride or groom who makes confession and receives absolution shows that disciples know he or she is a sinner in need of God's mercy.

There is a custom not mentioned in the rubrics where the bride and sometimes the groom, after Holy Communion or the exchange of rings, places a bouquet of flowers before a statue of the Blessed Mother. This custom is a sign of devotion to Mary and a witness to a life of prayer. However, it is an act of personal piety. It is not an act of the assembly. Rather than insert a private devotion into the public liturgy, the devotion to Mary may take place outside the liturgy at another time such as during the wedding rehearsal. The devotion to Mary during the wedding rehearsal would contribute toward the bridal party's prayerful preparation for the celebration of matrimony.[31]

---

30. As noted previously, when Mass is not celebrated and Holy Communion is distributed, the rite concludes with either the solemn form or the simple form of blessing (OCM 116). When Mass is not celebrated and Holy Communion is not distributed, the minister blesses the people using the simple form, saying, "And may almighty God bless all of you, who are gathered here, / the Father, and the Son, and the Holy Spirit," to which the people reply, "Amen" (OCM 116, 141).

31. In considering these customs not mentioned in the rubrics, the OCM directs that "attention should also be given . . . to local customs, which may be observed if appropriate" (OCM 29). The OCM states that the Conferences of Bishops are to make adaptions to accommodate customs and needs of their region (OCM 39).

Similarly, the unity candle is another custom not mentioned in the rubrics. The liturgical sign for unity, however, is Holy Communion. The bridal parties, families, and assembly take part in Communion so that they become one Body, one spirit in Christ. Even in the ceremony without Holy Communion, the common action and prayer of the assembly builds up the unity of all present. Instead of lighting a unity candle as part of the liturgy, a better place would be the wedding reception. As part of the custom of the introduction of the bridal party, the parents could light the side candles followed by the bride and groom. The unity candle gives the reception dignity and meaning beyond a banquet with a band. It speaks to Jesus' command that his disciples, now joined in the sacrament of matrimony, shine as a joyful light in the world for all to see. Having received the light of Christ in baptism, the newly married couple surrounded by family and friends at the reception shines all the more brightly.

Strategy for Preaching

*Scriptural Texts: *Tobit 8:4b-8; Psalm 112; Romans 12:1-2, 9-18; Matthew 5:13-16*

Liturgical Texts: Collect OCM 189; Nuptial Blessing OCM 205

The gospel text of Matthew 5:13-16 is directed toward disciples. It has two metaphors about disciples-in-action—"salt of the earth" and "light of the world"—followed by the hoped-for response from those who see disciples in action. A homily following the structure and intent of the text could encourage the assembly to claim their discipleship especially in the married life. A focus statement might be, "The world depends on us." A function statement might be, "Your light must shine."

A good place to begin the homily is to begin where the gospel text begins. In this text, it begins with salt and light. The phrases, "salt of the earth" and "light of the world," so familiar that they mean little, would benefit from some discussion.

First, salt seasons food. Salt makes food taste good. A man was told by his heart doctor to give up salt. Meal after unsalted meal, eating tasteless food, the man wondered if life was worth living without salt. Salt makes food taste so much better. Besides flavoring, what else does salt do? Salt preserves food. Before refrigerators, people rubbed salt into hams and fish to keep the meat from rotting. Salt preserved the meat for months at room temperature. Salt was so valuable that Roman soldiers were paid a sum of money with which to buy salt for themselves. The Latin word for "salt" is *sal*. The salarium, or "salt money," is the root of our word "salary." Finally, besides making food taste good and preserving food from rotting and being as valuable as money, salt is necessary to life. Each molecule of table salt is made up of a sodium atom and a chlorine atom. Once dissolved in the body, the sodium and chlorine become electrolytes. They are necessary to osmosis so that cells get the nutrients they need. Simply put, without salt, people die. Jesus said, "You are the salt of the earth."

Similarly, the homily can help us hear with new ears, "You are the light of the world." Light makes the difference between stumbling in a dark bedroom or visiting the bathroom with toes intact, getting lost in the woods at night or having a great camping trip, and driving blind at night or arriving home safe and sound. The light of the Olympic torch makes the difference between another athletic competition or sixteen days of world peace disguised as a sports event. Light makes all the difference in the world. Not for nothing, Jesus said, "You are the light of the world."

Talking at length about salt and light, besides breathing new life into these clichés, builds suspense. The listener wants to know why the preacher is going on at such length about salt and light at a wedding! A temptation for the preacher to avoid is to ping-pong between marriage and salt or marriage and light. Comparisons such as, "Just as salt makes food taste better, marriage makes life better," followed closely by, "Just as salt preserves food, marriage preserves love," position the listener as a spectator watching the homilist volley back and forth. They may watch with interest one comparison after another yet have no stake in the game. The way to avoid this temptation is to delay explanation of what salt and light have to do with the marriage ceremony taking place. After all, before telling his disciples to give witness through their deeds, Jesus first talked at length about the importance and function of salt and light.

The homily next turns to the marriage. Without making direct comparison to what was said about salt and light, the homily can drop clues. The wedding in the church building, as mentioned in the previous section about liturgy, is not the same as a wedding in a hotel. The difference goes beyond the presence of a priest and organist and a long aisle. The wedding in the church building means that their marriage is part of the church itself. The two-becoming-one lives out the baptism of every disciple to give witness to Christ. Married in the church, the Christian couple lives differently than a couple married in the park. Christian couples pray together, even on their wedding night (see Tob 8:4-8). Christian couples make a lifelong commitment even as Christ has made an eternal commitment to us. Christian couples honor their marriage bed. They put their marriage first before work or kids. The Christian marriage, like the church wedding, stands out for all to see.

The end of the gospel text envisions others becoming disciples themselves when they see the deeds of disciples. Following its lead, the homily envisions what happens when others see a Christian marriage in action. Here, an illustration is important to add strength to the message that the world depends on us just as it depends on salt and light. A story that comes to mind is a man who had been away from the church ever since college. God did not mean anything to him. Engaged to a Catholic woman, he went with her one Sunday to Mass. He wanted to see the church she had chosen for their wedding. Something happened. He kept coming to Mass. Like a moth to a flame, his attraction to his girlfriend grew into a living relationship with the Lord. Through his marriage preparation and after the wedding, he came back to faith. Eventually he was ordained a permanent deacon. Thanks to his girlfriend, who let her light shine, he went through a deep conversion and, in doing so, glorified our heavenly Father. His faith depended on her witness. The message that the world depends on us disciples ennobles the marriage taking place.

Up to this point, the focus has been on the witness of the disciple. The good news, though, is always about what God has done and is doing. It is well worth noting that the Lord is the Light that shines in the darkness. The life of a disciple, whether married or not, is like the moon, a reflection of the God of Light. The halos of the saints pictured in Catholic art symbolize the radiance given to them by God for all to see his glory.

A natural conclusion to the homily is one that leads to the rite of marriage about to take place. Playing off the questions before the consent, the preacher could rhetorically question the assembly if they are prepared that their Christian witness shine for all to see. He could ask the bride and groom if they are willing for their marriage to be salt of the earth. The reminder that salt must be consumed to be of any value could hint at the self-sacrifice of such a pledge. Christian marriage is not just an important moment in the lives of a man and woman. Like salt and light, their Christian marriage is essential to the life and well-being of the world.

OCM 180. Matthew 7:21, 24-29 (or Short Form 7:21, 24-25)

"A wise man built his house on rock."

Readings from the Ambo

"Everyone who listens to these words of mine / and acts on them / will be like a wise man who built his house on rock" (Matt 7:24). With these words, Jesus ends the Sermon on the Mount. He tells us not only to listen to his teaching. We must act on it.

The saying is preceded by his warning, "Not everyone who says to me, 'Lord, Lord,' / will enter the Kingdom of heaven, / but only the one who does the will of my Father in heaven." In other words, it is not enough to hear Jesus teach, "Be reconciled with your brother" (Matt 5:24). Before you can offer the sign of peace at Mass, you have to make peace. It is not enough to know the saying, "Turn the other cheek" (Matt 5:39). Instead, "Love your enemies, and pray for those who persecute you" (Matt 5:44). We are to listen to his teaching and act on it.

The one who listens and acts on his words is compared to a wise man who built his house on rock. When the storm came, the house did not collapse. In contrast, those who listen but do not act on Jesus' words are compared to a fool who built his house on sand. When the storm came, the house collapsed.[32]

An Old Testament reading that emphasizes action is the picture of domestic bliss painted in Proverbs (OCM *149). The proverbial worthy wife brings her husband good, not evil. Indifferent to deceptive charm and

---

32. The gospel text given in *The Order of Celebrating Matrimony* skips from verse 21 to verse 24, omitting the reference to the day of judgment when many will say, "'Lord, Lord, did we not prophesy in your name? Did we not drive out demons in your name? Did we not do mighty deeds in your name?' Then I will declare to them solemnly, 'I never knew you. Depart from me, you evildoers'" (Matt 7:22-23). The omission refers to those who heal and do good deeds in the name of Jesus yet are corrupt and evil. The omission of these verses in the OCM loses this nuance that our actions must be backed up by Christian character. Instead, the edited selection focuses us on the importance to act on Jesus' teaching in the Sermon on the Mount.

fleeting beauty, the woman who fears the Lord weaves cloth, gives to the poor, and extends her arms to the needy. On the Thirty-Third Sunday in Ordinary Time, Year A, the Proverbs text is paired with Psalm 128, "Blessed are those who fear the Lord" (OCM *171) and the parable of the Talents (Matt 25:14-30). In the parable, a rich man going on a journey entrusted his possessions to his servants. At the accounting on his return, one servant had doubled his five talents as did the servant with two talents. The servant with one talent had dug a hole in the ground and buried his master's money out of fear. The demanding master threw him out into the darkness where there will be wailing and grinding of teeth. The Lectionary link between Proverbs and the parable of the Talents adds a dimension to the worthy wife. Rather than a prize to win her husband praise at the city gates, the worthy wife is like the worthy servant who doubled his master's possessions. Her household routine and concern for the poor double what the master has given her. As an allegory, Matthew's parable insists that, at the final judgment, the Lord holds us accountable for our deeds that let the kingdom come. Faith, not fear, frees us to act like the worthy servant and the worthy wife, so that we may hear the words, "Come, share your master's joy." The daily work of marriage for the family and for the poor shows us what it means to be a worthy servant who doubles the possessions of the master.

A New Testament reading from *The Order of Celebrating Matrimony* that similarly emphasizes action over words is 1 John 3:18-24 (OCM 164). "Children, let us love not in word or speech / but in deed and truth. . . . [W]e keep his commandments." In addition, it adds a relational element that complements Matthew 7. "And his commandment is this: / we should believe in the name of his Son, Jesus Christ . . . Those who keep his commandments remain in him, / and he in them." Johannine theology highlights the importance of the disciple's belief in Jesus. Like a branch and vine, remaining connected to Christ is essential to bearing fruit that remains. You cannot act in his name fruitfully unless you have a living relationship with him.

For a responsorial psalm, Psalm 112 stresses the keeping of the commandments. The refrain is, "Blessed the man who greatly delights in the Lord's commands." One of its verses sings the praise of such a man. "It goes well for the man who deals generously and lends, / who conducts his affairs with justice. . . . Openhanded, he gives to the poor." The psalm tells us that the man who fears the Lord does more than listen to the Lord. He does more than delight in his commandments. In his dealings with others, the God-fearing man lives the commandments of the Lord. Another verse in Psalm 112 brings to mind the house built on rock compared to the house built on sand. We are told that the man who delights in the Lord's command has built on rock. "He will never be moved; . . . he will see the downfall of his foes" (OCM 170).

Connecting the Bible and the Liturgy

These Scripture readings may be especially appropriate for a wedding that is a convalidation.

In a convalidation, a marriage that took place outside the church is brought into the church. The convalidating spouses make a new and free act of consent in the wedding ceremony. While acknowledging the couple's shared life, convalidation is not a blessing of an existing union or a renewal of vows. The man and woman give their consent to a marriage that is lifelong, exclusive, and open to children.

A common situation leading to a convalidation is that the couple married outside the church because of a previous marriage for one or both of them. For the convalidation to take place, the partner in the previous marriage must have died or the church must have given a declaration of nullity, often called an annulment, of the previous marriage. Another common situation is that the couple married in another church as a "neutral territory," a compromise between one spouse who is Catholic and the other spouse who is active in another faith.

For whatever reason for the earlier marriage outside the church, your preaching depends on knowing why they desire that their marriage is convalidated. Often, a non-Catholic spouse is becoming Catholic. If their marriage took place outside the church, the convalidation is necessary before the reception of the non-Catholic spouse into full communion with the church. For them, the convalidation might be a "check the box" requirement.[33] Another reason for the convalidation might be that the Catholic spouse is coming back to the church after years away. If they have had children together or have brought children into a blended family, they might want their children to become active in the church and receive

---

33. The hope is that, along the way toward full communion and with marriage preparation suited to their situation, the convalidating couple is formed so that the convalidation becomes something they desire in and of itself.

the sacraments. They might have recognized that something has been missing from their family. For them, the convalidation is a homecoming.

Practically, the liturgy for a convalidation is often less of a production than a wedding for a young couple never married. Having already had the big wedding and the blow-out reception, the convalidating couple is usually less concerned about the long aisle, the limousine, and the coordinated tuxedo and bridal gown. A suit and a nice dress are all the special clothes thcy require for the special day. They are usually happy with an intimate liturgy surrounded by family and friends. With less cultural pressures for a certain kind of wedding, the liturgy can more faithfully celebrate the deeper meanings of the marriage.[34]

The Scripture readings from the Gospel of Matthew and the other suggestions given above are well suited for a convalidation. Instead of Scripture readings that gush with love (see 1 Cor 13), the couple may well be ready for meat and potatoes. One teachable moment is the fact that their previous wedding took place outside a Catholic Church building. It might have been in a non-Catholic church, in a scenic gazebo, on the beach, or in their backyard. Getting married in the church means that they get married in a Catholic church building. It is their spiritual home. For this reason, special permission is required for Catholics to marry in a place other than their parish church. The church building is where they normally celebrate the sacraments. As marriage signifies the union of Christ and his church, it rightly takes place in the house of God surrounded by the people of God.

For the collects, the Collect OCM 188 mentions the importance of deeds.[35] We pray "that what they receive in faith they may live out in deeds." It relates to the gospel text where Jesus teaches us that we are to do more than listen to his words. We are to act on them. Or again, "Children, let us love not in word or speech / but in deed and truth" (1 John 3:18-24). Actions speak louder than words.

---

34. Convalidation of a civil marriage is often celebrated using the Order of Celebrating Matrimony without Mass. If both are Catholic, a nuptial Mass should take place. In a nuptial Mass, the newly married spouses may bring forward the bread and wine to the altar for the preparation of the gifts (OCM 70). Their children may participate as well in various ways such as bringing forward the gifts.

35. The rubric for Collect OCM 188 notes that it may not be used in the same celebration as the first Nuptial Blessing (OCM 74, 105).

Strategy for Preaching

Scriptural Texts: *Proverbs 31:10-13, 19-20, 30-31; Psalm 112; 1 John 3:18-24; Matthew 7:21, 24-29

Liturgical Texts: Collect OCM 188; Nuptial Blessing OCM 207

A focus statement, the one thing you want them to know, might be "Christ is our rock." It plays on Matthew's image of a house built on rock. The function statement, what you want the listener to do about it, might be "Build your life together on Christ." Bear in mind that while you are speaking to the wedding couple, you are in reality speaking through them to the friends and family. They need to hear the Good News, too! To bring this message home, the preaching for a convalidation can make three moves.

The first move begins where they are, having their marriage brought into the church. It acknowledges their existing union and their life together. You can talk about how they met, where they were married (more on this in the next move), if they have any children, and the friends they have made along the way together. With their permission, you can share the reasons for their convalidation, such as the non-Catholic person becoming Catholic and his or her faith journey. Their story can be a witness to their family and friends. What you do not want to say at a convalidation is anything that suggests that the couple has seen the error of their ways and is finally returning to the fold. The wedding is not an opportunity to scold. It is an opportunity to evangelize.

The second move breaks open the Word. The organizing image taken from the Scriptures is that the teaching of Christ is bedrock. How important is bedrock? The mighty towers of New York City are built on superstrong mica schist that lies close to the surface for much of the island of Manhattan. The steel girders reach down to the solid rock so that they can support fifty or even a hundred stories of offices and apartments and hotel rooms. In contrast, Superstorm Sandy in October 2012 pushed the surf so high into the dunes along the Eastern Seaboard that houses along the beach collapsed. The surf had eaten away the sand, and the houses were ruined. Bedrock is the difference between strong skyscrapers and ruined homes.

The teaching of Christ is bedrock. It is the difference between building a house on rock or building it on sand. We can build our lives on it.

Here, you can offer two teachings that are relevant to the wedding liturgy. The first teaching is on marriage. Our culture considers marriage to be a matter between two adults. If it does not work out, they get a divorce. The church, in contrast, considers marriage to be more than a matter between a man and a woman. Marriage signifies the union of Christ and his church. How N. and N. love each other—faithfully, for life, bearing fruit and children—shows us how Christ loves us. A second teaching is that getting married in the church means that you are literally married in the church building. In this particular place, we gather for Sunday Mass to celebrate the memorial of the death and resurrection of Jesus Christ. We stand here on holy ground. What better place to sanctify and strengthen the union of N. and N.? The teaching of the church has endured over two thousand years because its foundation is the teaching of Jesus Christ. We put his words into action. We build our lives together on him.

The third move goes deeper. It invites us to know not just the teachings. It invites us to know the Teacher. A married couple is faithful in good times and bad, in sickness and health all the days of their lives not because Jesus teaches them to do so. When you are in love and committed to your spouse more than to life itself, it is what you naturally want to do. The teaching protects and nurtures the underlying relationship. The same applies to a friendship. You have a friend's back not because of an unwritten rule of friendship, but because you care about the friend. Going deeper than the teachings and knowledge about the Teacher, you hit bedrock. A living relationship with the risen Christ is bedrock.

You can show us what it might look like when we have a relationship with Christ. A negative example is an inmate who spoke with me when I was preparing for Mass in a prison. "Father, I did something really bad." I thought that he meant his crime. But he continued, "I did not pray." His greatest failing was that he did not know the Lord. If he had had a living relationship with the Lord, his life and the lives of others might have been very different. A positive example might be the contrast between the big wedding expected by our culture and the simpler liturgy taking place. With wisdom and faith, we are better able to trust in the Lord and love one another and not become so distracted with nonessentials. Friends and families can find a home in a life built together on Christ.

In the transition to the exchange of consent, note that what is taking place is more than a blessing or renewal of vows. N. and N. give a new consent. They make a once and forever free act of consent to a marriage that is lifelong, exclusive, and open to children. Their consent given before the Lord and his church anchors everything that has gone before and everything that is to come. The foundation is Jesus Christ.

Section III: Preaching Matrimony between a Catholic and a Catechumen or a Non-Christian

Section III of this commentary is for use with chapter 3: The Order of Celebrating Matrimony between a Catholic and a Catechumen or a Non-Christian. This is the case when the bride or groom is Catholic while the other is Jewish, Muslim, Hindu, or otherwise unbaptized. Another probability in our secularizing milieu is that the non-Catholic bride or groom or much of the assembly might be a "None," baptized but belonging to no religion. While chapter 3 of *The Order of Celebrating Matrimony* may not have envisioned its use with the Nones, we will explore its possibilities to stir the faith present.

The preacher before an assembly of non-Christians or Nones may presume that most present are unfamiliar with Catholic tradition. They may respect believers and appreciate the beauty of the liturgy, but Catholic liturgy is a foreign tongue outside their ways of thinking and doing. The rite of reception in chapter 3 accounts for the gap in Christian faith as the rubrics omit the sign of the cross and the greeting such as, "The Lord be with you."[36] It recognizes that the non-Christians present in the assembly might not authentically make the sign of baptism or respond, "And with your spirit." As mentioned earlier, if circumstances such as cultural reasons so suggest, the Blessing and Giving of Rings may be omitted (OCM 131). If the non-Christian spouse does place the ring on the other's finger, he or she may say nothing or simply, "N., receive this ring / as a sign of

---

36. Even the rite of reception may be omitted if circumstances so suggest. The celebration of marriage with a non-Christian may instead begin with the Liturgy of the Word (OCM 119–121). The sign of the cross and the greeting remain the norm in the celebration within Mass (OCM 51) and in the celebration without Mass (OCM 86).

my love and fidelity." If he or she is a Christian, they may add, "In the name of the Father, and of the Son, / and of the Holy Spirit" (OCM 132).

In this third section of the commentary, the common ground in the liturgy where the Nones, non-Christians, and Christians can meet is in the themes of unitive love and fidelity. The selection from Mark (OCM *183), declaring "what God has joined together, / no human being must separate," is often chosen along with one of the two Genesis readings on the creation of man and woman. The pairing, even prior to conscious faith, speaks to the yearning for unity and fidelity common to the human heart. Relying heavily on the Genesis text, this essay is especially appropriate when those of Jewish or Muslim faith are present. The remaining three essays are more appropriate for liturgy when those of no religious affiliation or the Nones are strongly represented. The theme of love finds voice in the pericope with the double commandment in Matthew, "You shall love the Lord, your God . . . [and] your neighbor as yourself" (OCM 182). Jesus' commandments to "remain in my love" (OCM 185) and "love one another" (OCM 186) are directed to his disciples during the Last Supper Discourse, but their proven appeal to the unchurched is an opportunity to stir faith into flame. For these celebrations of matrimony where mature Christian faith is not certain, we favor readings and prayers with themes of unity, fidelity, and fruitfulness.

OCM 182. Matthew 22:35-40

"This is the greatest and the first commandment. The second is like it."[37]

Readings from the Ambo

Whether the bridal party and guests are deeply committed disciples or cultural Catholics or Nones, all would agree that love is at the heart of the marriage. The question is, of course, what do we mean by the word "love"? Two of the most popular readings in *The Order of Celebrating Matrimony* share this all-important word. Their selection gives an opportunity to move

---

37. This essay is best suited for the Nones. Its reflection on the cross of Christ would have little meaning for devout non-Christians, such as Jews, Muslims, and Hindus, and could be misunderstood as Christian triumphalism.

the assembly from believing that love is defined by the lover to seeing that real love is defined by God.

The setting for Matthew 22:35-40 (OCM 182) is the temple area in Jerusalem. Jesus, in the days leading up to his crucifixion, is teaching the astonished crowds and debating the religious leaders. Confronted by a Pharisee to name the greatest commandment in the Law, Jesus combines the commandments to love God (Deut 6:5) and neighbor (Lev 19:18). "The whole law and the prophets depend / on these two commandments." What exactly does love of God and neighbor look like? The Gospel of Luke follows the commandment to love God and neighbor with two stories. The story of the Good Samaritan illustrates love of neighbor, while the story of Martha and Mary hosting Jesus illustrates love of God (see Luke 10:25-42). In contrast, the account in Matthew has no such immediate illustration but soon enters into the account of the passion and death of Jesus, the ultimate demonstration of God's love for us. For the Thirtieth Sunday in Ordinary Time, Year A, the Lectionary joins Matthew 22:34-40 with Exodus 22:20-26. The selection from the covenant code dealing with sojourners, widows, orphans, and the destitute suggests concrete ways that we are to love our neighbor. Love in the Bible is not a feel-good word. It leads one to serve the least and the last and even suffer and die for them, as Jesus Christ did for us.

The New Testament reading often chosen with Matthew 22:35-40 is 1 Corinthians 12:31–13:8a that famously tells us, "Love is patient, love is kind" (OCM 157). Corinth was a Greek city with various cults, a commercial center, games, and theater. Paul wrote to the church in Corinth to urge them to have no divisions among them, as the Body of Christ is one body with many parts. Some of the issues causing division were ideological: idolatry, the denial of the resurrection of the dead, and the meaning of the Eucharist. Some of the issues causing division were practical: those spiritually "in the know" or spiritually gifted over those who were not, and sexual behavior, marriage, and gender.

In the cultural context of the church in Corinth, the encomium on love in chapter 13 is not a philosophical statement on love as much as an exhortation toward unity. While the Gospels of Matthew, Mark, and Luke consider love as a verb and something you do toward your neighbor, Paul considers love a noun, something you have. Without love, as verses 1-3 state, you have only noise, futility, and loss. "If I . . . do not have love, I am nothing." Beginning with "Love is patient," verses 4-7 personify love and offer seven positive and eight negative descriptions of love that bring out the power of love to unify.[38] "Love never fails." An Old Testament reading that is often chosen in this vein is the love poetry in the Song of Songs (OCM 150). It declares, "For stern as death is love."

Unchurched listeners unfamiliar with religious language or uncomfortable with the demands of discipleship can easily separate Matthew 22 and 1 Corinthians 13 from their original intent. These Scripture readings from Matthew, 1 Corinthians, and Song of Songs are so familiar that they likely play like an old song whose lyrics you no longer hear. The challenge is replaced by nostalgia. Given these Scripture readings, it remains for the liturgy and the preaching to move the assembly toward Christian love.

Connecting the Bible and Liturgy

In marriage, the cross and the couple are intimately connected. There is a seed of truth in the humor that marriage is a cross. Pope Francis in his apostolic exhortation *On Love in the Family* wrote, "Christian marriage is a sign of how much Christ loved his Church in the covenant sealed on the cross" (*Amoris Laetitia*, 73). He reiterated that conjugal love "is a reflection of the unbroken covenant between Christ and humanity that culminated in his self-sacrifice on the cross" (*Amoris Laetitia*, 120). He cites John Paul II's apostolic exhortation *The Role of the Christian Family in the Modern World*: "The married couple are therefore a permanent reminder for the Church of what took place on the cross" (*Familiaris Consortio*, 13). Pope Benedict described marriage as an icon. "Marriage based on exclusive and definitive love becomes the icon of the relationship between God and his people and vice versa" (*Deus Caritas Est*, 11). Marriage reveals, however imperfectly, God's way of loving his people through the cross.

The crucifix during a wedding is not background decoration. Brought to the assembly's attention, it becomes a check on our cultural notions of married love. Where society exalts self-expression and self-fulfillment, the cross exalts self-sacrifice. The married couple, taking up their crosses and following Christ, rises again after they have fallen, forgives one another, bears one another's burdens, is subject to one another, and loves one another with supernatural, tender, and fruitful love.[39] The truth that authentic love

---

38. Pope Francis reflects extensively on these verses from 1 Corinthians 13 and their relevance to married life and family in *Amoris Laetitia*, 90–119.

39. *Catechism of the Catholic Church*, 1642.

bears fruit, especially in the gift of children, corrects the perception that love is about personal satisfaction. As the cross brought eternal life into the world, so does marriage bring life into the world. Christian love bears fruit.

Besides the crucifix present in the sanctuary, the sign of the cross is part of wedding liturgy. The first action of the gathered assembly is normally to sign itself with the sign of baptism, "In the name of the Father and of the Son and of the Holy Spirit."[40] (The sign of the cross at the beginning of the liturgy also gives the presider a quick count of the number of Catholics present.) The sign of the cross is repeated before the reading of the gospel. It is made over the blessing of the wedding rings, *arras*, and *lazo*. The last action of the presider is to bless the assembly with the sign of the cross. Another possible presence of the cross might be the shape of the church. A cruciform floor plan shapes the Body of Christ into its most profound form, the cross.

Among the liturgical options, the selection of the gospel acclamation "God is love. / Let us love one another, as God has loved us" (OCM 175, from 1 John 4:8b and 11) repeats that God's love is the measure of our love. The Collect OCM 193 praises God "who since the beginning of the world / have blessed the increase of offspring," reminding us of the fruitfulness of authentic love. The collect asks God to bless the couple "so that in the union of Marriage / they may be bound together / in mutual affection, / in likeness of mind, / and in shared holiness." It envisions a loving union that is more than simply mutual affection. There is likeness of mind and shared holiness, which means shared life with God.

Strategy for Preaching

*Scriptural Texts: Song of Songs 2:8-10, 14, 16a; 8:6-7a; *Psalm 128; 1 Corinthians 12:31-13:8a; Matthew 22:35-40*

Liturgical Texts: Collect OCM 193; Nuptial Blessing OCM 209

1 Corinthians 12:31-13:8a is to weddings what Psalm 23, "The Lord is my shepherd," is to funerals. Popular and familiar, its recitation as-

---

40. As noted previously, the rubrics in chapter 3: The Order of Celebrating Matrimony between a Catholic and a Catechumen or a Non-Christian omit the sign of the cross and the greeting such as "The Lord be with you" (OCM 119–121). This discussion encompasses the uses of the sign of the cross throughout all three orders of celebrating matrimony.

sures the assembly that all is right with the ceremony. The text tempts the preacher to elaborate on several of the qualities of love enumerated by Paul. Making points about love, though, runs counter to the human experience. We do not dream in points, work in points, struggle in points, or play in points. Why love in points? As St. Paul said, "But I shall show you a still more excellent way."

A strategy for preaching "Love is patient" is to move the assembly's understanding of married love from the familiar to the unfamiliar, from cultural conventions to church teaching, from a Valentine's heart to the cross of Christ. Eugene Lowry, in his book *The Homiletical Plot*, proposes a five-stage sequence or "loop" that serves the strategy for preaching 1 Corinthians 13.[41]

The first step of Lowry's loop is "Oops." It upsets the status quo. To hear the familiar Corinthian reading with new ears, the preacher makes a change in the text. You can repeat Paul's litany, replacing the word "love" with the word "I" as in "me." For example, you would say, "Love is patient," and all respond, "I am patient." You continue so that "love is kind" is repeated as "I am kind," "love is not jealous" becomes "I am not jealous," and "love bears all things" is now "I bear all things." This simple, engaging exercise helps us to grasp that we do not always bear all things patiently or respond with kindness. We do not always love.

The second step of Lowry's loop is "Ugh." As we explore why we do not always love, the hole we have stepped into grows deeper. A paraphrase of the first part of 1 Corinthians 13 tells us that preaching and speaking without love is just noise, knowing all things and having great faith without love is nothing, and sacrificing all that we have, yet without love, gains nothing. For lack of love for creation and our common home, countless species are going extinct and our vast oceans have become a smoldering garbage dump. For lack of love, tens of millions of refugees have been forced from their homes as war makes them victims of disease and exploitation. For lack of love, workers struggle in an economy ruled by greed and fear to provide dignity for their families. The lack of love is not simply an occasional oversight. It has cosmic consequences.

A diagnosis of our lack of love may suggest that it is the consequence of settling for . . . wait for it . . . being patient, kind, and never jealous!

41. Eugene L. Lowry, *The Homiletical Plot: The Sermon as Narrative Art Form*, expanded ed. (Louisville, KY: Westminster John Knox Press, 2001), 26.

The Blind Side is a movie based on the true story of a rich white Memphis family who took in Big Mike. He was a poor black man-child more than big enough to play football. The Tuohy family gave him the first bed he'd ever had in his life. They took him shopping for clothes that fit his big-and-tall frame. They gave Big Mike a family that he had never had before. One day at a luncheon, some friends complimented Leigh Ann Tuohy for her Christian generosity. "You are changing his life," they said over the salad. Leigh Ann replied, "No. He is changing our lives." That's love. Love is not safe. Contrary to the idea that love is only about being patient, kind, and never jealous, real love changes your life in ways that are not always planned or appealing. The diagnosis may point toward our fear to love truly.

The third step in the Lowry loop is "Aha!" A clue to resolving this situation appears. In the context of the celebration of marriage, the clue is the miraculous exchange of consent about to take place. The bride and groom say to each other, "I promise to be faithful to you, / in good times and in bad, / in sickness and in health, / to love you and to honor you / all the days of my life." They make this unconditioned promise knowing full well that at times the other person is not always patient, not always kind, plays it safe, and can be afraid of the demands of love. Though the other person does not always love, they promise to love each other no matter what. The couple's mutual self-giving love turns upside down our conditioned and controlling love. It is the clue that sets us on the path to love as God loves.

The fourth step in the Lowry loop is "Whee!" The clue is revealed as nothing less than the Good News. We experience the freeing power of the Gospel. In the bride and groom's promise to one another, we glimpse how the Lord God loves us. Come what may, the Lord gives himself to us, knowing full well that we are not always patient or kind, sometimes jealous, sometimes playing it safe, and sometimes resistant to becoming love. From the cross, God shows his love.

The fifth and final step in the Lowry loop is "Yeah!" This step anticipates how life can now be lived. It helps us to imagine the consequence of the gospel alive in the world. By now, the assembly recognizes that real love does not look like a Valentine's heart. The fullness of love looks like Christ on the cross. In making their promise to each other, the bride and groom make a promise to the world so desperate for real love. They promise not to play life safe. They promise to give witness to God's amazing, saving love, beginning right now before our very own eyes.

OCM *183. Mark 10:6-9

"They are no longer two, but one flesh."[42]

Readings from the Ambo

If the verse "they are no longer two but one flesh" sounds familiar in this commentary, that is because the same verse is found in another gospel selection, Matthew 19:3-6 (OCM *181). Jesus had been asked about divorce. Rather than legislate a new teaching, he went back to an old teaching. In both versions of Matthew and Mark provided by *The Order of Celebrating Matrimony*, Jesus quotes from the first chapter of Genesis when God made them male and female. He quotes from the second chapter of Genesis where a man shall leave his father and mother to be joined to his wife. An interpretive distinction that the OCM makes between the nearly identical versions in Matthew and Mark is in the verse highlighted for each. For Matthew 19:3-6, it chose the final verse of the pericope, "Therefore what God has joined together, / no human being must separate." The emphasis is on separation. For Mark 10:6-9, it chose, "So they are no longer two but one flesh." The emphasis is on union (OCM *183).

The quoted verse, "So they are no longer two but one flesh," is the punch line in the creation story in Genesis 2:18-24 (OCM *145). While the first creation story in the first chapter of Genesis tells us that God created humanity in his image, "male and female he created them," the second creation story in the second chapter of Genesis tells us that man and woman were made for each other. The story begins with the Lord God, having made the man, stating, "It is not good for the man to be alone." Not content with merely noting the state of affairs, the Lord takes steps to fix it. "I will make a suitable partner for him." Pope Francis remarks that the suitable partner created by the Lord, more literally, "a helper fit for him," is able to lighten man's solitude in a way that the animals and creation cannot. He notes that the original Hebrew suggests a direct encounter, face-to-face, eye-to-eye (*Amoris Laetitia*, 12). After the Lord God built up into a woman the rib that he had taken from the man, the man said, "This

---

42. The book of Genesis is shared by Christianity, Judaism, and Islam. This essay, reflecting on the second chapter of Genesis, is especially appropriate when those of Jewish or Muslim faith are present.

one, at last, is bone of my bones / and flesh of my flesh." The encounter explains why a man leaves his father and mother and clings to his wife.

Pope Francis, continuing in *Amoris Laetitia*, reflects that the phrase "to be joined" or "to cleave," in the original Hebrew, "bespeaks a profound harmony, a closeness both physical and interior, to such an extent that the word is used to describe our union with God found in Psalm 63, 'My soul clings to you.'" The two become one flesh in the union of their bodies, hearts, and lives. The encounter by Adam, who is also the man of every time and place, not only relieves his solitude. The encounter leads to their union, and their union gives rise to the family (*Amoris Laetitia*, 13). Through divine mathematics, the two-become-one-flesh becomes three, four, five, or more.

Psalm 128 is a favored responsorial psalm for weddings and also linked in the Sunday Lectionary to Genesis 2:18-24.[43] Psalm 128 envisions the blessings upon the reverent householder. He shall prosper, his wife like a fruitful vine, and his children like shoots of the olive plants around his table. Blessed by the Lord from Zion, his blessings extend to his children's children and implicitly upon generations to come. Showing its pride of place among the psalm options for weddings, Psalm 128 is the only psalm with an asterisk (OCM *171). Further, Pope Francis devotes the first chapter of his apostolic exhortation *On Love in the Family* to Psalm 128 and uses the psalm to structure *Amoris Laetitia*.

Connecting the Bible and the Liturgy

The theme of union can be found in the Collect OCM 189. "O God, who in creating the human race / willed that man and wife [*sic*] should be one, / join, we pray, in a bond of inseparable love . . . so that, as you make their love fruitful, / they may become, by your grace, witnesses to charity itself."[44] The collect nearly outlines Genesis 2:18-24: God created the man and then the woman, the two became one, and their bond bore fruit in their family. The Collect OCM 192 similarly evokes creation, union, and fruitfulness when we pray, "[U]phold / what you have established for the

43. See the Twenty-Seventh Sunday in Ordinary Time, Year B. Mark 10:2-15 is the gospel reading.
44. The Collect OCM 189, instead of referring to "man" and "woman" as in Genesis, upsets the scriptural equality with the cultural phrase "man and wife."

increase of the human race, / so that the union you have created / may be kept safe by your assistance."

The choice of the Nuptial Blessing depends on the circumstances of the particular ceremony. All three Nuptial Blessings begin with some reference to the creation stories in the book of Genesis. The first Nuptial Blessing includes, "O God, who . . . formed man and woman in your own image, making the woman an inseparable helpmate to the man, that they might no longer be two, but one flesh, and taught that what you were pleased to make one must never be divided. . . ." (OCM 205B). The second Nuptial Blessing adds that marriage is a calling, as we pray, "Holy Father, who formed man in your own image, male and female you created them, so that as husband and wife, united in body and heart, they might fulfill their calling in the world . . ." (OCM 207).

The third Nuptial Blessing offers two versions that accommodate the non-Christian. One version prays, "Holy Father, maker of the whole world, who created man and woman in your own image . . . " (OCM 209). The second version (OCM 139) has the same beginning but changes several phrases. "[W]ho are joined today in the Sacrament of Matrimony" becomes "who are joined today in the Marriage covenant." The phrase "they may (adorn their family with children and) enrich the Church" becomes "they may be known for the integrity of their conduct / (and be recognized as virtuous parents)." The second version of the third Nuptial Blessing drops entirely the phrase "let them pray to you in the holy assembly and bear witness to you in the world." The second version is given in chapter 3 of OCM, for celebrating matrimony between a Catholic and a catechumen or a non-Catholic. In sum, the changes avoid mention of the sacrament, the church, and the holy assembly. It would be appropriate to use the Nuptial Blessing OCM 138 in the wedding where one spouse is not baptized such as a Jew or Muslim or Hindu, or where one spouse is a None with no religious frame of reference.

The blessing and placing of the *lazo* or the veil is a custom provided in the OCM 71B, 103B, 137 that resonates with the theme of union. The custom in Spanish cultures including the Philippines is to place a rope or wedding garland around the bride and groom's shoulders in a figure eight. The *lazo* or lasso ropes them together. Or instead of the *lazo*, a veil can be placed over the head of the wife and the shoulders of the husband, symbolizing the bond that unites them. Godparents, whose presence links baptism to matrimony, are traditionally designated to place the *lazo*. The blessing takes place after the consent, rings, and Universal Prayer, and before the Nuptial Blessing.

Strategy for Preaching

*Scriptural Texts: *Genesis 2:18-24; *Psalm 128; *1 Peter 3:1-9; *Mark 10:6-9*

Liturgical Texts: Collect OCM 189; Nuptial Blessing OCM 138

Preaching for the unchurched and the non-Christian should avoid church jargon such as "conjugal covenant." It cannot presume their familiarity with Scripture, including the Scripture read in the Liturgy of the Word. On the other hand, "the two become one" is a common phrase that paints a picture.[45] Put into a message statement, the one thing that you want your targeted listener to know, it might read, "The two become one is very, very good." The targeted listeners would be those who struggle with loneliness and perhaps divorce. The response you might want to evoke is the desire for a committed connection with others and God.

A strategy for preaching "The two become one is very, very good" can follow the "four pages" structure. Paul Scott Wilson, in his book *The Four Pages of the Sermon*, uses the metaphor of four pages or four distinct moments of preaching. Page One is Trouble in the Bible. It considers a tension or conflict in the Bible in its own time. Page Two, Trouble in the World, looks at similar sin or human brokenness in our time. Page Three, God's Action in the Bible, identifies what God is doing in the biblical text about the tension or conflict. Page Four is God's Action in the World where the preaching points to God's gracious action in our world today that deals with Page Two, Trouble in the World.[46] Using analogy in its structural design, the "four pages" structure connects Scripture and God's action today. The Four Pages can organize a wedding homily using Genesis 2:18-24 into four preaching moments that connect Scripture and God's action. In sketching a homily using the Four Pages, you can literally

---

45. As a bonus toward interreligious hospitality, "the two become one" is straight from the book of Genesis, which is part of the Scriptures of Judaism and Islam.

46. Paul Scott Wilson, *The Four Pages of the Sermon: A Guide to Biblical Preaching* (Nashville, TN: Abingdon Press, 1999).

use four sheets of paper, each headed by a simple statement of one idea. The Four Pages flow ultimately toward the faith response that you want your targeted listener to have, in this case, a committed connection with others and God.

Page One, Trouble in the Bible: It is not good to be alone. To set up the tension in the text, you can remind the assembly that, when the Lord God made the earth and the heavens, he formed the man out of the dust of the ground. He blew into his nostrils the breath of life. Thanks to divine CPR, the man became a living being. God placed the man in a garden in Eden. The garden had every kind of tree delightful to see and delicious to eat. A river watered the garden. It was paradise, almost. Besides the situation with the tree of the knowledge of good and evil, which is another homily for another day, something was missing from paradise. The man was alone. The Lord himself said, "It is not good for the man to be alone." The loneliness of the human condition is more than a psychological state. Without going too deep into trinitarian theology, you can simply state that, in the Christian faith, God himself is not alone. God the Father, God the Son, and God the Holy Spirit are three Persons in perfect communion. If the Father stopped talking to the Son, they would cease to be God. What makes God be God is three divine Persons being in complete communion. When God made humanity in his image and likeness, he made us to be like him, in perfect communion with him and others. He created us for relationship. For the man to be alone was not good at all.

Page Two, Trouble in the World: Yet despite our best efforts, we are alone. God said it, and you know it is true. "It is not good for the man to be alone." You can say it again: it is not good to be alone. What is more miserable than a teenager with no friends? Why else for all those dating websites? Here, you can add experiences of loneliness that speak to your assembly, such as the nights in hotel rooms when traveling for work or the empty weekend hours after a divorce. You want them to recognize their futile attempts to fill the loneliness with projects, the internet, work, house, food, drink, vacations, children, or shopping. In their extreme, these distractions can become addictions. Yet none prove suitable. At the end of the day, there is still a deep-down dissatisfaction.

You can help them see that our culture makes it worse. Our electronics give us the illusion of connection while reducing relationships to 140 characters easily deleted. We glorify the self-made man and the lone ranger hero. The normal maturation from a child dependent on his or her parents to an interdependent adult living for others is stuck at the teenager's drive for independence. You can name pertinent examples where life is better together, such as corporations that accomplish more than individuals on their own or that child raising takes a village and a nearby grandmother. The desire you want to cultivate in the assembly is the desire to move from going it alone to going it together. It is no good to be alone. Yet despite our best efforts, we are alone.

Page Three, God's Action in the Bible: God took action to end humanity's loneliness. The reading from Genesis makes the move from going it alone to going it together. Adam, newly minted by God, looked at all created things in the garden to fill his loneliness. The Lord brought to him wild animals and birds of the air, but none took away his loneliness. Finally, God made the woman. Adam exclaimed, "At last! Bone of my bone and flesh of my flesh" (Gen 2:23). No more lonely nights in the garden. The two became one and lived happily ever after. Or did they? Raising an oral eyebrow, the question creates suspense. Rather than answer it right away, you can promise the listener, "More on that in a minute."

In the meantime, in an appeal to the idealism of the young, you can bring in the gospel story from Mark. When asked about the grounds for divorce, Jesus doubled down. Jesus did not water down God's plan for man and woman. He did not give in to popular opinion to reduce the marriage covenant to a contract. Once joined by God, Jesus said, the two become one flesh. That's it, end of discussion.

You can describe God's plan from the beginning of creation, that man and woman unite in a faithful, lifelong, and fruitful relationship. God does not want us to be lonely and alone. His gift of love is much more than emotional satisfaction. He wants us to be one with him and with one another, even as God is three divine Persons yet one God. God made us like peanut butter and chocolate. Each is delicious in itself. Together, though, chocolate and peanut butter become a delicious new food that is very good. God made Adam a helpmate, and the two became one flesh. God took action to end humanity's loneliness. The two become one was very, very good.

Page Four, God's Action in the World: Marriage connects us with one another and God. Earlier, the homily left hanging the fairy-tale ending,

"The two became one and lived happily ever after. Or did they?" The listener is waiting to hear what happens next.

To make the two become one, God made us sexual. Or as Pope St. John Paul II put it, we are an incarnate spirit made for love (*Familiaris Consortio*, 11). Here is the question: Is the cure worse than the disease? Are we worse off being alone or being sexual?

A log in the fireplace is beautiful. It warms body and soul. It draws us together. We instinctively gather around the fireplace. It can even be romantic. The same log burning on a couch can burn down the house. In other words, it matters whether the lit log is in the fireplace or on a couch. In the same way, our sexuality is very powerful. Uniting Adam to Eve, it can make lonely Adam the happiest man on earth. Our sexuality can also lead us, as the song goes, to look for love in all the wrong places. Human sexuality is abused to sell everything from beer to boats. Like a flaming log on the couch, it can destroy health, marriages, and families. What was God thinking?

Our sexuality does three things. First, it connects us to others. Despite being terrified of rejection, a teenager almost against her will finds herself stepping up to that certain boy to say, "Will you go out with me?" Miracles happen every day. Second, our sexuality commits us to another. A husband says, "That's my wife." She grimaces but agrees, "For better or for worse, that's my husband." They belong to one another. The bond of marriage is the deepest commitment that a man and woman can make. Sexual intimacy is the gorilla glue of marriage. Third, our sexuality gives life. Through sexual intimacy, a married couple literally creates life when it conceives a child. God's gift of love keeps on giving when we give ourselves in caring and committed relationships. Husband and wife become cooperators with God for giving life to a new human person (*Familiaris Consortio*, 14).

Our sexuality connects, commits, and creates. The communion of spouses leads to the community of the family in which each person lives for the others. Marriage is like the fireplace at the center of the home. What was God thinking? He created us in love and created us for love. He made us sexual so that the two became one and saw that it was very, very good.

Transition to the Celebration of Matrimony. Up to this point, you have been addressing the assembly. You have spoken to their fear of loneliness and awakened desire for a committed connection with God and others. To make the transition to the exchange of consent, you now address the couple. Turning from the Genesis story, you do not summarize everything you just said. Nor do you introduce new ideas. Instead, you extend an invitation. Evoking what life looks like when the couple lives as one, you simply speak about what happens next. "N. and N., God who created each of you in love now creates a sacred bond between you. In this union, you two become one. From this moment, your life together shows a lonely world that we are not made to be alone. Your marriage shows that we are created to be for each other, body and soul. For the two of you to become one witness to how God loves us, come forward."

OCM 185. John 15:9-12

"Remain in my love."[47]

Readings from the Ambo

The Order of Celebrating Matrimony gives two gospel options from chapter 15 of the Gospel of John: John 15:9-12 (OCM 185) and John 15:12-16 (OCM 186). Before diving into them, it pays to see their larger context. In John 13–17, Jesus is at the Last Supper. After washing the feet of his disciples and anticipating his arrest and crucifixion, he gives his final words to his disciples. In John 15:1-17, he gives two related teachings, abide in Christ and love one another. These uplifting themes are followed by a warning: prepare to be hated. Expect persecution when you abide in Christ and love one another (John 15:18-16:4a). As Father Ray Brown reflected, the intimate love between Jesus and his followers is contrasted with the hatred of the world for his followers.[48] Jesus himself was crucified by such hatred. The expectation of real resistance to the Christian way of life grounds the verse "remain in my love" so that it does not become a warm and fuzzy but abstract tribute to love. "Remain in my love" has a cost.

Looking more closely at the gospel text John 15:9-12, "Remain in my love" (NIV, NABRE) can also be translated, "Abide in my love" (NRSV).

---

47. This essay is best suited for the Nones, rather than for devout non-Christians such as Jews, Muslims, and Hindus. The "Jesus-Others-You" in the "Strategy for Preaching" is intended to stir faith in the Nones who have no religious affiliation.

48. Raymond E. Brown, *The Gospel and Epistles of John: A Concise Commentary* (Collegeville, MN: Liturgical Press, 1988), 83.

It sums up the allegory of the branch connected to the vine. Jesus is the true Vine. We are the branches. Just as a branch cannot bear fruit apart from the vine, neither can we. Our response is an absolute dependence on Christ even as the branch depends on the vine to have life. As he has kept his Father's commandments and remains in his love, so will those who keep Jesus' commandments remain in his love and bear fruit. In other words, keeping his commandments keeps his disciples abiding/remaining in his love. The goal of Christ's words and actions is our joy. He draws us into the divine communion of love "so that my joy might be in you / and your joy might be complete" (John 15:11).

For a New Testament reading, consider OCM 164 or OCM 165 from the First Letter of John. They are discussed in the essay about John 15:12-16. For a gospel acclamation, "Whoever remains in love, / remains in God and God in him" is from 1 John 4:16 (OCM 177). Picking up the theme of remaining/abiding, it connects the love that the couple has for each other and for family and friends with the love of God, for "God is love."

These Scripture readings from the Gospel of John and the First Letter of John are teachings. They do not have images or tell a story. The Old Testament story of Isaac and Rebekah can put flesh on these teachings. We read from the book of Genesis 24:48-51, 58-67 how Isaac came to marry Rebekah (OCM *146). Abraham, the father of Isaac, sent a servant on a long journey to his ancestral homeland to the family of Laban in order to find a wife for Isaac. The proposed marriage was not simply a matter between Isaac and Rebekah. It affected two extended families headed by Abraham and Laban. In the story, Abraham and Laban each played a role. God guided the path toward marriage. Yet Rebekah must give her consent, "I do." Only then, "Isaac took Rebekah into his tent; / he married her, and thus she became his wife." In his love for his wife, we are told, Isaac found solace after the death of his mother, Sarah. Their marriage was bigger than the couple. It was bigger than the union of two families. It had become part of the fulfillment of God's promise to make the descendants of Abraham as countless as the stars in the sky.

Connecting the Bible and the Liturgy

In the gospel reading, Jesus makes clear his desire for our joy. "I have told you this so that my joy might be in you / and your joy might be

complete" (John 15:11). The Questions and the Consent in the Celebration of Matrimony establishes a faithful, lifelong, and fruitful commitment. Each spouse gives consent without any conditions to the marriage.
This moment in the wedding is a prophetic witness for our culture. Our
culture believes that freedom of choice is the way to happiness. Our wedding liturgy holds the opposite. Namely, commitment is the way to joy.

The rite of reception at the very beginning of the marriage ceremony
sets the tone. It directs the priest to go with the servers to the door of
the church where he receives the bridal party and warmly greets them.
After all go to the places prepared, the one who presides addresses the
couple, "N. and N., the Church shares your joy / and warmly welcomes
you" (OCM 53, 88, 120). The Liturgy of the Word follows.

After the homily, all stand for the Celebration of Matrimony. The
presider asks the bride and groom three questions about their freedom,
fidelity, and acceptance and upbringing of children. They do not respond
"We have" or "We are." Speaking for themselves, each responds separately
"I have" or "I am." Like Rebekah who said "I do," the couple freely enters into marriage. For this reason, the custom of the father walking the
bride down the aisle "giving the bride away" is not part of the rite. The
bride freely gives herself. The groom freely gives himself. No one gives
them away or speaks for them. Similarly, the Catholic ceremony does
not include the Hollywood moment, "If anyone can show any just cause
why they may not be lawfully joined together, let him now speak, or else
hereafter forever hold his peace." The marriage preparation has already
determined their freedom to marry.

After the Questions, the presider invites the bride and groom to join
their right hands.[49] The bridegroom says, "I, N., take you, N., to be my
wife. / I promise to be faithful to you, / in good times and in bad, / in
sickness and in health, / to love you and to honor you / all the days of my
life" (OCM 62, 96, 127). The bride makes the same promise to him.[50] In

49. The rubrics do not mention the custom where the father of the bride gives
her hand to the groom, a custom reflecting an older practice where the father gave
the bride in exchange for property.
50. An alternative form of the consent from long-standing English tradition may
be used. "I, N., take you, N., for my lawful wife, / to have and to hold, from this day
forward, / for better, for worse, / for richer, for poorer, / in sickness and in health, /
to love and to cherish / until death do us part."

the Latin text, they do not merely promise fidelity and love. They promise to be faithful in order to love and honor the other. In other words, their faithfulness gives rise to their love.[51] For pastoral reasons, the presider may obtain their consent through questions. "N., do you take N. to be your wife? / Do you promise to be faithful to her / in good times and in bad, / in sickness and in health, / to love her and to honor her / all the days of your life?" The two question forms follow closely the words of the consent given in declaration form.[52]

The presider receives their consent, saying, "May the Lord in his kindness strengthen the consent / you have declared before the Church, / and graciously bring to fulfillment his blessing within you. / What God joins together, let no one put asunder" (OCM 64, 98, 129). The presider's second option puts it more poetically, "the God who joined together our first parents in paradise . . ."

After the Reception of the Consent and before the Blessing and Giving of Rings, there is an acclamation. The presider invites all present to praise God, "Let us bless the Lord." All reply, "Thanks be to God" (OCM 65, 99, 130). There is no mention in the OCM about applause at the end of the ceremony, nor is there mention of a presentation of the newly married couple. Instead, the moment of marriage is the place for applause. Like an exclamation point, the acclamation directs our joy in the sacramental moment to the praise of God.

Strategy for Preaching

Scriptural Texts: *Genesis 24:48-51, 58-67; Psalm 103; 1 John 4:7-12; John 15:9-12

Liturgical Texts: Collect OCM 190; Nuptial Blessing OCM 209

The Scripture verses "remain in my love" and "that your joy be complete" are true, beautiful, and forgettable. A device to avoid teaching timeless but forgettable truth is the mnemonic, The Tiny Dog Now Is

---

51. Turner, *Inseparable Love*, 94.

52. The OCM is silent about the practice where the bride and groom repeat the words of consent after the presider. As they are the ministers of the sacrament, the ideal is that they speak the words unassisted.

Mine. Paul Scott Wilson explains the memory aid in his book, *The Four Pages of the Sermon*.[53] Let's look at each.

The—one Text. Choose one text to preach from. It can be a scriptural reading from the Liturgy of the Word where you use the other readings for further insight. It can be a liturgical text such as the Questions and Consent. The assembly is not interested merely in the readings neatly linking together. They want a link to life. For our purposes, our Text is John 15:9-12 (OCM 185).

Tiny—one Theme. Craft one declarative statement that will shape everything you say. Also known as a sermon-in-a-sentence, the focus statement, or simply the message, the Theme is like an anchor to a harbor buoy. The homily can move and shift within the length of the anchor chain. The Theme must be good news about what God is doing. Our Theme is "We are created for joy."

Dog—one Doctrine. Discover one truth. The index to the *Catechism of the Catholic Church* under "Marriage" lists dozens of teachings from conjugal fidelity to indissolubility. You can muse on covenant, creation, evangelization, the family, holiness, or vocation. One teaching, though, not three or five, gives depth to the Theme. Our Doctrine for this particular preaching is God's Plan.

Now—one felt Need. Form a question that the Theme and Doctrine answer. The felt Need is not the need of the preacher, such as, "They need to know the true meaning of marriage." The felt Need is the need of the assembly. Otherwise, why should they care? We have assumed that the assembly for this homily is unchurched Nones. Their hungers arise out of the human condition—the need to love and be loved, to belong, to have purpose and hope. Our Theme, "We are created for joy," answers the question, "Am I just carbon atoms with attitude?" Our Doctrine, God's plan, speaks to the felt Need to have purpose and know: "Why am I alive?"

Is—one Image. Choose one dominant Image. Many images in a homily take the mind's eye on a blurring tour. In contrast, one recurring image or a main story serves to unify. An Image from the liturgy might be the Questions and Consent. The couple's personal story could be related to the story from the book of Genesis where Rebekah and Isaac come together. Considering the unchurched listener, our Image for this homily is from daily life: a child's play blocks with the letters J, O, and Y.

53. Wilson, 33–57.

Mine—one Mission. Have in mind a particular response to the Theme "We are created for joy." Do you want the assembly to think more about why they exist? Desire more joy in their life? Write down their life goals? The Mission is where the homily is taking us. As the homily is integral to the liturgy, its purpose should be consistent with the liturgy's purpose. Recall that the purpose of the marriage liturgy is twofold: establish a lifelong partnership and celebrate the mystery of unity and fruitful love between Christ and the church (OCM 1, 8). Similarly, the wedding homily should do the "rite" thing. It should work overall toward the same purpose as the liturgy. The purpose or Mission implicit in this homily is for the listeners to ask God the Father to make them persons of joy.

With this particular "The Tiny Dog Now Is Mine," you can outline a three-move homily that describes a path to j-o-y, envisions joy, and takes a step on the path toward joy.

For the first move of the homily, you can assert that the joy of the wedding is not just for one day. Joy is not only for N. and N. God made all of us to live in joy each and every day. Here, you take out a play block with the letter J. J is for Jesus.[54] In our confusing age, many honestly seek meaning but do not know whom to trust or where to commit their lives. Christians are those people who, in the midst of suffering and struggle, trust in Jesus Christ.[55] As personal witness has credibility, your own witness to the assembly is important. Telling briefly how you have known Jesus and his joy supports your statement that joy through Jesus is God's plan for us. You might also play the music, "Jesu, Joy of Man's Desiring." Composed by J. S. Bach almost three hundred years ago, its solemn yet uplifting melody has become the theme music of many weddings. You can hear a solid step in triplet time, a dance that moves you before you are aware. The title of the piece reveals that its joy directs us to our heart's deepest desire, Jesus. We are created for joy. J is for Joy in Jesus. Put Jesus first.

O is for Others. Showing the second play block, you can tell a story about how serving others is so important to you that it takes priority over your own comfort. The Catholic way is to feed the hungry and give

54. See the preparatory catechesis for the 2015 World Meeting of Families titled, *Love Is Our Mission: The Family Fully Alive.* The first chapter "Created for Joy" lays out the meaning of the church in terms of personal journey.

55. The word "trust" may be a better choice than the word "believe," which secular culture might equate with magical thinking.

drink to the thirsty. We do this not because they are Catholic. We do this because we are Catholic. We take responsibility for the Other, be they Muslim, Jew, Hispanic, immigrant, or poor, deserving or undeserving, innocent or guilty. No matter. That's what Jesus did. The way to joy is to put others next. O is for Others.

Y is for You. The third and final play block is the letter Y. Airline flight attendants tell us to put on our oxygen mask first in order to take care of others. We take care of ourselves—eat right, exercise, get a good education, work—in order to take care of others. Rearranging the play blocks, you can point out that Y-O-J is nonsense. The letter Y has a place in joy, but it is not first. The final letter in the word "joy" is Y.

You can sum up the first move of the homily with an analogy: joy is to the climate as happiness is to the weather. Some days are stormy, some days are sunshine. What does not change is the climate. God made us to live in his joy. Jesus said as much at the Last Supper. "I have told you this so that my joy may be in you and your joy may be complete" (John 15:11). Then he suffered and died for us. His desire for our joy had a cost. God made a way for all of us to live in joy each and every day, and that way begins with Jesus.

The second move of the homily is to envision joy. Having asserted that joy is spelled Jesus-Others-You, your listeners need flesh on the bones. The story from the first reading tells how Rebekah and Isaac come together. More than a matter of their individual lives, their marriage brought together two families. It gave consolation to Isaac mourning his mother. It made good on God's promise to Abraham, the father of Isaac, to make his children as countless as the stars in the desert night. Isaac and Rebekah together were something bigger than Isaac and Rebekah apart. They became part of God's plan for our joy. There is joy in being part of God's plan.

The third and final move of the homily is to give direction to the assembly. Bringing them to the present moment, you can talk about the couple's wedding registry, wishing for his and her bicycles, a Weber grill, board games, a frying pan, and a serious vacuum cleaner. Then pose the question, "Why not ask for the things that really matter?" We want patience, health, a good job. Today, this wedding day, why not shoot for the moon? Why not make your ask as high as the heavens? The joy of the wedding is not just for one day. Joy is not only for N. and N. God made a way for us to live in joy each and every day. Before witnessing N. and N. being joined in joy, close your eyes and ask God the Father to make you a person of j-o-y.

OCM 186. John 15:12-16

"This is my commandment: love one another."[56]

Readings from the Ambo

Jesus' double command to love God and love neighbor appears twice in *The Order of Celebrating Matrimony*. In the Gospel of Matthew, a scholar of the law tested Jesus in a tense scene. "Teacher, which commandment in the law is the greatest?" To which Jesus replied, "You shall love the Lord, your God . . . You shall love your neighbor as yourself." He adds, "The whole law and the prophets depend / on these two commandments" (OCM 182). In contrast to the controversy in Matthew, the Gospel of John sets the love command in the intimacy of the Last Supper. Teaching his disciples for the last time, Jesus simply commands, "[L]ove one another as I love you" (OCM 186).

The next verse in the passage clarifies that the love Jesus has in mind is to lay down one's life for one's friends. Such a love is not distinctly Christian. One does not have to be a Christian to drop everything to help a friend. One does not have to be baptized to set aside a career to care for a loved one. What distinguishes Christian love is that it is modeled on Jesus. "To lay down one's life" reminds us of the Good Shepherd who laid down his life for his sheep. The hired man who is not a shepherd and whose sheep are not his own runs away from the wolf. In contrast, a good shepherd knows his sheep by name. He freely lays down his life for his sheep (John 10:11-18). "Love one another as I love you."

Earlier during the Last Supper, after he had humbled himself and washed the feet of his disciples, Jesus said, "I give you a new commandment: love one another. As I have loved you, so you also should love one another" (John 13:34). In Latin, the word *mandatum* was the origin of the term Maundy Thursday, or Holy Thursday. Washing the feet of his disciples as well as the feet of Judas, his betrayer, foreshadowed his crucifixion that cleansed them from sin. He died on the cross for his disciples.

---

56. As with the preceding essay, this essay is best suited for the Nones as well as Millenials. The discussion "Connecting the Bible and Liturgy," addressing the place in the wedding ceremony of the kiss, acclamation, and applause, gives insight to the ceremony that applies equally to Christians and non-Christians. The "Strategy for Preaching," however, focuses on developing a relationship with God in Jesus Christ and may not be appropriate to non-Christian believers.

"Love one another as I love you" meant humble self-sacrifice. The command also appears as the gospel acclamation for the Twenty-Fourth Sunday in Ordinary Time, Year A, to introduce the parable of the king who wished to settle accounts. In the parable, the king forgave the huge debt of a debtor. Yet that same servant in turn choked and imprisoned a fellow servant who owed him a much smaller amount. The parable illustrated Jesus' instruction to Peter to forgive his brother not seven times but seventy-seven times (Matthew 18:21-35). "Love one another as I love you" meant forgiving seventy-seven times. Jesus in his humility, self-sacrifice, and forgiveness is the standard of Christian love.

Only God could give a new commandment. In giving the commandment, "Love one another as I love you," Jesus revealed himself as God. Jesus made clear that he was not giving a suggestion or a guideline. It was a divine decree charged upon his people. The point of the commandment was not to lay a burden. Just the opposite. The commandment gave a share in God's life. "If you keep my commandments, you will remain in my love." In the passage preceding this selection, Jesus told his disciples that he himself kept his Father's commandments and remained in his love. As his disciples love one another as he loved them, with humble self-sacrifice and forgiveness, they remain in his love (OCM 185). Love of one another leads to abiding with God. Marriage marked by humility, self-sacrifice, and forgiveness leads the spouses to dwell with the Lord.

The OCM offers two New Testament selections from the First Letter of St. John that complement the command, "love one another as I love you." One selection, 1 John 4:7-12, states, "Beloved, if God so loved us, / we also must love one another." The love of God embodied in Jesus is the Christian understanding of love. In loving one another as God loves us, God remains in us and his love is brought to perfection in us. The three themes taken together—the love commandment, remaining in God, and Christ's love for us—are one piece. One does not exist without the other (OCM 165).[57] The other selection in the OCM from the First Letter of St. John is 1 John 3:18-24. It has the same themes as 1 John 4:7-12, beginning, "Children, let us love not in word or speech / but in deed and truth." It adds that our hearts can rest easy knowing that God is greater than our

---

57. 1 John 4:7-12 accompanies the gospel reading from John 15:9-17 on the Sixth Sunday of Easter, Cycle B.

weakness. The just person who keeps his commandments has even more confidence before God, whose commandment is to love one another and believe in the name of his Son, Jesus Christ (OCM 164).

It is worth noting that three of the four gospel acclamations in *The Order of Celebrating Matrimony* come from 1 John 4:7-12 (OCM 165). "Everyone who loves is begotten of God and knows God" (OCM 174, 1 John 4:7b); "God is love. / Let us love one another, as God has loved us" (OCM 175, 1 John 4:8b and 11); and "If we love one another, / God remains in us / and his love is brought to perfection in us" (OCM 176, 1 John 4:12). The composers of the OCM Lectionary must have thought highly of 1 John 4. It connects the love of one another with God's love for us. In a word, "God is love."

For those unfamiliar with Catholic liturgy, you can show hospitality and guide them through the liturgy. For example, to help us engage in the liturgy, the Roman Missal allows that the presider may introduce the faithful to the Liturgy of the Word.[58] After the collect and everyone has settled into their places, the presider can say a few words. For example, "Now we listen to God's word to us" prepares the listeners to know what next to expect. The presider might say a word that gets the assembly to listen for something particular in the Scripture reading, such as, "The second reading from Scripture is from the First Letter of John. It gives us a commandment. Notice what the commandment is." Such an introduction plants a seed that grows in the homily.

Connecting the Bible and the Liturgy

A cultural custom to conclude the wedding ceremony is the kiss. At the end of the ceremony, the minister typically announces, "I now introduce to you Mr. and Mrs. N. and N. You may kiss the bride!" To the applause of the assembly and with cameras flashing like fireworks, the newlyweds embrace and plant a big kiss before making their grand exit down the aisle.

The kiss, however, is not part of the liturgy. The couple is married and adult. They do not need the minister's permission to kiss each other. Instead, at the conclusion of the celebration, the priest or deacon blesses the people. He makes the sign of the cross and says, "May almighty God bless

58. Roman Missal, 128.

all of you, / who are gathered here, / the Father, and the Son, and the Holy Spirit." All respond, "Amen."[59] The red rubrics commend the praiseworthy practice to end the celebration with a "suitable chant." The only other instruction in the conclusion is that the witnesses and the presider sign the marriage record; it is not to be done on the altar (OCM 141–143). That's it. No mention of Mendelssohn's "Wedding March" from *A Midsummer Night's Dream*. No kiss.

The big moment for applause and photographs envisioned by the liturgy is the Consent. After the bridegroom and bride declare their consent to enter the covenant of holy matrimony before God and his church, promising to be faithful in good times and in bad all the days of their life, they are married.[60] The presider receives their consent and adds, "[W]hat God joins together, no one may put asunder." The presider invites all present to praise God with an acclamation, "Let us bless the Lord." All reply, "Thanks be to God."[61] The acclamation, new to the second edition of the OCM, is the assembly's response to the moment of marriage.

Similarly, after the Blessing and Giving of Rings, a hymn or canticle of praise may be sung by the whole community (OCM 68, 102, 134). This moment of praise is also new to the second edition of the OCM. As mentioned earlier, the custom where the couple lights a unity candle while a singer performs a solo is in contrast to the OCM vision that the whole community sing in praise to God. The OCM makes no mention of a unity candle.

The acclamation and praise intended in the celebration of matrimony recall the acclamation in the celebration of baptism. Immediately after the immersion in water and the words "I baptize you in the name of the Father, and of the Son, and of the Holy Spirit," the rubric states that it is appropriate for the people to sing a short acclamation. The same spontaneous applause that accompanies baptism belongs to the moment of consent. In practice, the people, especially those unfamiliar with a Catholic wedding, need help to claim their part. A participation aid can point out their response. The cantor can cue the people to repeat a musical

---

59. The rubrics in the ceremony between a Catholic and a catechumen or non-Christian omit the liturgical greeting "The Lord be with you," as the greeting presumes a gathering of Christian faithful. The final blessing uses the simple form and never the solemn threefold form.

60. It is at this point that the rubrics first mention the husband and wife instead of the bride and bridegroom (OCM 132).

61. Another acclamation may be sung or said (OCM 65, 99, 130).

acclamation such as an Alleluia. The bottom line is that the big moment for the people's acclaim is the marriage moment.

Strategy for Preaching

Scriptural Texts: *Genesis 1:26-28, 31a; Psalm 33; 1 John 4:7-12; John 15:12-16

Liturgical Texts: Collect OCM 191; Nuptial Blessing OCM 209

"Know your audience" is the first rule of public speaking. What kind of audience might you expect for a wedding? The 2014 U.S. Religious Landscape Study by the Pew Research Center found that over one in three Millennials born 1981–1996 is religiously unaffiliated.[62] In comparison, only one in five Baby Boomers born 1946–1964 describe themselves as atheist, agnostic, or nothing in particular. Millennials are much more likely than Baby Boomers to be religious Nones. As many of those who attend a wedding are young adults, you can safely assume that more and more of those you are preaching to do not believe in God, heaven, or hell; seldom or never pray or attend a religious service or read Scripture; favor same-sex marriage; and turn to common sense and science instead of religion for moral guidance. They consider themselves spiritual but not religious. In short, they are not impressed by verses from Scripture, quotes from the pope, or citations from the *Catechism*.

What many still respond to is personal experience. *Fulfilled in Your Hearing*, the 1982 statement on preaching by the United States Conference of Catholic Bishops, advises accordingly that the homily normally begin with a contemporary human situation. After connecting with the lived personal experience of the assembly, the homilist can turn to Scripture to show how God is present and active in this human situation. A structure grounded on lived experience speaks more authentically to the lives of the religious Nones than, "In today's readings . . . this reminds us . . . therefore let us . . . " Such a three-part pattern tends to interpret

---

62. The unaffiliated Millennials grew from 31 percent in 2007 to 35 percent in 2014 among all Millennials. The trend toward unaffiliation is growing. For more survey results, see Pew Research Center, 2014 U.S. Religious Landscape Study. Accessed at http://www.pewforum.org/religious-landscape-study/religious-tradition/unaffiliated-religious-nones/.

Scripture in such a way as to draw out an ethical demand ("we should . . .") and impose a burden on the listeners summed up in two words, "Try harder." This pattern may offer good advice, but is rarely Good News. It hardly invites those in attendance to come back and hear more. Connecting life and faith does.[63]

How do you preach to the Nones? Andy Stanley, in his book *Communicating for a Change*, emphasizes personal experience through a five-part format: Me-We-God-You-We.[64] Preaching from John 15:12-16, "Love one another as I love you," the one thing we might want them to walk away with is the message, "Rules protect relationships." For the Millennials who distrust religion, its rules and its rule makers, such a message presents a challenge. While "rules protect relationships" talks about something they care deeply about (relationships), the message sets up a tension (rules) that needs resolution. This tension drives the homily home.

The first part, ME, is not really about me. It is about finding common ground. The assembly has to trust the messenger before it trusts the message. Your personal experience shared with sincerity and conviction goes a long way toward earning their trust. To ease into the main message, "Rules protect relationships," start with some personal examples on the topic "My friendships have rules." You might iterate rules for your own friendships, such as to return phone calls and messages, remember birthdays, spend time hanging out doing nothing in particular, be loyal, never talk bad about a friend, keep their secrets a secret, be honest but not critical, listen and open up, and forgive and ask forgiveness when the rules are broken. After you name some of the unspoken rules of your own friendships, note the payoff: You have real friends. The rules strengthen your friendships.

The next part, WE, builds on the first part ME to include the assembly. It continues to consider that rules (ugh!) can be a good thing (huh?). "My friendships have rules" segues nicely to the topic at hand, "Marriages have rules." Rules for the couple: Never yell at each other unless the house is on fire. Never bring up mistakes of the past. No ultimatums—ever. Date

63. James Wallace, ed., *Preaching in the Sunday Assembly: A Pastoral Commentary on* Fulfilled in Your Hearing (Collegeville, MN: Liturgical Press, 2010), 81.

64. Andy Stanley and Lane Jones, *Communicating for a Change* (Colorado Springs, CO: Multnomah Books, 2006), 120–31.

night is sacred. Fool around (with each other). No difficult conversations after 10 p.m. (not only is it harder to solve problems when you're tired, but being tired is often the problem). Kiss good night for six seconds. Long kisses often lead to something even better than conversation. The rules, once again, pay off. The rules strengthen the marriage.

The third part, GOD, turns toward faith. It starts to resolve the tension by pointing toward God. In this case, what does God have to do with rules? To an assembly slowly recognizing the value of rules and relationships yet suspicious of God and church, the statement "God gave us a new rule" challenges their belief that God and rules are oppressive. You can tell them that God gave us a new rule, "love one another." At first glance, who cares about such a bland command? In itself, it is meaningless. The good news is the second half of the verse, "as I love you." Put "love one another" together with "as I love you" and God's new rule says, "Love one another as I love you." Here, tell the story of Jesus to describe how he loves us. Born in Bethlehem two thousand years ago, God Most High became a baby. He taught and healed. In the last week of his life, he loved us to the end. He washed the feet of his followers, even the feet of Judas who betrayed him. He was tortured, suffered, and died on the cross. Three days later he rose from the dead. He did all this because he loves us.

The story of Jesus, as wonderful as it is, is an abstraction to the unchurched Nones. They need an image. A banana is such an image. A banana has two parts, the skin and the fruit. No one eats the skin. Yet who would buy a banana without a skin? Without a skin, the banana fruit quickly becomes mush. It spoils and smells. The skin protects and preserves the fruit. In the same way, the rules protect our relationships. As the banana skin protects and preserves the fruit, the rules protect and preserve our bananas—friendships and marriage. Jesus did something new. Jesus gave us a new rule, "Love one another as I love you," to protect a new banana, our relationship with him. That's the payoff: friendship with Christ.

The fourth part, YOU, is the application to the assembly. It answers the assembly's unspoken questions, "So what?" and "Now what?" Speaking to the couple and at the same time speaking through them to all who aspire to marriage, you tell them that there are three rules for marriage. The first rule is to be faithful. The couple gives their unconditional consent to put their marriage first. They promise not to have inappropriate relationships or use pornography. They promise to put the marriage before their children, work, house, travel, parents, retirement, or any other matter, as good as these things might be. The next rule builds on the first. The rule is to be faithful all the days of their life. No matter what happens to their looks, their health, or their fortunes, they pledge their lifelong fidelity. "All the days" means each and every day, whether they feel like it or not. Not just on weekdays, not just during the summer, but all the days of their lives they promise fidelity. The third rule is to be open to accept children lovingly from God and to bring them up according to the rule of Christ and his church, namely, to love one another as Christ loves us. Just as strong and healthy roots cannot help but burst into a tree trunk and canopy giving cool shade and tasty fruit, a faithful, lifelong relationship cannot help but give life. Children are the fruit of marriage. These three rules are what make a marriage a marriage. They are the banana skin that preserves and protects the marriage. Love does not sustain the marriage; marriage sustains the love.

The fifth and final part, WE, is the moment of inspiration. Paint a picture of what it looks like when we do the fourth part, YOU. When a married couple keeps the three rules of marriage, what happens? Great things happen! The two become one. They build a bond that can survive sickness, failure, unemployment, and disappointment. Loving one another as Christ loves them, they lay down their lives for each other. In this fifth part, you dream on behalf of all present. Help them imagine what would happen if we live the rule "Love one another as I love you." Selfishness would give way to sacrifice, friends can ask forgiveness, and marriages would accept suffering with joy. We discover new rules, such as the truth that chastity is the path to intimacy and that thanks and praise belong to the Lord. The rules become so much a part of us that it's no longer about the rules. It's about the banana. The fifth part, WE, inspires the assembly to feel "Wheee!" There is no need to exhort them to be faithful all the days of their lives. You have planted in them the desire to love one another as Christ loves them.

Appendix I: Various Texts to Be Used in the Rite of Marriage

I *Biblical Readings*

(Note that at least one reading designated with an asterisk [*] must be used in the wedding liturgy)

Readings from the Old Testament (see Lectionary for Mass, 801)

*144. Genesis 1:26-28, 31a. Male and female he created them.

*145. Genesis 2:18-24. The two of them become one body.

*146. Genesis 24:48-51, 58-67. In his love for Rebekah, Isaac found solace after the death of his mother.

*147. Tobit 7:6-14. May the Lord of heaven prosper you both. May he grant you mercy and peace.

*148. Tobit 8:4b-8. Allow us to live together to a happy old age.

*149. Proverbs 31:10-13, 19-20, 30-31. The woman who fears the Lord is to be praised.

150. Song of Songs 2:8-10, 14, 16a; 8:6-7a. Stern as death is love.

*151. Sirach 26:1-4, 13-16. Like the sun rising in the Lord's heavens, the beauty of a virtuous wife is the radiance of her home.

152. Jeremiah 31:31-32a, 33-34a. I will make a new covenant with the house of Israel and the house of Judah.

Readings from the New Testament (see Lectionary for Mass, 802)

153. Romans 8:31b-35, 37-39. What will separate us from the love of Christ?

154. Romans 12:1-2, 9-18 (or Short Form 12:1-2, 9-13). Offer your bodies as a living sacrifice, holy and pleasing to God.

155. Romans 15:1b-3a, 5-7, 13. Welcome one another as Christ welcomed you.

156. 1 Corinthians 6:13c-15a, 17-20. Your body is a temple of the Spirit.

157. 1 Corinthians 12:31–13:8a. If I do not have love, I gain nothing.

158. Ephesians 4:1-6. One Body and one spirit.

*159. Ephesians 5:2a, 21-33 (or Short Form 5:2a, 25-32). This is a great mystery, but I speak in reference to Christ and the church.

160. Philippians 4:4-9. The God of peace will be with you.

161. Colossians 3:12-17. And over all these put on love, that is, the bond of perfection.

162. Hebrews 13:1-4a, 5-6b. Let marriage be held in honor by all.

*163. 1 Peter 3:1-9. Be of one mind, sympathetic, loving toward one another.

164. 1 John 3:18-24. Love in deed and in truth.

165. 1 John 4:7-12. God is love.

166. Revelation 19:1, 5-9a. Blessed are those who have been called to the wedding feast of the Lamb.

Responsorial Psalms (see Lectionary for Mass, 803)

167. Psalm 33:12 and 18, 20-21, 22. The earth is full of the goodness of the Lord.
168. Psalm 34:2-3, 4-5, 6-7, 8-9. I will bless the Lord at all times. Or: Taste and see the goodness of the Lord.
169. Psalm 103:1-2, 8 and 13, 17-18a. The Lord is kind and merciful. Or: The Lord's kindness is everlasting to those who fear him.
170. Psalm 112:1bc-2, 3-4, 5-7a, 7b-8, 9. Blessed the man who greatly delights in the Lord's commands. Or: Alleluia.
*171. Psalm 128:1-2, 3, 4-5ac and 6a. Blessed are those who fear the Lord. Or: See how the Lord blesses those who fear him.
172. Psalm 145:8-9, 10 and 15:17-18. How good is the Lord to all.
173. Psalm 148:1-2, 3-4, 9-10, 11-13a, 13c-14a. Let all praise the name of the Lord. Or: Alleluia.

Alleluia Verses and Verses before the Gospel (see Lectionary for Mass, 804)

174. 1 John 4:7b. Everyone who loves is begotten of God and knows God.
175. 1 John 4:8b and 11. God is love. Let us love one another, as God has loved us.
176. 1 John 4:12. If we love one another, God remains in us and his love is brought to perfection in us.
177. 1 John 4:16. Whoever remains in love, remains in God and God in him.

Gospel Readings (see Lectionary for Mass, 805)

178. Matthew 5:1-12a. Rejoice and be glad, for your reward will be great in heaven.
179. Matthew 5:13-16. You are the light of the world.
180. Matthew 7:21, 24-29 (or Short Form 7:21, 24-25). A wise man built his house on rock.
*181. Matthew 19:3-6. What God has united, man must not separate.
182. Matthew 22:35-40. This is the greatest and the first commandment. The second is like it.
*183. Mark 10:6-9. They are no longer two, but one flesh.
*184. John 2:1-11. Jesus did this as the beginning of his signs at Cana in Galilee.

185. John 15:9-12. Remain in my love.
186. John 15:12-16. This is my commandment: love one another.
187. John 17:20-26 (or Short Form 17:20-23). That they may be brought to perfection as one.

II Collects

188. O God, who consecrated the bond of Marriage by so great a mystery . . .
189. O God, who in creating the human race willed that man and wife should be one . . .
190. Be attentive to our prayers, O Lord, and in your kindness pour out your grace . . .
191. Grant, we pray, almighty God, that these your servants . . . may grow in the faith . . .
192. Be attentive to our prayers, O Lord, and in your kindness uphold what you have established . . .
193. O God, who since the beginning of the world have blessed the increase of offspring . . .

III Prayers for the Blessing of Rings

194. Bless, O Lord, these rings, which we bless in your name . . .
195. Bless and sanctify your servants in their love, O Lord, . . .

IV Prayers over the Offerings

196. Receive, we pray, O Lord, the offering made on the occasion . . .
197. Receive in your kindness, Lord, the offerings we bring . . .
198. Show favor to our supplications, O Lord . . .

V Prefaces

199. The dignity of the Marriage covenant.
200. The great Sacrament of Matrimony.
201. Matrimony as a sign of divine love.

VI Commemoration of the Couple in the Eucharistic Prayer

202. in Eucharistic Prayer I
203. in Eucharistic Prayer II
204. in Eucharistic Prayer III

VII *Other Prayers of Nuptial Blessing (with Music)*

205. Also 74, 105. O God, who by your mighty power created all things
     out of nothing . . .
207. Holy Father, who formed man in your own image, . . .
209. Holy Father, maker of the whole world, . . .

VIII *Prayers After Communion*

210. By the power of this sacrifice, O Lord, . . .
211. Having been made partakers at your table, we pray, O Lord, . . .
212. Grant, we pray, almighty God, that the power of the Sacrament . . .

IX *Blessings at the End of the Celebration*

213. May God the eternal Father keep you of one heart . . .
214. May God the all-powerful Father grant you his joy . . .
215. May the Lord Jesus, who graced the marriage at Cana by his pres-
     ence, . . .

Appendix II: Formularies for the Celebration of Marriage in the Roman Missal

The Roman Missal gives three ritual Masses for the celebration of marriage "for the sake of convenience." From among the options for the
various prayers, Formulary A takes the first option of each prayer, Formulary B takes the second option of each prayer, and Formulary C takes
the third option of each prayer. The rubric specifies that all texts may be
exchanged, if appropriate, with others. The numbers indicate *The Order
of Celebrating Matrimony*.

Formulary A in the Roman Missal

Collect	190. Be attentive to our prayers, O Lord, / and in your kindness / pour out your grace . . . , or: 189. O God, who in creating the human race / willed that man and wife should be one . . .
Prayer over the Offerings	196. Receive, we pray, O Lord, / the offering made on the occasion . . .
Preface	199. The dignity of the Marriage covenant.

Nuptial Blessing	205. Also 74, 105. O God, who by your mighty power created all things out of nothing . . .
Prayer after Communion	210. By the power of this sacrifice, O Lord, . . .
Solemn Blessing	213. May God the eternal Father keep you of one heart . . .

Formulary B in the Roman Missal

Collect	190. Be attentive to our prayers, O Lord, / and in your kindness / pour out your grace . . . , or: 188. O God, who consecrated the bond of Marriage / by so great a mystery . . .
Prayer over the Offerings	197. Receive in your kindness, Lord, / the offerings we bring . . .
Preface	200. The great Sacrament of Matrimony.
Nuptial Blessing	207. Holy Father, who formed man in your own image, . . .
Prayer after Communion	211. Having been made partakers at your table, / we pray, O Lord, . . .
Solemn Blessing	214. May God the all-powerful Father grant you his joy . . .

Formulary C in the Roman Missal

Collect	191. Grant, we pray, almighty God, / that these your servants . . . may grow in the faith . . . , or: 193. O God, who since the beginning of the world / have blessed the increase of offspring . . .
Prayer over the Offerings	198. Show favor to our supplications, O Lord, . . .
Preface	201. Matrimony as a sign of divine love.
Nuptial Blessing	209. Holy Father, maker of the whole world, . . .
Prayer after Communion	212. Grant, we pray, almighty God, / that the power of the Sacrament . . .
Solemn Blessing	215. May the Lord Jesus, / who graced the marriage at Cana by his presence . . .

Bibliography

Ritual Books

Book of Blessings, 1989.
Catechism of the Catholic Church, 2nd ed., 1997.
The Order of Celebrating Matrimony (OCM), 2nd ed., 2016.
The Roman Missal, Third Edition, 2010.

Selected Church Teaching on Matrimony

Benedict. *God Is Love (Deus Caritas Est)*. Encyclical Letter. December 25, 2005. Accessed at http://w2.vatican.va/content/benedict-xvi/en/encyclicals /documents/hf_ben-xvi_enc_20051225_deus-caritas-est.html.

Francis. *On Love in the Family (Amoris Laetitia)*. Post-Synodal Apostolic Exhortation. March 19, 2016. Accessed at http://m.vatican.va/content /dam/francesco/pdf/apost_exhortations/documents/papa-francesco _esortazione-ap_20160319_amoris-laetitia_en.pdf.

John Paul II. *The Role of the Christian Family in the Modern World (Familiaris Consortio)*. Apostolic Exhortation. November 22, 1981. Boston: Pauline Books and Media, 2015.

———. *Letter to Families (Gratissimam Sane)*. February 2, 1994. Manchester, NH: Sophia Institute for Teachers, 2015.

United States Conference of Catholic Bishops. *Marriage: Love and Life in the Divine Plan*. Pastoral Letter. November 17, 2009. Accessed at http://www .usccb.org/issues-and-action/marriage-and-family/marriage/love-and-life /upload/pastoral-letter-marriage-love-and-life-in-the-divine-plan.pdf.

———. *For Your Marriage*. Website. Accessed at http://www.foryourmarriage.org/.

World Meeting of Families. *Love Is Our Mission: The Family Fully Alive*. A preparatory catechesis for the World Meeting of Families. Philadelphia: World Meeting of Families, 2014.

Commentaries on Scripture

Brown, Raymond E. *The Gospel and Epistles of John: A Concise Commentary*. Collegeville, MN: Liturgical Press, 1988.

Byrne, Brendan. *A Costly Freedom: A Theological Reading of Mark's Gospel*. Collegeville, MN: Liturgical Press, 2008.

———. *Life Abounding: A Reading of John's Gospel*. Collegeville, MN: Liturgical Press, 2014.

———. *Lifting the Burden: Reading Matthew's Gospel in the Church Today*. Collegeville, MN: Liturgical Press, 2004.

Harrington, Daniel J. *The Gospel of Matthew*. Edited by Daniel J. Harrington. Vol. 1. Sacra Pagina series. Collegeville, MN: Liturgical Press, 1991.

Kysar, Robert. *Preaching John.* Minneapolis, MN: Fortress Press, 2002.

Commentaries on the Rite of Matrimony

Champlin, Joseph M., with Peter A. Jarret. *Together for Life.* Fifth edition. Notre Dame, IN: Ave Maria Press, 2011.
Turner, Paul. *Inseparable Love: A Commentary on* The Order of Celebrating Matrimony *in the Catholic Church.* Collegeville, MN: Liturgical Press, 2017.
———. *One Love: A Pastoral Guide to* The Order of Celebrating Matrimony. Collegeville, MN: Liturgical Press, 2016.

Homiletics

Francis. *The Joy of the Gospel (Evangelii Gaudium).* Apostolic Exhortation. November 24, 2013. Accessed at http://w2.vatican.va/content/francesco/en/apost_exhortations/documents/papa-francesco_esortazione-ap_20131124_evangelii-gaudium.html.
Lowry, Eugene L. *The Homiletical Plot: The Sermon as Narrative Art Form.* Expanded edition. Louisville, KY: Westminster John Knox Press, 2001.
Stanley, Andy, and Lane Jones. *Communicating for a Change.* Colorado Springs, CO: Multnomah Books, 2006.
The Sunday Website of St. Louis University. Accessed at http://liturgy.slu.edu/.
United States Conference of Catholic Bishops. *Website for Homiletics.* Accessed at http://www.usccb.org/prayer-and-worship/homiletics/index.cfm.
———. *Preaching the Mystery of Faith: The Sunday Homily.* Washington, DC: United States Conference of Catholic Bishops, 2012.
———. *Preaching the Social Doctrine of the Church in the Mass, Year A.* Washington, DC: United States Conference of Catholic Bishops, 2013.
Untener, Ken. *Preaching Better: Practical Suggestions for Homilists.* New York: Paulist, 1999.
Wallace, James A., ed. *Preaching in the Sunday Assembly: A Pastoral Commentary on* Fulfilled in Your Hearing. *Commentary and Text.* Collegeville, MN: Liturgical Press, 2010.
Wilson, Paul Scott. *The Four Pages of the Sermon: A Guide to Biblical Preaching.* Nashville, TN: Abingdon Press, 1999.

Other

Pew Research Center. *2014 U.S. Religious Landscape Study.* Accessed at http://www.pewforum.org/religious-landscape-study/religious-tradition/unaffiliated-religious-nones/.
Wilbricht, Stephen S. *Rehearsing God's Just Kingdom: The Eucharistic Vision of Mark Searle.* Collegeville, MN: Liturgical Press, 2013.

PREACHING FUNERALS

Francis L. Agnoli

Why celebrate funerals? And, more to the point, given the focus of this book, why preach at them? According to the general introduction to the *Order of Christian Funerals*[1] (OCF), in its funeral rites "the Church intercedes on behalf of the deceased . . . and ministers to the sorrowing and consoles them . . . with the comforting word of God and the sacrament of the eucharist" as well as offers "worship, praise, and thanksgiving to God for the gift of a life which has now returned to God" (OCF 4–5). The heart of the OCF is the paschal mystery (OCF 1).

The Scriptures are given particular prominence in the celebration of these rites. The general introduction reminds us that the "readings proclaim to the assembly the paschal mystery, teach remembrance of the dead, convey the hope of being gathered together again in God's kingdom . . . encourage the witness of Christian life . . . [and] tell of God's design for a world in which suffering and death will relinquish their hold on all whom God has called his own" (OCF 22). The psalms are held in special esteem because they are able to give voice to "the suffering and pain, the hope and trust" of those gathered for the funeral rites (OCF 25).

Why preach? The OCF (27) holds up the homily, required at the funeral liturgy and permitted (though presumed; see 61 and 77) at the vigil, as an exercise of pastoral ministry. The preacher is called to be "attentive to the grief" of those gathered, to "dwell on God's compassionate love and on the paschal mystery" of Christ, and to see how this mystery was present in the life of the deceased and in their own lives. To console, to strengthen, to give thanks, to proclaim hope: this is why we preach, and why we preach a homily—and never a eulogy (OCF 27).[2]

---

1. *Order of Christian Funerals*, in *The Rites of the Catholic Church: Volume One* (Collegeville, MN: Liturgical Press, 1990). All references are to this edition.

2. A friend or member of the family may speak in remembrance of the dead at the end of both the vigil (80, 96) and the funeral (170, 197). Some might refer to this as a

Preaching, including funeral preaching, involves multiple dialogue partners: the Scriptures, the cultural and liturgical contexts in which the preaching takes place, the assembly, and the preacher. While this latter topic cannot be explored in depth here, it is important to at least mention that we preach out of who we are: our history of loss as well as our theology of suffering, death, and dying will affect how we approach the task of funeral preaching. Preachers bring themselves into the pulpit, with their own particular stories of grief and loss. Some of these losses may have been mourned well, but old wounds may be reopened by the particularities of a given funeral. Other losses might still be raw and not yet integrated. Either way, preachers will preach out of these experiences, just as preachers will preach out of their theology—whether it has been made explicit and critically reflected upon or not. The less aware we are of our losses and theology the more we risk preaching in a way that harms the assembly.

Context: The *Order of Christian Funerals*

Funeral preaching takes place in a particular liturgical context: the celebration of the rites found in the OCF. [3] While the OCF offers rites for the funerals of adults as well as of children, I am limiting myself here to the former.

The OCF presumes three rites, separated by two processions: the vigil, the funeral liturgy (within or outside of Mass), and the rite of committal. The vigil focuses on the present, on accompanying mourners in their bewilderment, shock, and grief, and helping them to "express their sorrow and to find strength and consolation" in the paschal mystery of Christ (OCF 52). While the funeral liturgy still remains attentive to the mourners, these rites focus primarily on giving "praise and thanks to God for Christ's victory over sin and death" and on commending "the deceased to God's tender mercy and compassion" (OCF 129). The funeral, with its emphasis on anamnesis, recalls the past in order to comfort in the

---

"eulogy," though the OCF does not use that term (and so neither do I). A eulogy in the sense of exaggerated praise for the deceased would be out of place at a Christian funeral.

3. The term "funeral rites" refers to all the rites contained in the OCF, and especially to the three major rites (vigil, funeral, committal). The term "funeral liturgy" refers to the second station of the three, and may be celebrated within Mass or outside of Mass.

present and open up a new future. By viewing the great deeds of God in the past through the lens of the life of the deceased, God's promises can once again be appropriated. Finally, the focus of the rite of committal shifts to the future, to relinquishment with a sense of hope in the face of the reality of death (OCF 206, 209).

In other words, the OCF might be considered as a "rite of passage." The sequence of rites attends to separation (vigil), to traversing the liminal state (funeral), and to reintegration (committal). The present loss is named honestly, the past is remembered with gratitude, and the future is approached with a sense of hope and meaning.

Context: Grief

General

Grief and mourning are complex human experiences; not everyone mourns in the same way or experiences the same reactions to loss. That being said, some generalizations are helpful.[4] The immediate reaction to loss may be characterized in the acute phase by denial, numbness, disbelief, and physical symptoms such as shortness of breath, throat tightness, sighing, and loss of appetite. Here, the individual is faced with the immediacy of separation from a loved one. Pastoral care in this acute setting most often centers on practical assistance and support as mourners express their feelings of loss. After this acute phase, mourners begin to experience the distress that comes from the reality of the separation. Bargaining, anxiety, yearning, and anger may all be experienced. It is not unusual at this time for mourners to want to tell stories about the deceased; pastoral care revolves around encouraging such remembrances and active listening. Eventually, if all goes well, one moves from denial to acceptance—not as a single moment, but more as a gradual shift over time. Here, pastoral care has the goal of assisting the bereaved in the task of reintegration.

4. Coval B. MacDonald, "Loss and Bereavement," in *Clinical Handbook of Pastoral Counseling*, vol. 1, expanded ed., ed. Robert J. Wicks, Richard D. Parsons, and Donald Capps, 539–58 (New York: Paulist Press, 1993); Paul K. Maciejewski, Baohui Zhang, Susan D. Block, and Holly G. Prigerson, "An Empiric Examination of the Stage Theory of Grief," *JAMA* 297, no. 7 (Feb. 21, 2007): 716–23; and Vamik D. Volkan and Elizabeth Zintl, *Life After Loss: The Lessons of Grief* (New York: Charles Scribner's Sons, 1993).

Of course, not everyone experiences the same complex of feelings, in the same order, and without revisiting previous phases. But the general pattern is helpful to keep in mind: separation, transition (liminality), and incorporation. Honesty in the face of loss, gratitude for the past (remembrance), hope in the future (meaning-making): these are also the hallmarks of healthy mourning. The OCF provides the mourners a road map to follow; it points them—even while they are still early in their journey—in the right direction.

Particularity

Every funeral is particular. While the OCF forbids that the homily be a eulogy, this does not mean that funeral preaching is to be impersonal or generic. Rather, it may be helpful to think of the funeral homily as communal meaning-making that flows from the intersection of three stories:[5] God's story (as reflected in *these* Scriptures and liturgical texts), the story of *this* deceased person, and the story of *these* bereaved persons. In weaving these stories together we are able to name the particular loss and how it is being experienced, we are able to give thanks for a particular person and point out where Christ has been present in his or her life and death and in the life of the assembly. As a result, we can help move *these* people toward a hopeful future. Generic preaching that ignores the particularity of the deceased, the bereaved, or even of God in this situation falls far short of what the OCF envisions for the funeral homily. Such preaching is lifeless, has no impact, and is a disservice to the mourners.

A homily that overemphasizes the story of the deceased becomes a eulogy; there is no room for the grief of the mourners or for proclaiming either God's abiding presence and care or the Christian hope of salvation.[6] An overemphasis on the mourners turns the funeral into grief therapy;

---

5. Robert A. Hughes, *Trumpet in Darkness: Preaching to Mourners*, Fortress Resources for Preaching (Philadelphia: Fortress Press, 1985): 22, 80.

6. Perhaps this phenomenon is reflected in the increasing use of the term "celebration of life" for funerals, implying that only positive memories (the past) of the deceased are permissible. Present loss and future hope are marginalized, if not excluded. In commenting on the "'celebration of life' craze," my coauthor, Fr. David Scotchie, offered this admonition: "Can we correct this cultural hijacking of our liturgy and return to the celebration of the life, death, and resurrection of Jesus Christ as the core of our funeral rites? As for the deceased, we give thanks for the gift of

the deceased is displaced and there is no room for God. Finally, even an overemphasis on "God's story" can be detrimental, leading to a generic homily that, while perhaps theologically exact, ignores the particularities of both deceased and mourner. That being said, we do need to finally turn our attention to "God's story" as revealed in the readings and prayers chosen for a particular funeral.

Texts: A Method of Correlation

"A careful selection and use of readings from Scripture for the funeral rites will provide the family and community with an opportunity to hear God speak to them in their needs, sorrows, fears, and hopes" (OCF 22). How does one make such a careful selection, given that if there are two readings and a responsorial psalm before the gospel, there are 31,350 possible combinations of readings that might be used at the vigil or funeral liturgy for an adult?

Groups of Readings

A number of authors have offered various ways to organize the funeral readings. For example, both Reginald Fuller and Donald Senior group the readings according to themes. Paul Turner does the same, and adds groupings according to key words. Robert Hughes suggests readings based on the cause of death and what would likely be the predominant emotion among the mourners. Funeral preachers may find any or all of these approaches to be quite helpful. I offer a different approach, starting with the gospel and then correlating it with other readings and prayer texts, as well as the liturgical setting.[7]

A Method of Liturgical Correlation

The gospel readings seem like a reasonable place to start. On the one hand, the liturgy assigns the gospel pride of place. On the other hand, if

---

their life in the context of the paschal mystery; we don't celebrate their life in the same sense that we celebrate the memorial of the death and resurrection of Christ."

7. One aspect of the liturgical setting that the preacher should consider is the liturgical season. While space precludes exploring this issue here, see, for example, the work of Barbara Schmitz.

family members are going to have a part in choosing the readings, they will likely be most familiar with those texts and be willing to choose at least that reading. With that choice made, the gospel reading is paired with or correlated to other readings and prayers. These suggestions can help guide the preacher, or even the family, in selecting the other liturgical texts.

That being said, it may be that the family is unfamiliar with the Scriptures, or rather than choosing a gospel reading asks that another text, such as Psalm 23, be used. Or it may be that they defer these choices to the preacher. In the former situation, the method of correlation that I propose may still be used, but starting with the non-gospel text. For example, if the family wishes to use Psalm 23, then by referring to table 3 below, the preacher could see with which gospel (and, therefore, with what other readings and prayers) that psalm might correlate. In the latter situation, the preacher might pick a particular gospel based on one's own knowledge of the situation, or relying on insights from other authors,[8] and then use the method of correlation that I describe here.

According to the rubrics found in the OCF (see 343–344, as well as 73, 89, 156, and 360), the readings used at the funeral rites are to come from the funeral Lectionary (found in part III of the OCF and in volume IV of the *Lectionary for Mass*).[9] There is no provision given for selecting other texts (unlike the *Rite of Baptism for Children*, which allows broad leeway in choosing readings; cf. 44, 81, 112). However, some argue that if the pastoral needs of the mourners are not met by the readings found in the funeral Lectionary, another reading may be chosen as long as it is found in the *Lectionary for Mass*.

Obviously, not every possible combination of readings and prayers can be explored here. What I offer is an approach. The reader may find other fruitful combinations, or wonder at the pairings that I propose. In the end, the funeral preacher must discern which combination of readings and prayers is most appropriate, most helpful, in a given pastoral situation.

---

8. Such as Fuller, Senior, Turner, and Hughes, as mentioned above.

9. Regarding the choice of readings, the OCF says, "As a general rule, all corresponding texts from sacred Scripture in the funeral rites are interchangeable. In consultation with the family and close friends, the minister chooses the texts that most closely reflect the particular circumstances and the needs of the mourners" (344). Therefore, for example, those New Testament texts identified as readings during Eastertime may be used outside of that season.

Structure of Each Essay

Starting Point: The Gospels

In the essays that follow, I will use the nineteen gospel texts found in the OCF as my starting point. I will offer a commentary on each of these texts, and note whether it may better fit the tenor of the vigil (with its emphasis on the reality of death/mourning; separation; the present) or the funeral (emphasis on the paschal mystery/anamnesis; transition; future hope). Of course, this division is somewhat artificial. There may be the occasion (perhaps after a long illness) where relief and joy are dominant emotions rather than shock and grief; in such circumstances, the texts labeled for use at the funeral may also be used at the vigil. Likewise, in the case of a sudden or violent death, texts identified as appropriate for the vigil may also be helpful at the funeral.

Table 1 lists the gospel readings used at funerals, and suggests for which of the rites it might be most appropriate (V = vigil, F = funeral liturgy). In what follows, the readings will be referred to using the numbers from the OCF, which also correlates with the essay number. The table also gives the reference to the texts as given in volume IV of the *Lectionary for Mass*.

Table 1: Gospel Readings

Gospel Readings			
OCF # (Essay #)	Use	Text	Lectionary Volume IV #
1.	F	Matt 5:1-12a	1016.1
2.	V,F	Matt 11:25-30	1016.2
3.	V	Matt 25:1-13	1016.3
4.	F	Matt 25:31-46	1016.4
5.	V,F	Mark 15:33-39; 16:1-6 (or 15:33-39)	1016.5
6.	F	Luke 7:11-17	1016.6
7.	V	Luke 12:35-40	1016.7
8.	V	Luke 23:33, 39-43	1016.8

Table 1: Gospel Readings (cont.)

OCF # (Essay #)	Use	Text	Lectionary Volume IV #
9.	V,F	Luke 23:44-46, 50, 52-53; 24:1-6a (or 23:44-46, 50, 52-53)	1016.9
10.	F	Luke 24:13-35 (or 24:13-16, 28-35)	1016.10
11.	F	John 5:24-29	1016.11
12.	F	John 6:37-40	1016.12
13.	F	John 6:51-58(59)	1016.13
14.	V	John 11:17-27 (or 11:21-27)	1016.14
15.	F	John 11:32-45	1016.15
16.	F	John 12:23-28 (or 12:23-26)	1016.16
17.	V	John 14:1-6	1016.17
18.	F	John 17:24-26	1016.18
19.	V,F	John 19:17-18, 25-30(39)	1016.19

First Correlation: The Other Readings

For each of the gospel readings, I will then propose which texts from the Old and New Testaments might best accompany it, whether in terms of images used or theology expressed. I would note here that because different denominations hold to different canons, in assemblies that include members of other traditions the presider/preacher might wish to consider not using deuterocanonical texts.

As mentioned above, in the essays that follow, the readings will be referred to using the numbers from the OCF. Table 2 also gives the listing of the readings in volume IV of the *Lectionary for Mass*. The essay(s) in which the text is referenced will be noted in this table and in tables that follow. If the reference is boldface, that text forms part of the "preaching strategy" explored in that essay.

Table 2: Non-Gospel Readings from the Roman Catholic Funeral Lectionary

Old Testament			
OCF #	Text	Lectionary Volume IV #	Essay #
1.	Job 19:1, 23-27	1011.2	#1,8,**10,12**
2.	Wis 3:1-9 (or 3:1-6, 9)	1011.3	#1,2,6,7,8,**9,13**,14,16,19
3.	Wis 4:7-15	1011.4	#3,4,**6**,7,11,14
4.	Isa 25:6a, 7-9	1011.5	#1,**2**,4,6,7,8,**15**,16,17,18
5.	Lam 3:17-26	1011.6	#**5,6,19**
6.	Dan 12:1-3	1011.7	#**1**,3,4,7,**11**,12,13,14,16,19
7.	2 Macc 12:43-46	1011.1	#**4**,7,11,**16,18**,19

New Testament			
OCF #	Text	Lectionary Volume IV #	Essay #
1.	Acts 10:34-43 (or 10:34-36, 42-43)*	1012.1	#2,4,10,11,**13**,16,19
2.	Rom 5:5-11	1014.1	#5,9,13,16,19
3.	Rom 5:17-21	1014.2	#5,**9**,16,19
4.	Rom 6:3-9 (or 6:3-4, 8-9)	1014.3	#**10**,11,13,14,16,19
5.	Rom 8:14-23	1014.4	#**2**,8,14,16,18,19
6.	Rom 8:31b-35, 37-39	1014.5	#2,**8,14**,18,19
7.	Rom 14:7-9, 10b-12	1014.6	#3,**4**,7,11,16
8.	1 Cor 15:20-28 (or 15:20-23)	1014.7	#**1**,8,10,14
9.	1 Cor 15:51-57	1014.8	#**3**,7,8,10,**12**,14
10.	2 Cor 4:14-5:1	1014.9	#2,6,8,9,12,14,16,17,18,19
11.	2 Cor 5:1, 6-10	1014.10	#4,6,7,8,**11**,12,13,17,18
12.	Phil 3:20-21	1014.11	#8,11,16,**17**,18,19

Table 2: New Testament (cont.)

OCF #	Text	Lect. Vol. IV #	Essay #
13.	1 Thess 4:13-18	1014.12	#2,3,**6**,7,11,13,14
14.	2 Tim 2:8-13	1014.13	#1
15.	1 John 3:1-2	1014.14	#2,8,**18**
16.	1 John 3:14-16	1014.15	#4,11,**16**,18,19
17.	Rev 14:13*	1012.2	#1,4,**7**
18.	Rev 20:11-21:1*	1012.3	#1,4,7,11,14
19.	Rev 21:1-5a, 6b-7*	1012.4	#1,2,4,12,**15**,17,18,**19**
These are intended for use during Eastertime.			

In general, I would recommend the lament psalms for the vigil and the other psalms for the funeral, but more specific suggestions will be made if appropriate. The responsorial psalms are listed in table 3.[10]

Table 3: The Responsorial Psalms

Responsorial Psalm				
OCF #	Psalm	Genre[9]	Lectionary Volume IV #	Essay #
1.	Ps 23	Confidence	1016.1	#1,**2**,7,8,10,**13**,16,19
2.	Ps 25	Lament	1016.2	#3,4,6,8,9,11,14
3.	Ps 27	Confidence (vv. 1-6) Lament (vv. 7-14)	1016.3	#4,**9**,14,**17**,18
4.	Ps 42/43	Lament	1016.4	#7,**8**,**10**,**15**,17,18,19
5.	Ps 63	Lament or Confidence	1016.5	#1,7,10,**12**,13,16,19
6.	Ps 103	Hymn	1016.6	#1,4,6,**16**,**18**,19

10. Irene Nowell, *Sing a New Song: The Psalms in the Sunday Lectionary* (Collegeville, MN: Liturgical Press, 1993).

OCF #	Psalm	Genre	Lectionary Volume IV #	Essay #
7.	Ps 116	Thanksgiving	1016.7	#**4,6**,10,19
8.	Ps 122	Song of Zion	1016.8	#8,**11**,17,18
9.	Ps 130	Lament	1016.9	#2,**5**,11,14
10.	Ps 143	Lament	1016.10	#9,11,**14,19**

Second Correlation: Prayers and Other Liturgical Texts

The second section of each essay will focus on correlating the readings with the prayer texts found in the OCF and, in the case of the funeral liturgy within Mass, the Roman Missal. Both the OCF and the Missal include a collection of "general" prayers for the deceased (and, in the case of the vigil in the OCF, for mourners) as well as a collection of prayers that refer specifically to the state in life of the deceased or the circumstances surrounding the death; these may be more appropriate in a given situation.

Outside of Mass, the prayers are typically taken from the OCF. One may, if desired, use the collects from the third edition of the Roman Missal. Even outside of Mass, these have pride of place. Within Mass, however, the texts (if available) in the Missal must be used. If a prayer found in the OCF (398) does not have an equivalent in the Missal (see table 4 below), it may be used at Mass.

The Order of Christian Funerals (OCF)

In the essays that follow, I will refer to texts from the OCF by section number. When it comes to a text taken from part V of the OCF, the prayers for the dead (398) and the prayers for the mourners (399), I will also use the number assigned to the prayer. For example, the first prayer listed under the prayers for the dead would be 398, #1. The following tables list the collects found in OCF 398 and 399, where they are also located in the body of the OCF, their equivalent in the Roman Missal (for 398), and the essays in which they are referenced.

Table 4: Collects from the OCF 398 and Roman Missal (for Adults)

Prayers for the Dead OCF 398	Roman Missal 3	Essay #
1. General		#3,6,7,10,12,13,14,17,18,19
2. General (= 88A)		#3,**5**,6,7,8,10,12,**14**,18,19
3. General		#1,3,4,7,10,11,12,14,**17**,18,19
4. General		#2,4,6,**7**,8,**9**,15,18
5. General (= 164A; 190A)	I. For the Funeral / A. Outside Easter Time / first option	#1,2,4,5,6,7,8,9,14,19
6. General (= 72B)		#5,**8**,9,14,19
7. General		#1,5,6,9,10,11,13,14,19
8. General (= 164D; 190D)	I. For the Funeral / C. During Easter Time / first option	#6,14
9. General		#1,3,4,7,10,11,12,13,14,17,18
10. General (= 96A)		#6,11,13,14,15,17,18
11. General		#**13**,15
12. General (= 164B; 190B)	I. For the Funeral / A. Outside Easter Time / second option	#2,4,5,6,7,11,17,18,19
13. General (= 164C; 190C)	I. For the Funeral / B. Outside Easter Time / first option	#6,10,12,14,15,16,17,18,19
14. A pope	IV.1. For a Pope / A	
15. A diocesan bishop	IV.2. For a Bishop / A. For a Diocesan Bishop	
16. Another bishop	IV.2. For a Bishop / B. For Another Bishop	
17. A priest	IV.3. For a Priest / A	
18. A priest	IV.3. For a Priest / B	
19. A priest	n/a	
20. A deacon	IV.4. For a Deacon	

Prayers for the Dead OCF 398	Roman Missal 3	Essay #
21. A deacon	n/a	
22. A religious	IV.5. For a Religious	
23. A religious	n/a	
24. One who worked in the service of the gospel	IV.6. For One Who Worked in the Service of the Gospel	
27. A young person	IV.7. For a Young Person	#6,14
28. A young person	n/a	#6,14
29. Parents	IV.11. For the Priest's Parents	
30. Parents	n/a	#**17**
31. A married couple	IV.10. For a Married Couple (first collect)	
32. A married couple	n/a	
33. A married couple	n/a	#17
34. A wife	IV.10. For a Married Couple (second collect)	
35. A husband		
36. A deceased non-Catholic married to a Catholic	n/a	
37. An elderly person	n/a	
38. An elderly person	n/a	
39. One who died after a long illness	IV.8. For One Who Suffered a Long Illness	#2,14
40. One who died after a long illness	n/a	#2,14
41. One who died after a long illness	n/a	#2,14
42. One who died suddenly	IV.9. For One Who Died Suddenly	#3,7,14
43. One who died accidentally or violently	n/a	#**3**,7,14

Table 4 (cont.)

Prayers for the Dead OCF 398	Roman Missal 3	Essay #
44. One who died by suicide	n/a	#3,14
45. One who died by suicide	n/a	#3,14
46. Several persons	III. Various Commemorations / B. For Several Deceased Persons or for All the Dead / 7. Other Prayers	
47. Several persons	III. Various Commemorations / B. For Several Deceased Persons or for All the Dead / 9. Other Prayers	

Table 5: Collects from the OCF 399 (for Adults)

Prayers for Mourners OCF 399	From the Vigil for the Deceased	Essay #
1. General		#1,5,6,9,18,19
2. General	80A, 88B	#1,5,8,9,12,**14**,16,19
3. General		#**7**,8,14,15
4. General	72A	#2,3,4,5,6,7,10,11,13,17,18,19
5. General	80B, 96B	#1,**5**,6,15
6. General		#2,3,5,6,7,**8**,17,18
7. General		#1,**3**,6,7,14,19

Finally, table 6 references other prayers and texts from the OCF and elsewhere, and where they are mentioned in the essays that follow.

Table 6: Other Texts

Prayer / Text	Essay #
Missal: Eucharistic Prayer I	#4,11
Missal: Eucharistic Prayer II	#4,10,11,**13,16,19**
Missal: Eucharistic Prayer III	#4,10,11,**13,16**,19
Missal: Invitation to Communion (132)	#**13**
Missal: Preface, Third Sunday of Lent	#19
Missal: Preface, Fifth Sunday of Lent	#15
OCF 71 (= 87)	#3,**4,10**,11,**13,17,18**,19
OCF 81 (= 97)	#**4,7**,12
OCF 83-84 (= 160–161; 185–186)	#**10,11**,13,14,19
OCF 175 (= 202; 231; 404)	#1,2,**9**,10,12
OCF 218A; 405	#16
OCF 224 and 402.2	#**9**
OCF 401 #1, #3	#10,13,19
RCIA 154	#19
RCIA 175	#15

The Roman Missal

In making correlations to the readings, I will also make use of texts taken from the Roman Missal (3rd ed.). In addition to the prefaces for the dead, I will refer to prayer texts from the section "Masses for the Dead." The Missal notes:

> Although for the sake of convenience, complete Masses with their own antiphons and prayers are given here, all the texts may be exchanged one for another, especially the prayers.[11] In these latter, however, changes should be made, according to circumstances, in gender and number.

11. For example, there are collections of texts identified for use in Eastertime. While these prayers might be especially appropriate in that season, the texts may be used outside of Eastertime and other texts may be used within Eastertime.

Similarly, if the prayers given here for funerals and anniversaries are used in other circumstances, the phrasing that appears less suited should be omitted.

The following table provides a listing of the prayers found there, as well as the essay in which the prayer is cited. In the essays that follow, I will refer to the prayers using the notation in the second column.

Table 7: Roman Missal: Masses for the Dead (Adults)

Section	Mass (reference in text)	Prayers	Essay #
I. For the Funeral			
A. Outside Easter Time	I.A.	Collect (C): 2 options Prayer over the Offerings (PO) Prayer after Communion (PC)	#1,4,5,6,7,8,9, 11,13,15,17,18,19
B. Outside Easter Time	I.B.	Same	#1,4,6, 11,12,14, 15,16,17,19
C. During Easter Time	I.C.	Same	#2,3,6,7,8,12, 16,17,18,19
D. Other Prayers for the Funeral Mass	I.D.	C, PO, PC	#10,11,12,13,14, 16,19
II. On the Anniversary			
A. Outside Easter Time	II.A.	C, PO, PC	#11,13,14,16,19
B. Outside Easter Time	II.B.	Same	#10,11,13,14, 17,18,19
C. During Easter Time	II.C.	Same	#5,9,11,13,14,16,19
D. Other Prayers on the Anniversary	II.D.	Same	#12,17,18,19
E. Other Prayers on the Anniversary	II.E.	Same	#7,8,12,17,18,19

Section	Mass	Prayers	Essay #
III. Various Commemorations			
A. For One Deceased Person			
Set 1	III.A.1.	C (2 options), PO, PC	#**1**,2,4,5,6,8,9,10,11 12,**13**,15,17,18,19
Set 2	III.A.2.	C, PO, PC	#7,10,15,16,17, 18,19
Set 3 (Other Prayers)	III.A.3.	C, PO, PC	#2,3,**6**,7,10,12,16, 17,18,19
Set 4 (Other Prayers)	III.A.4.	C, PO, PC	#11,12,13,14,**18**,19
Set 5 (Other Prayers)	III.A.5.	C, PO, PC	#5,7,9,12,13,15,19
B. For Several Deceased Persons or for All the Dead			
Set 1	III.B.1.	C, PO, PC	#7,11,**12**,13,14, 17,18,19
Set 2	III.B.2.	C, PO, PC	#**1**,2,4,**6**,10,11, 16,19
Set 3	III.B.3.	C, PO, PC	#1,2,4,6,7,**11**
Set 4	III.B.4.	C, PO, PC	#7
Set 5	III.B.5.	C, PO, PC	#**15**,**18**,19
Set 6	III.B.6.	C, PO, PC	#12,16
Set 7 (Other Prayers)	III.B.7.	C, PO, PC	#11,13,14,19
Set 8 (Other Prayers)	III.B.8.	C, PO, PC	
Set 9 (Other Prayers)	III.B.9.	C, PO, PC	#1,3,**4**,7,10,11, 17,18,19

Table 7 (cont.)

Section	Mass	Prayers	Essay #
IV. Various Prayers for the Dead			
1. For a Pope			
Set A		C, PO, PC	
Set B		C, PO, PC	
Set C		C, PO, PC	
Set D		C, PO, PC	
2. For a Bishop			
A. For a Diocesan Bishop		C, PO, PC	
B. For Another Bishop		C, PO, PC	
3. For a Priest			
Set A		C, PO, PC	
Set B		C, PO, PC	
4. For a Deacon		C, PO, PC	
5. For a Religious		C	
6. For One Who Worked in the Service of the Gospel		C	
7. For a Young Person	IV.7.	C	#6,14
8. For One Who Suffered a Long Illness	IV.8.	C	#2,14
9. For One Who Died Suddenly	IV.9.	C	#3,7,14
10. For a Married Couple		C: 2 options, the second if only one spouse is deceased	
11. For the Priest's Parents		C, PO, PC	
12. For Relatives, Friends, and Benefactors		C, PO, PC	

Table 8: Prefaces for the Dead

Prefaces for the Dead	Essay #
The hope of resurrection in Christ	#1,**2**,3,6,7,8,**10**,**12**,15,17,**18**,**19**
Christ died so that we might live	#5,**9**,**16**,19
Christ, the salvation and the life	#5,9,11,14,**15**,19
From earthly life to heavenly glory	#2,3,5,7,9,**11**,14,19
Our resurrection through the victory of Christ	#**1**,3,**4**,5,**6**,7,9,11,19

Third Correlation: Preaching Strategy

The final section of each essay will focus on a preaching strategy to be used with a particular collection of texts. This strategy will contain the outline of a possible homily, including a "focus" and "function" statement. A "focus" statement summarizes in one sentence what the preacher is trying to say. A "function" statement summarizes in one sentence what the preacher wants the homily to do or to have happen for the assembly.[12]

A Note on Homiletic Form and Content

The homily is part of the liturgy; in this case, of a particular funeral rite. Therefore, it should reflect the purpose and theology of the rite. One way to reflect this correlation is to structure the homily in such a way that it reflects the overall structure of the OCF. In other words, the homily itself may be structured in three parts: naming the loss honestly, remembering the past with gratitude, and looking to the future with hope and meaning. In that way, the stories of the bereaved, of the deceased, and of God are woven together.

In this approach, the funeral homily begins with naming the present loss truthfully. Not only is the reality of death acknowledged, but the reality of *this* death is named, as are the feelings and questions of *these* mourners. This first move reflects Fred Craddock's insistence that induc-

---

12. Thomas G. Long, *The Witness of Preaching* (Louisville, KY: Westminster John Knox Press, 1989), 86.

tive preaching be grounded in experience.[13] In the second move, the focus shifts to the past. The glimpses of the life of Christ revealed in and through the life of the deceased are recalled. The liturgical and scriptural texts provide the way to name the grace and connect the story of the deceased to the paschal mystery, and help to move the assembly to thanksgiving.[14] Those in the congregation are primary participants in this act of remembering. In the third move, the mourners are pointed toward a future with hope. Just as recalling the Good News points to the grace evident in the life of the one who has died, it is in and through the promise of the paschal mystery that the bereaved can be helped to find meaning and hope, reorientation in the midst of disorientation. Because of the grace we have experienced in the past, in the particular life of the deceased and in our relationships with him or her, as well as in the history we share as a community of faith as revealed in the readings and prayer texts, we can hope; we can trust in the promises given by God. However, such trust calls for relinquishment, for "letting go," as crucial to integration of the loss. It is in this trustful abandon that the questions and feelings raised by this death by these people can find, not answer, but direction. The preacher points, suggests, encourages; but it is the listener who "completes the sermon"[15] by engaging in and completing the journey of grief.

Other forms of inductive preaching, such as Paul Scott Wilson's "Four Pages" and Eugene Lowry's narrative preaching or "Loop," are also appropriate approaches to take in structuring the funeral homily. In addition, authors such as Robert Krieg and Robert Hughes have suggested other ways to structure the funeral homily. Please see the bibliography at the end of this chapter.

1. Matthew 5:1-12a

Readings from the Ambo

The gospel. The Beatitudes serve as part of the introduction to the Sermon on the Mount. The mountain setting (in contrast to the Lukan

---

13. Fred B. Craddock, *As One Without Authority*, rev. (St. Louis, MO: Chalice Press, 2001), 52.

14. James A. Wallace, ed. *Preaching in the Sunday Assembly: A Pastoral Commentary on* Fulfilled in Your Hearing (Collegeville, MN: Liturgical Press, 2010), 84.

15. Craddock, *As One Without Authority*, 53.

version) evokes the biblical notion that such places are privileged locations for an encounter with the divine. In both form and content, the Beatitudes allude to the Old Testament, especially the Wisdom literature and Isaiah. In the context of Matthew's community—increasing conflict with other Jews—the Beatitudes might be seen as an exposition of those attitudes that Christians ought to manifest in the face of suffering.

Application to funerals. The preacher may choose to address the Beatitudes to the present moment: blessed are *you* who mourn, for you will be comforted. Such comfort, while reaching its ultimate fulfillment in the eschaton, begins here and now. It is mediated through the love and support of family and friends, and through the ministry of the church. If the Beatitudes are read at the vigil, this orientation to present loss would be most appropriate. Preachers should keep in mind that an overly positive approach, and emphasis on words of blessing, may not be heard if spoken while mourners are still early in their journey of grief. Therefore, the vigil may be too soon to emphasize future blessing as a result of present mourning and loss.

The preacher may also choose to use the Beatitudes as a lens through which to look at and give thanks for the life of the deceased. Of course, no one lives the Beatitudes perfectly. Just as we should avoid dwelling on the faults[16] of those who have died, we should also avoid overstating their virtues and "preaching them into heaven" or canonizing them. All are sinners; it is clear when the preacher's words are exaggerated. It is also clear when the words of the Scriptures and liturgy have been brushed aside, and the Good News is nowhere to be heard, leaving the mourners more embarrassed than consoled. But a preacher might profitably center on one or two of the Beatitudes or on how the Beatitudes formed a "rule of life" for the deceased. The preacher could speak to how grace was manifested in one who tried to live this way, albeit imperfectly. Of course, one should also be careful not to give the impression that by living the Beatitudes one has earned God's love or the reward of heaven. A grace-filled life is first and foremost a gift.

Finally, the preacher may wish to emphasize the Beatitudes as future promise. This passage proclaims that those who mourn are blessed, and that faith in Christ—while ridiculed by the world—will be rewarded.

---

16. Speaking the truth does not mean revealing that which should remain confidential. If brokenness is to be revealed it is to show the grace operative in the dead person's life. If in doubt, "speak only well of the dead."

While still acknowledging the reality of loss, the future orientation of the reading suggests its use in the funeral liturgy. We are promised life where all tears will be wiped away; but to see that promise requires a vision that can see beyond the present loss.

Other readings. The eschatological thrust of the Beatitudes recommends a number of readings from the Old Testament. The reading from Job (OT #1) has often been interpreted by Christians as referring to the bodily resurrection of the dead. In the midst of suffering, Job proclaims his faith that he is not abandoned. The preacher can proclaim the same faith to mourners: you are not alone. Isaiah 25:6a, 7-9 (OT #4) is taken from Isaiah's apocalypse (chaps. 24–27). The mountain image connects to the setting of the Beatitudes. In the sixth reading from the Old Testament (Dan 12:1-3) we read another apocalyptic vision. At the end of time, the dead shall awaken to everlasting life (or horror). Those who have given evidence of God's presence (wisdom) in this life by living according to the Beatitudes will be like stars shining in the firmament in the next life. Words of hope written in the face of persecution become words of hope spoken in the face of death. The theme of hope in the midst of suffering, blessing in sorrow, is also expressed in Wisdom 3:1-9 (OT #2). What seems like the finality of death is an illusion (foolish). Though the dead may have suffered in this life, in God no torment shall touch them. Instead, grace and mercy will attend them.

This reading does raise an important issue. Preachers may be tempted to claim special knowledge of God's will regarding both the death of the individual and his or her salvation. Attempts to try to explain tragedies and defend God, as if God needed to be protected from blame, will inevitably fail. For example, to use the reading from Wisdom to explain death, any suffering leading up to it, or, indeed, the present suffering of the mourners as God's "punishment" is for the preacher to claim knowledge to which he or she has no access. Explanations and defenses treat death and suffering as a problem to be solved; the bereaved are encountering death and suffering as a mystery.

This mystery, the paradox of life in death, blessing in suffering, finds expression in a number of readings from the New Testament. In 1 Corinthians 15:20-28 (NT #8), Paul reminds his audience of Christ's ultimate victory over death: as Christ, the firstfruits, so the believer. Mourners are blessed now because they have this hope, this promise, that death itself will be destroyed (v. 26), a sentiment shared with the reading from Isaiah. They will be blessed because one day they too will share in the resurrection, as the readings from Job and Daniel, and even Wisdom, claim. In 2 Timothy 2:8-13 (NT #14), Paul, as he seeks to encourage Timothy in the midst of suffering, reminds the reader of this promised resurrection. The call to "remember" and the encouragement to "persevere" are aptly spoken to those who mourn, whose grief might tempt them to forget the hope of the Christian life.

Three selections from Revelation are offered as readings during Eastertime: 14:13 (NT #17); 20:11–21:1 (NT #18); and 21:1-5a, 6b-7 (NT #19). Revelation 14:13 speaks of being at rest, echoing Wisdom's (OT #2) claim that the dead are at peace. At the same time, mourners are also "in the Lord" and so can find a measure of peace in the midst of their sorrows. The second selection refers to judgment, which is also a theme in the reading from Daniel (OT #6). The preacher will need to be careful not to take the imagery literally, and to balance judgment with mercy. In addition, the promise of a new heaven and earth may be seen in Isaiah's (OT #4) vision of the new Jerusalem. Isaiah's assurance that tears will be wiped away and that death will be no more finds expression in the third selection from Revelation.

If the preacher wishes to focus on banquet imagery, then Psalms 23 and 63 would reflect those ideas. Psalm 103 focuses on the kindness and mercy of God, making a helpful contrapuntal to the theme of judgment.

Connecting the Bible and the Liturgy

The OCF. The eschatological language in a number of the prayers for the dead (OCF 398) suggests their use with the readings above. Prayer #3 speaks of "a place of refreshment, light, and peace" (OT #2). Prayer #9 makes reference to the "great day of judgment" (OT #6, NT #18) and dwelling with Abraham, holding that "in death our life is changed, not ended." Prayer #5 refers to "firstfruits" (NT #8) and being at rest (NT #17). That the paradox of the Beatitudes is found in the mystery of the cross is brought out in prayer #7.

The gospel claims that mourners are blessed. Among the prayers for the mourners (OCF 399), that they be comforted is specifically mentioned in prayers ##1, 2, and 5; prayer #7 asks that the mourners be surrounded by God's love.

The Missal. The two collects offered under Mass III.A.1 are fitting texts to match with the readings above. The first collect highlights the paradox, the mystery, of the Beatitudes and the cross (see OCF 398, #7), and that we are saved together ("gathered into the company of your chosen ones"—those "written in the book" [Dan 12:1]). The second collect prays that the deceased may come to a place of "peace and light," using the same imaginal language as OCF 398, #3 and the reading from Wisdom (OT #2).

A number of prayers in the Missal mention eschatological judgment. Others stress God's mercy and compassion, which can serve as a context for the readings. For example, the prayer over the offerings I.A asks for God's mercy and refers to Christ as a "merciful Judge." The book of life (see NT #18) and God's mercy are mentioned in the second collect under Mass I.B. Collect III.B.9 refers to our hope of God's mercy. The notion of death as "sleep in Christ" is found in the prayer over the offerings III.B.2 and collect III.B.3; the reading from Daniel speaks of death this way (OT #6).

If the preacher is stressing the consolation of the mourners, then Preface I for the Dead picks up on that language, and on the eschatological language of hope ("life is changed not ended"). If the preacher wishes to stress Christ's victory over death (see OT #4, NT #8), then preface V echoes the same theme. The Eucharist itself foreshadows the eschatological banquet.

Strategy for Preaching

Scriptural Texts: Daniel 12:1-3; Psalm 103; 1 Corinthians 15:20-28;[17] Matthew 5:1-12a

Liturgical Texts: Collect III.A.1 (first option); Prayer over the Offerings III.B.2; Preface V for the Dead

The preacher's anchor is the second Beatitude: those who mourn, like those gathered for the funeral, are blessed because they will be comforted.

---

17. This is the way the text is referenced in volume IV of the *Lectionary for Mass.* The pericope in the OCF is listed as 15:20-23, 24b-28. However, the readings are the same.

The first comfort that they experience is in the present: the concrete comfort of family and friends, and the comfort of the church's ministry. Part of the church's ministry is to keep in front of the mourners the promise to which the deceased, as well as they, are heirs: the promise of resurrection. Paul is clear: as Christ, so the believer. We live in the in-between time now; death is still very real. We do not deny death, but put it in proper perspective. In the end, even death will be defeated. The *focus* of such preaching could be to proclaim the church's faith in the resurrection; the *function* could be to provide comfort by recalling that faith.

Judgment is part of our faith; but the preacher must touch on that subject carefully. He or she is not God, and may not make pronouncements about the ultimate fate of the deceased. That does not mean that the mourners should be left without comfort. The preacher is called to speak in terms of the "sure and certain hope" (OCF 175A) that we have in the resurrection. How can the mourners find hope that the deceased's name was written in the book of life (Dan 12:1)? By the way he or she gave evidence of such in this life. Here, without exaggeration, the preacher can make a connection to the way the deceased tried to live the Beatitudes, to give evidence of wisdom (see Dan 12:3). No one lives the Beatitudes perfectly. We must therefore hope in God's kindness and mercy (Ps 103; prayer over the offerings), compassion and grace that overcome sin (preface); these are the ultimate sources of comfort in the midst of sorrow and loss.

Even though they are in "distress" (Dan 12:1) now, by looking back with gratitude on a life that gave evidence of God's grace, mourners are comforted by knowing that in God's mercy and kindness there is the hope of resurrection life, not only for their loved one who has died but also for them. It is in that final resurrection that they will know true beatitude: being gathered into the company of God's chosen ones (collect).

2. Matthew 11:25-30

Readings from the Ambo

The gospel. The rejection of Jesus and his message is addressed in chapters 11–13 of Matthew's gospel. This particular passage is a combination of two wisdom sayings. The first saying (vv. 25-27), which is shared with

Luke (10:21-22), speaks of those who reject worldly wisdom for the true wisdom of Jesus as "childlike" (infants, simple, foolish).[18] Those counted as wise or learned are, in fact, the true fools while those to whom Jesus has revealed the Father are the real sages.

The second section (vv. 28-30) is unique to Matthew. Reflecting the milieu after the destruction of the temple, the "burdens" mentioned here may have originally referred to the opponents of Jesus whose interpretation of the law burdened (Matt 23:4) others. The image of the "yoke" returns us to the beginning of the passage. To a Jewish audience, a "yoke" would connote both the Torah and wisdom (see Sir 51:26-27).[19] Here, Jesus is presented as Wisdom incarnate.[20] Far from being burdensome, adherence to his teaching, his interpretation of the law, brings rest and refreshment.

Application to funerals. In the face of death, Christian hope—and even joy—can seem foolish to others. We live in an increasingly secular culture, one in which talk of life after death or hope in the resurrection seems more nonsense than good news. We are told that only the hard sciences provide true knowledge and wisdom. God's presence in the midst of loss and the hope found in the paschal mystery are "hidden" from many. However, those with the eyes of faith—those who have a "childlike" trust in and dependence on the Father—still see.

Rest and refreshment have long been common ways to speak of life after death. Especially if death has come after a prolonged illness or years of decline, it would be natural for mourners to hear the words of Jesus as being spoken to the deceased. At the same time, the mourners can hear those words spoken to them—as they bear the burden of grief and loss, or if they bore the burden of caring for someone in their dying.

Depending on the circumstances, this gospel passage might have a place at either the vigil or the funeral liturgy. The praise for childlike faith and the invitation to those burdened suggest this as an appropriate reading for the vigil: in the midst of loss, the mourners are called to renewed faith and trust. The gospel may also be appropriate for the funeral liturgy if death came after a long or debilitating illness. In this latter case, it is

18. Daniel J. Harrington, *The Gospel of Matthew*, Sacra Pagina series, ed. Daniel J. Harrington (Collegeville, MN: Liturgical Press, 2007), 167–68.

19. Ibid., 168.

20. Reginald H. Fuller, "Lectionary for Funerals," *Worship* 56, no. 1 (1982): 54.

both the mourners (especially caregivers) as well as the deceased who "find rest" now in Christ. In the face of death, Christ is the one to whom we can turn in confidence for both consolation and hope.

Other readings. Given the gospel's identification of Jesus as a wisdom figure, Wisdom 3:1-9 (OT #2) would make a good choice. On the one hand, the foolishness of the world is directly confronted (vv. 2-3). At the same time, the language of being at peace (vv. 1, 3) echoes the gospel's language of rest and being relieved of burdens. In its original setting, "torments" may have referred to suffering in this life.[21] While placing this reading in the funeral Lectionary may suggest a reference to suffering in the life to come, the original meaning is not lost. As mentioned above, if this reading is chosen, however, one would have to carefully address the suggestion that suffering is somehow a specific punishment (either of the deceased or of the mourners) from God. Perhaps a connection to suffering as a consequence of being in a fallen world (see Rom 8:14-23 below) could serve to prevent such a misappropriation. Another possibility for the first reading would be Isaiah 25:6a, 7-9 (OT #4). The destruction of death, the wiping away of tears, and the image of God's mountain as a place where suffering has come to an end again reflect the sentiments of the second half of the gospel reading.

Romans 8:14-23 (NT #5) speaks of the "sufferings of this present age" to be nothing in comparison to resurrection life. Suffering is presented as part of created reality, all of which "groans" in anticipation of redemption. In the midst of suffering, a more important truth is proclaimed: the believer is a child of God. The eternal glory that comes from adoption outweighs any temporary suffering that comes from creation's "slavery to corruption"—a sentiment that is echoed in 2 Corinthians 4:14–5:1 (NT #10). Therefore, if the past suffering of the deceased is paramount in the mourners' minds, these would be appropriate readings. One would need to be careful not to dismiss the feelings of the bereaved; while present sufferings are "nothing" if one is taking a cosmic perspective, they are "something" and very real at the personal level. On the other hand, if the mourners have expressed that they have felt abandoned by God because

---

21. Dianne Bergant and Robert J. Karris, eds., *The Collegeville Bible Commentary: Based on the New American Bible with Revised New Testament* (Collegeville, MN: Liturgical Press, 1989), 705.

of the prolonged suffering of their loved one, then Romans 8:31b-35, 37-39 (NT #6) could be used. Nothing can separate us from Christ's love.

In addition to Romans 8:14-23, 1 John 3:1-2 (NT #15) speaks of the believer as a child of God. Given the gospel reading's emphasis on child-like faith, this reading could also be used. If the preacher wanted to emphasize the first section of the gospel passage, with its proclamation of a hope hidden from the wise, then Paul's claim in 1 Thessalonians 4:13-18 (NT #13) that we are not to "grieve like the rest, who have no hope" would fit. If the Isaiah reading is chosen, one could also use Acts 10:34-43 (NT #1) to pick up on the theme of universality or Revelation 21:1-5a, 6b-7 (NT #19) for its reference to tears being wiped away and there being an end to death, mourning, wailing, and pain.

Among the responsorial psalms, the theme of rest and refreshment is especially clear in Psalm 23; it would work well at the funeral liturgy. Psalm 130, with its opening lament and eventual turn to trust, would work well at the vigil—especially if the second option for the antiphon ("I hope in the Lord, I trust in his word") is used.

Connecting the Bible and the Liturgy

The OCF. Among the prayers for mourners (OCF 399) used at the vigil, #4 (= 72A) speaks both of being "children of God" and of the hope that being such brings. In addition, reference to "this time of testing and pain" echoes Matthew's language of "burdens." The "hope" and *place* of salvation spoken of in Isaiah (OT #4) are also referred to in prayer #6; Isaiah's "mountain" is here God's "eternal kingdom."

Their references to rest and tears commend prayers for the dead (398) #4 and #5. The former is especially appropriate, and reads, in part: "The old order has passed away: / welcome him/her then into paradise, / where there will be no sorrow, no weeping nor pain, / but the fullness of peace and joy . . ." Hope and trust are mentioned in prayer #12 (= 164B). In addition, it should be noted that the OCF provides three collects for use at the funeral rites for "one who died after a long illness" (#39–#41). These prayers speak of the deceased "sharing the cross" of Christ by having suffered weakness and pain in patience—a suffering that has been mercifully brought to an end. That same mercy is invoked in hope of eternal life.

The Missal. The passage from Matthew's gospel, as a funeral reading, emphasizes rest and the laying down of burdens. Language that evokes this same sense of rest and rejuvenation after a time of suffering is found in a number of texts from the Roman Missal. Collect III.A.1 (second option) prays for the deceased to come to a "place of peace and light . . . in the company of [the] Saints." Collect III.A.3 refers to enjoying the "comfort" of God's eternal light, a contrast to the burdens of this life. Collect III.B.2 refers to the deceased as having been "freed from the bonds of mortality" while collect III.B.3 prays for the "souls of the faithful [to] find rest." The first option for collect I.C speaks of hope being strengthened, while the second option speaks of a God who "opens up the beginning of things to come" by "the ending of present things." The accompanying prayer after Communion refers to "a dwelling place of light and peace." Collect IV.8 (see OCF 398, #39) speaks of the deceased having "served" God by their suffering, what would certainly seem foolish to many, and prays that they enter into God's glory.

Hope and consolation are highlighted in Preface I for the Dead. Preface IV speaks of God's providence, which may be helpful to proclaim in the face of what might seem to some to have been meaningless suffering. Preface IV also has language that echoes Paul's words to the Thessalonians (NT #13): when God gives "the sign," then the redeemed will be raised.

Strategy for Preaching

Scriptural Texts: Isaiah 25:6a, 7-9; Psalm 23; Romans 8:14-23; Matthew 11:25-30

Liturgical Texts: Collect IV.8; Preface I for the Dead

As mentioned above, Matthew 11:25-30 offers words of hope and consolation that are applicable in a number of situations. On the one hand, this text could be used when preaching at the funeral of one who died after a long illness, in which case it is their burdens—and the burdens of their caregivers—that are being relieved. On the other hand, this gospel also speaks to the "burden" of acute grief and loss faced by those present at a funeral vigil. I imagine the former scenario here. The *focus* of such preaching could be that it is in God that we find rest and relief of our burdens;

the *function* could be to help the mourners experience the consolation that not only the deceased but they, too, are the objects of God's care.

The homily could be structured using Eugene Lowry's method, as described in his *The Homiletical Plot: The Sermon as Narrative Art Form*. In "Lowry's Loop," the homily begins by naming a bind or conflict. In this case, the context itself gives us the overarching bind: the loss of a loved one after a long illness and the myriad emotions and questions that this experience raises.

Lowry would then have the preacher delve into the bind, unpacking and exploring it. Typically, that would involve naming the "false" answers to the initial bind. At a funeral, the preacher could name the burdens that have been and are being faced by the mourners. For some, such as family members and friends who have not been involved in the day-to-day care of someone dying from a prolonged illness (such as cancer or Alzheimer disease), the acute grief may be the biggest burden—as well as possible guilt for not having been around and done more. For those who served as caregivers, and who have already grieved the acute loss as they experienced their loved one's decline, the burden may be more past than present. However, ambivalent feeling over the loss—such as a sense of relief—may be guilt inducing for some, and there may be anger at those who were not around. The burden may also be how to transition back to "normal" life without having to care for the deceased anymore. The burdens faced by the deceased will also need to be named honestly. Tears are part of life (Isa 25:8), part of creation (Rom 8:20-22).

It is into this sense of loss that the preacher, being careful not to deny the reality of the suffering experienced by the deceased and the mourners, can point in a direction of hope: our faith teaches us that these pale in comparison to the glory that awaits (Rom 8:18; collect). This reversal, or "aha moment," is the hallmark of Lowry's method.

What follows next is the proclamation of the Good News, the true answer to the dilemma posed at the beginning of the homily. Here, the preacher could name the ways that the mourners—as the children of God (Rom 8:16-17)—have already experienced God's presence; how God has relieved burdens through others. In this way, we avoid a dualistic message that this life is all suffering and God is absent, and that it is only in the next life that we experience God's presence. For example, one should mention the ways that the deceased, during life, lifted the burdens of others—and so helped to witness to Christ's presence. Then, the preacher could speak to how, in diminishment, the deceased also shared in the paschal mystery (collect). One could continue by naming the ways the caregivers, in turn, helped to carry the burdens of the deceased as he or she declined. Others who ran errands, visited, or provided respite care may have helped the caregivers themselves. Through all these examples, the preacher can proclaim God's abiding presence and care—showing that the lifting of burdens is not just a matter for the next life, but we enjoy a foretaste of it here as well—just as the Eucharist here is a foretaste of the banquet to come (Ps 23:5).

Finally, Lowry asks the preacher to name the implications of the Good News—in this case, of God's abiding presence and care, for both the bereaved and the deceased. On the one hand, God's presence to the mourners as they continue their way through grief needs to be mentioned. The mutual support of family and friends, of the church community, and even of helping professionals if needed, are ways in which God's abiding care is manifest. On the other hand, the preacher will also need to mention that the deceased is not abandoned either, because in Christ "the hope of blessed resurrection has dawned" (preface). Because the deceased was one who took on the yoke of Christ (Matt 11:30), we can proclaim the "sure and certain hope" (OCF 175A) of eternal life. Death does not have the final word (Isa 25:7-8). Instead, for those who have this childlike (Matt 11:25) faith in Christ (Rom 8:14-17, 19), in death "life is changed not ended" (preface). They inherit the promise that they will enjoy an "eternal dwelling" (preface) on God's holy mountain, where tears are dried, burdens lifted, and all have the hope of finding rest and refreshment, peace and light, and glory (Isa, Ps 23:2, 5, Matt 11:28, collect).

3. Matthew 25:1-13

Readings from the Ambo

The gospel. Chapters 24 and 25 in Matthew form an eschatological discourse, a series of sayings or parables by Jesus that focus on the coming of the kingdom of heaven (25:1). The parable of the Ten Virgins is usually read as an allegory of the sudden return of Christ. Believers are admonished to "stay awake" (25:13)—always watchful and ready for the

Parousia, especially given the apparent "delay" in Jesus' return. Luke also addresses this concern in chapter 12 of his gospel (see essay 7 below). Rather than ten virgins, this parallel pericope refers to servants who await their master's return from a wedding feast. However, the admonition is the same: be prepared!

Application to funerals. In the church's tradition, we speak not only of Christ's return at the end of history, a general Parousia, but also of one's particular encounter with Christ at death (*Catechism of the Catholic Church*, 1021–1022). In the context of a funeral, it is this latter encounter—for the one who has died, as well as eventually for those gathered for the liturgy—that is a more central concern. The emphasis in this reading on the suddenness of the advent of the kingdom, or of Christ's return, suggests that it might well be used in instances of sudden or unexpected death. This emphasis also recommends this gospel passage for proclamation at the vigil, when the acute nature of the loss is more pronounced. At the same time, juxtaposition of the suddenness of loss with the suddenness of Christ's arrival already provides for a glimmer of hope in the midst of loss.

Other readings. There are a number of readings that refer to the suddenness of death, either directly or by analogy. For example, Wisdom 4:7-15 (OT #3) begins: "The just man, though he die early, shall be at rest." This just man is described as "having become perfect in a short while" and having been "snatched away" before being overcome by evil. If this reading is selected, care must be taken not to "canonize" the individual or to blame God for this death ("He was so good that God took him"). If this reading is used, it would be helpful to put the passage in its wider context: an argument against the simplistic notion that the length of life correlates with how justly one lives.[22]

Daniel 12:1-3 (OT #6), with its apocalyptic concerns, might also be used. Among the psalms, the laments seem most appropriate. Psalm 25 in particular prays for an end to affliction and suffering. We see the same themes in 1 Corinthians 15:51-57 (NT #9) and 1 Thessalonians 4:13-18 (NT #13). It is worth noting that in these readings the suddenness of death is tempered with Paul's claim of death's defeat (1 Cor 15:54-55)

---

22. Fuller, "Lectionary for Funerals," 39; Donald Senior, *Loving and Dying: A Commentary on the Lectionary Texts for Weddings and Funerals* (Kansas City, MO: Celebration Books, 1979), 43–44.

and his words of hope and consolation (1 Thess). Romans 14:10 (NT #7) admonishes: "Why do you judge your brother? Or why do you look down on your brother?"—words that may be important to hear in the context of suicide or accident.

Connecting the Bible and the Liturgy

The OCF. There are a number of suitable choices from among the prayers for the dead (398). If the preacher desires to emphasize the eschatological imagery in a number of the readings (especially OT #6 and the NT readings), then prayers #3 and #9 would work well. Especially if death came suddenly and violently, the mention of passing "unharmed through the gates of death" and being in God's "safekeeping" until the day of judgment in prayer #3 would be appropriate. Prayer #9 also mentions the day of judgment. The notion of change in this prayer has a parallel in the reading from 1 Thessalonians (NT #13). On the other hand, if the preacher wishes to use the image of "rest" (OT #3) as a way to speak hope and comfort into a chaotic situation, then prayers #1–#3 would pick up on that idea with the metaphors of light and peace.

One of the blessings of the second edition of the OCF is the many prayers that address concrete pastoral situations. For example, among the prayers for the dead, there are four collects that speak to the situation being imagined here. Prayer #42 is intended for "one who died suddenly." There, the suddenness of the death, and the need for faith to be strengthened in the midst of such a tragedy, are acknowledged. Prayer #43 is intended for "one who died accidentally or violently" and speaks of the deceased having been "suddenly [and violently] taken" from the bereaved while imploring God's mercy on him or her and God's comfort on those suffering the loss. Finally, the OCF provides two prayers for use if one died by suicide (#44 and #45). While the prayers do not explicitly mention suicide, they do invoke God's mercy as well as petition for the mourners' consolation.

Among the prayers for the mourners (399), #4 mentions the "brevity of our lives on earth" while #6 prays for those "left behind" to mourn the absence of the deceased. Prayer #7 refers to the bereaved as being "overwhelmed by their loss," a common sentiment in situations of sudden or unexpected death. At the same time, these prayers also speak of the bonds that survive death (#4; see also OCF 71, 87), of living "in hope of the eternal kingdom" where all will be reunited (#6), and of the confidence and strength found in faith (#7). The reading from 1 Thessalonians (NT #13) shares the explicit theme of hope with these prayer texts. While 1 Corinthians 15:51-57 (NT #9) claims that death has been defeated, it will not feel that way to mourners, and the preacher will need to acknowledge this reality.

The Missal. Collect I.C (first option) prays for a strengthening of hope, which may be being tested in these circumstances. The suddenness of death is picked up in collect III.A.3, where the deceased is referred to as one "for whom the fleeting light of this world shines no more." Prayer after Communion III.B.9 prays that the Eucharist be "a plea for pardon, strength for the weak, a stronghold in danger"—all apt images in the face of sudden loss. Collect IV.9 is the Missal's version of the prayer found at 398, #42 in the OCF.

Among the prefaces for the dead, preface I emphasizes hope and consolation—especially important in the case of a sudden death, while IV speaks of God's providence, and the mention of a "sign" from God to usher in the resurrection echoes the "word of command" and trumpet blast mentioned in the reading from 1 Thessalonians (NT #13). However, the language used in preface IV ("at your command that we return, on account of sin, to that earth from which we came") may lead to a misunderstanding that the sudden (and perhaps violent) death was God's doing in general and a form of punishment in particular. Preface V may work: even though death is "our own fault," our compassionate God is able to bring victory even out of such loss. However, one must be careful not to use these words uncritically to suggest that the death was some sort of direct punishment by God. Such language may also be quite jarring in the situation of a death by suicide.

Strategy for Preaching

Scriptural Texts: 1 Corinthians 15:51-57; Psalm 25; Matthew 25:1-13

Liturgical Texts: Opening Prayer 399, #7; Concluding Prayer 398, #43

As mentioned above, the focus on the abruptness and surprise of Christ's coming suggests this reading for the vigil more so than the funeral liturgy, and especially in situations when death was sudden and unexpected. At the vigil, the homily ought to focus particularly on acknowledging the reality of the loss and consoling the bereaved. While Christian hope should not be absent, in the midst of overwhelming grief, if the preacher is not careful, the gospel can sound saccharine and false. Lament must precede praise and thanksgiving. The *focus* of the homily could be Christ's ultimate victory over death, even when everything the mourners are experiencing in the moment argues otherwise. The *function* could be to strengthen the faith of the mourners by first helping them name the reality and depth of the loss.

I would propose a homily in three moves. First, as in the lament psalms, the reality of the present loss must be acknowledged. In this case, it is not just the raw emotions of the bereaved that must be given voice but also the truth about the death of the deceased. Shock and anger (at God, at the deceased individual, at others) may predominate—especially in the case of an accidental or violent death, or death by suicide. With the sudden death of a younger person there is also the loss of a future that must be grieved, and this particular loss ought to be named. The sting of death is very real (1 Cor 15:55-56); the mourners plead for an end to their affliction and suffering (Ps 25), for comfort (398, #43).

Once the present truth is named, the homilist can begin to look to the past and name with gratitude aspects of the deceased's life and their relationship with the bereaved. In particular, naming grace[23]—how Christ was present in that life and in those relationships—opens the way to begin to look forward with hope. How might the deceased have been like the wise virgins, and prepared for Christ's coming? Where is the evidence for victory over death as seen in the lives of the deceased and the bereaved?

In the third move, the preacher can begin to gently point toward hope. Like the psalmist, the bereaved are waiting for consolation, and no one who waits for God "will ever be put to shame" (Ps 25; R. 3a). Our faith assures us of Christ's victory (1 Cor 15:57). While that victory will come into its fullness at the end of time (Matt 25), the confidence and strength (399, #7) found in faith is a foretaste of that ultimate victory. It is in one another and in the church that the bereaved will be supported when faith seems hard to come by.

---

23. See Mary Catherine Hilkert, *Naming Grace: Preaching and the Sacramental Imagination* (New York: Continuum, 1997).

4. Matthew 25:31-46

Readings from the Ambo

The gospel. In its original context, this section from Matthew's gospel probably referred to the Gentiles (the "nations") being judged for the way they treated the disciples of Jesus (the "least brothers"). That there would be separate judgments for Jews and Gentiles has support in both Jewish tradition (both in the Old Testament and elsewhere; see 2 Bar 72:4-6 in particular) and in other New Testament texts (Matt 19:28; Rom 2:9-10; 1 Cor 6:2-3; and 1 Pet 4:17). In other words, the question that this text addresses is how do non-Jews and non-Christians enter the kingdom of heaven—a pressing theological issue in our time as well.[24]

However, this text has been interpreted more broadly over time. The judgment scene in Matthew is typically taken to be about how important the care of the poor is for gaining eternal life. In such an approach, the "nations" refers to all humanity and "the least" are any in need. Therefore, *all* will be judged on whether or not they provided care for those in most need. It is this use of the passage that figures in the *Catechism*'s treatment of the Last Judgment (1038).

Application to funerals. Most preachers at a funeral will follow the more common interpretation: those who care for those in need in this life (and therefore also care for Christ) will be rewarded in the next. On the one hand, it is appropriate to remind the listeners of the demands of the Christian life, and note how in the life of the deceased such grace was manifest. On the other hand, the preacher needs to be careful not to fall into the trap of Pelagianism[25]—or of canonizing the deceased as a perfect exemplar of Jesus' call. Instead, there is an opportunity here to present the church's eschatology as a source of hope and not dread: we do all these things, we live and die, united to Christ (Rom 14:8). It is in that union—manifested in how we live—that we place our hope.

---

24. Harrington, *The Gospel of Matthew*, Sacra Pagina, 357–59.

25. See Pope Francis, *Gaudete et Exsultate*, apostolic exhortation (19 March 2018), 47–62. In addition, the Lutheran-Catholic *Joint Declaration on the Doctrine of Justification* provides a helpful and nuanced discussion of "faith/grace" and "good works" in salvation.

Either interpretation, which connects resurrection life and caring for those in need regardless of an explicit profession of faith in Christ,[26] makes this gospel passage helpful in situations when there is significant religious plurality among the friends and family of the deceased. In such situations, this gospel may be used to preach a message of hope to those who do not share the Christian faith, while still upholding the unicity of Christ. In either case, the poor and those in need are portrayed as those who are recipients of Christ's special care. Therefore, the preacher may make a connection to the mourners—and name them in their sorrow as also being beneficiaries of Christ's particular care.

Other readings. A number of readings in the funeral Lectionary speak of a final judgment. Second Maccabees 12:43-46 (OT #7) mentions prayer for the dead in hopes of eventual resurrection and reward for those "who had gone to rest in godliness" (2 Macc 12:45). Such prayer is evidence of the ongoing relationship between the living and the dead, what we might call the communion of saints. The reading from Daniel (OT #6) speaks of the final judgment in similar terms as the gospel. Those who awake from death are separated into two groups: the "wise" and "those who lead the many to justice" who "shall live forever," and those who "shall be an everlasting horror and disgrace" (Dan 12:2-3). Wise and just living may be connected to the care of those in need, the hidden Christ, in the gospel reading. Wisdom 4:7-15 (OT #3) speaks tangentially of judgment, in the sense that the one who died early is referred to as having pleased God and become perfect. While this reading may be appropriate at the funeral of a younger person, great care must be taken not to apply the reading uncritically. No one is perfect (v. 13), and the preacher has no way of knowing that God "snatched" the deceased away before he or she could sin (vv. 11, 14). As noted in essay 3 above, one needs to remember that this passage is intended as an argument against the idea that length of life is correlated with how justly one lives.

Romans 14:7-9, 10c-12 (NT #7) states that we all shall stand in judgment before God, and therefore should not presume to judge others. The Christian is to live and die "for the Lord" (v. 7)—such living (and dying to oneself) is evidenced in the care given to others (Matt 25:35-36). Acts 10:34-43 (NT #1) speaks of the resurrected Christ as the one appointed by God to render this judgment. Second Corinthians 5:1, 6-10 (NT #11)

---

26. See *Ad Gentes,* 7, *Dignitatis Humanae,* 1, and *Lumen Gentium,* 16.

also states that we "must all appear before the judgment seat of Christ" and receive our reward based on our deeds (v. 10). Revelation 20:11–21:1 (NT #18) most closely resembles the gospel text by its reference to the dead being judged by their deeds and divided into two groups: those "thrown into the pool of fire" (20:15) and those welcomed into the new heaven and earth. The preacher will need to make sure not to fall into a Pelagian earning of heaven by one's deeds, but rather encourage his or her listeners with the claim that grace-filled deeds are a manifestation of the deceased's living relationship with the Lord and Judge of all. As the *United States Catholic Catechism for Adults* puts it: "Perfect love will make possible entrance into heaven, imperfect love will require purification, and a total lack of love will mean eternal separation from God."[27] That we already share in eternal life because of our love for others, our laying down our lives for others, is brought out in 1 John 3:14-16 (NT #16).

If a preacher wanted to focus on the more universal aspects of the gospel text, he or she could pair the gospel with the reading from Isaiah (OT #4). The prophetic texts refers to "all" people being provided for on God's holy mountain and benefitting from the destruction of death. The same idea can be brought forth by using the reading from Revelation 21:1-5a, 6b-7 (NT #19). Likewise, Peter's observation in Acts 10:34 (NT #1) that "God shows no partiality" also fits with this focus. Revelation 14:13 (NT #17) states that the works of the deceased accompany them, and so they are able to rest (see OCF 81, 97).

While the lament psalms better reflect the focus of the vigil, Psalms 25 and 27 speak well to the theme of judgment and so may be appropriate for the funeral liturgy as well. In Psalm 25, there is comfort in hearing that no one who waits for the Lord is put to shame (antiphon). The psalm stresses God's compassion and kindness. Psalm 27 speaks of God as a refuge, so there is no need to fear. God's kindness and mercy is also stressed in Psalms 103 and 116; the latter also mentions that God's presence is encountered in this life.

Connecting the Bible and the Liturgy

The OCF. If the Maccabean text is used, the ongoing relationship that we have with those who have gone before us can be highlighted using two

---

27. United States Conference of Catholic Bishops, *United States Catholic Catechism for Adults* (Washington, DC: USCCB, 2006), 153.

related texts from the vigil. In the Invitation to Prayer, the minister states that the "ties of friendship and affection which knit us as one throughout our lives do not unravel with death" (71, 87). Likewise, option A for the opening prayer states that "death is not the end, / nor does it destroy the bonds / that you forge in our lives" (72; cf. 399, #4).

The eschatological concerns and focus on judgment in the gospel and other readings recommend a number of texts from OCF 398. Prayers #3 and #9 ask God to raise the deceased up "on the great day of judgment." The prayers also speak of God's mercy and forgiveness, making it clear that salvation is not earned. In like manner, prayer #12 asks that the deceased receive the "eternal reward" promised those who hope and trust in God. The emphasis is on one's relationship with God. The preacher may also wish to make a connection to the text from the blessing at the end of the vigil (81, 97) that speaks of the relationship between deeds in this life and rest in the next: "Blessed are those who have died in the Lord; let them rest from their labors for their good deeds go with them" (see NT #17). If the Isaiah reading is used (OT #4), then the fourth and fifth prayers in this section that also mention tears being wiped away would fit.

The Missal. If the Funeral Liturgy within Mass is celebrated, then Preface V for the Dead, with its focus on God's compassion and grace, on Christ's victory, and on the promise of resurrection helps put judgment in the proper perspective. If the less common interpretation of the gospel is followed, the preacher could make a connection to the eucharistic prayer, noting that we pray for all the dead, not just Catholics or other Christians. For example, Eucharistic Prayer II intercedes for "all who have died in [God's] mercy" (Missal 105) and Eucharistic Prayer III prays for those "who were pleasing to [God] at their passing from this life" (Missal 113, 115).

A number of prayers in the Missal mention eschatological judgment, as noted in essay 1 above. In addition, the company of the saints (see the comments on the Maccabean text above) is mentioned in the second collect under Mass III.A.1 and in collect III.B.9. If the reading from Daniel (OT #6) is chosen, then prayers that refer to death as "sleep in Christ," such as the prayer over the offerings III.B.2 and collect III.B.3, may be appropriate. Eucharistic Prayer I uses similar language: "Grant them, O Lord, we pray, and all who sleep in Christ, a place of refreshment, light and peace" (Missal 95).

Strategy for Preaching

Scriptural Texts: 2 Maccabees 12:43-46; Psalm 116; Romans 14:7-9, 10c-12; Matthew 25:31-46

Liturgical Texts: Collect III.B.9; Preface V for the Dead; Prayer over the Offerings I.A; OCF 71

The emphasis on judgment in these readings may seem off-putting at first. After all, judgment is a topic that seems to be anathema these days. How often have we heard (or been texted), "DJM! Don't judge me!" from others? How often have we heard that there is no such thing as objective rights and wrongs, but that it is only one's subjective feelings that matter in issues of morality? Preachers are not immune from this pressure. Perhaps as an overcorrection to an emphasis on God's justice (often presented in harsh terms), preachers today seem more apt to preach the deceased into heaven than to raise the issue of prayer for those "in" purgatory.

It should come as no surprise that those gathered for a funeral will hear the word "judgment" through a variety of filters. For some, the term will call to mind the cold and distant God of their childhood. Others may be antagonistic to the very idea and to the church that dares to speak in such terms. And some may be all too ready to point their fingers. It is into this situation that the preacher can offer the good news that God is the only judge (we are not), and the Judge is merciful. Therefore, the *focus* of the homily could be on God's judgment not as a source of terror, but of hope. By recovering what the Christian tradition has to say about eschatology, the *function* could be to help foster such hope, as well as trust in God's mercy and compassion, in the listeners.

The preacher could begin with how uncomfortable we are with the idea of judgment, acknowledging that there is some truth to that sentiment—as Paul makes clear in his letter to the Romans. No human may judge (Rom 14:10), but because in life or in death "we are the Lord's" (Rom 14:8), it is the Lord alone who judges. The good news is that while this judge is just, God is also gracious and merciful (prayer over the offerings I.A and Ps 116:5). God's mercy is indeed good news because no person is perfect. The deceased was not perfect, but did strive to "live in the Lord" (Rom 14:8) as evidenced by the care he or she provided to others (Matt 25:35-36). It is not that the deceased "earned" heaven by actions, but that those good actions showed us that Christ was part of his or her life (Rom 14:8)—hidden, as Christ was hidden in those in need whom he or she served (Matt 25:40). We meet God's presence in this life: in those most in need and in those who serve them in love. So here is our hope: We do all these things, we live and die, united to Christ. It is in that union—manifested in how we live—that we place our confidence. The gift of grace that made the care of others possible is the same gift of grace that makes salvation possible. In other words, because of what the mourners saw in the life of the deceased here ("godliness"—2 Macc 12:45), they can hope in resurrection life for their loved one (and themselves).

Finally, the preacher can remind the mourners of the words used at the vigil the night before: the "ties of friendship and affection which knit us as one throughout our lives do not unravel with death" (OCF 71, 87). By weaving in the reading from Maccabees and the collect, the preacher can further explore this ongoing relationship, and especially our ongoing prayer on behalf of the deceased. Such prayer reflects trust in God's mercy and compassion, rather than belief in a "God" who either does not care or is severe and punitive.

5. Mark 15:33-39; 16:1-6 (or 15:33-39)

Readings from the Ambo

The gospel. Mark's gospel lacks many of the details found in the other Synoptics. That, and the use of "and" (*kai*) and "immediately" or "right away" (*euthys*) to connect clauses, sentences, and sections, give Mark a sense of urgency absent from Matthew and Luke.[28] Mark's account of the passion is stark. Everything, in Jesus' life and in the narrative itself, is stripped away. In the midst of his suffering, Jesus cries out in the words of Psalm 22. Lament psalms, while giving voice to suffering, are also cries of confident trust and hope. The life of Jesus in Mark's gospel is one of service and suffering; this is the path to glory (Mark 10:45).

Application to funerals. This reading (especially in the shorter form), with its emphasis on the death of Christ and his cry of abandonment, is well suited for the vigil when the reality of death is at its most raw. The

---

28. John R. Donahue and Daniel J. Harrington, *The Gospel of Mark*, Sacra Pagina series, ed. Daniel J. Harrington (Collegeville, MN: Liturgical Press, 2002), 17.

mourners may very well share in Jesus' lament, feeling abandoned in their loss, whether by God or by their loved one. Their lives have become covered in darkness. At the same time, the cries of mockery become a challenge to faith: Christ did not come down from the cross (15:32). So will mourners give in to hopelessness, or find meaning in the loss they have suffered?[29] Will they be able to follow Jesus, giving honest voice to both their sorrow and their faith? Hope comes from knowing that, like Jesus, we are not, in the end, abandoned.

The longer form, which includes the account of the empty tomb and the annunciation of the resurrection, could also be used at the funeral liturgy, when the liturgical focus broadens to more intentionally include a look toward future hope. This reading speaks of Jesus' death, burial, and resurrection. The funeral rites are celebrated in the midst of the same transition: the person has died, they are being buried, and the resurrection is anticipated with hope. It is unfortunate that 15:40-47, with its account of the ministrations of the women, is omitted; those who have assembled for the funeral rites may have performed similar service for their deceased family member or friend and could have heard echoes of their experiences in the story.

Other readings. The book of Lamentations is considered to have been written in the aftermath of the fall of Jerusalem in 587 BCE. This collection of five poems, traditionally ascribed to the prophet Jeremiah, expresses both the grief of the community as well as their faith and hope in God. The reading used in the funeral Lectionary is taken from the third poem, which is a more personal reflection than an account of the destruction of David's city. Like a lament psalm, Lamentations 3:17-26 (OT #5) begins with a cry of anguish but ends in an expression of hope. Thus, this reading can be seen to echo Jesus' cry on the cross as well as the feelings of those gathered for the funeral rites. While any of the lament psalms included in the funeral Lectionary could be used with these readings, Psalm 130 in particular follows this pattern of anguished cry leading to an expression of hope.

The cross figures prominently in the two readings from Romans 5 (NT #2 and #3); but both readings also speak of justification and salvation. "Christ died for us" (Rom 5:8), "one righteous act" (Rom 5:18) on

---

29. Bergant and Karris, *Collegeville Bible Commentary*, 934.

the behalf of sinners. This act has justified us (made us righteous before God) and reconciled us to God here and now; as a result, we can look forward to our future salvation. All this, because of God's love for us (Rom 5:5). While "death is the finalization of fallen humanity's wrong relation with God,"[30] it has been defeated by Christ's action on the cross, by grace (Rom 5:2, 15, 17). It is this hope in the midst of the cross of grief that the funeral rites proclaim.

Connecting the Bible and the Liturgy

The OCF. There are a number of prayers from the OCF that might be paired with these readings. From OCF 398, prayer #2 has lament-like qualities, and would be especially appropriate if the reading from Lamentations (OT #5) was also used: "Are you not the God of love who open your ears to all?" OCF 399, #5 asks God to be "attentive to the voice of our pleading"—also a lament-like cry.

As seen in the second half of that same reading, laments eventually turn to hope, suggesting the use of prayers #4 and #6 from 399, as well as 398, #12. Prayers #5–#7 in 398 emphasize the cross, using Pauline language also heard in the readings from Romans (NT #2, #3). Prayers #1 and #2 from 399 also emphasize the cross and rising from the dead.

The Missal. The collects found in Funeral Mass I.A correspond to 398, #5 and #12. Reflecting the Pauline readings, both the collect ("underwent death in the flesh") and the prayer over the offerings ("in the Blood of Christ") from II.C are also appropriate. The "mystery of the Cross" is also mentioned under III.A.1 (first collect) and Christ's blood in the prayer over the offerings III.A.5.

Pauline language, echoing the Romans 5 readings, is also found in a number of the prefaces for the dead. In preface II, our corporate personality in Christ is highlighted, making a connection to the Adam-Christ typology in Romans 5:17-21 (NT #3). Preface III speaks of Christ as life and salvation. Paul's belief that death results from sin finds expression in preface IV. Grace and redemption through Christ's victory (NT #3) are mentioned in preface V.

30. Fuller, "Lectionary for Funerals," 43.

Strategy for Preaching

Scriptural Texts: Lamentations 3:17-26; Psalm 130; Mark 15:33-39; 16:1-6

Liturgical Texts: Opening Prayer 399, #5; Concluding Prayer 398, #2

I imagine this as a homily preached at the vigil, using Paul Scott Wilson's "Four Pages" as the form. As Wilson details in his *The Four Pages of the Sermon: A Guide to Biblical Preaching*, the preacher begins by pointing out the "trouble" or crisis in the biblical text (Page One) and then drawing out an analogous "trouble" in the world of the assembly (Page Two). The preacher then points out "God's action" or grace in the Scriptures (the good news, or grace) in response to the crisis (Page Three), and concludes by announcing that same good news into today's situation (Page Four): how God is active in the here and now. In the case of funeral preaching, it may be helpful to reverse the first two "pages," beginning with the "trouble in the world" (the situation of the mourners) and then drawing the connection to the Scriptures ("trouble in the Bible"). Wilson also holds that only one text should be used for preaching. Here, while the core text is the gospel, images and language from the other readings and liturgical texts are woven into the homily. The *focus* would be to proclaim that the mourners are not abandoned in their sorrow. The *function* would be to allow the opportunity to lament and then begin to move toward hope.

The preacher begins by naming the crisis or trouble being experienced by the assembly. In the case of a funeral, this is the death of a loved one. More specifically, this gospel passage is especially appropriate in situations where mourners are feeling abandoned, either by God (because prayers for recovery were not answered, for example) or by their loved one. In such a situation, the preacher could begin by putting Jesus' words on the lips of the mourners. The language from the first part of the reading from Lamentations (3:17-20) can be used to name the feelings being experienced by those who have gathered for the vigil: they are deprived of peace . . . have forgotten happiness . . . the future is lost. They, too, plead (399, #5) for God to hear them. In the second "page" of this homily, the preacher can make the connection between the mourners' feelings of abandonment and Jesus' cry from the cross. The language from Psalm 22:2-3 and Psalm 130:1-2 can be used to name the "trouble in the Bible."

In the third page, the preacher holds out the reason to have hope, as announced in the Scriptures: God's mercies are not spent (Lam 3:22). Here, the preacher can mention that Jesus' cry from the cross is the beginning of Psalm 22. By putting Psalm 22 on the lips of Jesus, Mark wants his readers to follow the logic of lament: the recalling of God's faithfulness leads to renewed hope. Laments, as can be seen in the latter half of Psalm 130, are expressions of trust in God, who has acted on behalf of God's people in the past. If the longer form of the gospel reading is used, the preacher can help make that hope more explicit by recounting the finding of the empty tomb (Mark 16:5-6). In the fourth and final page, the hope proclaimed in the gospel, and echoed in the other readings, is brought to bear on the situation of the mourners. The mourners are encouraged to turn to God (398, #2) and remember (Lam 3:21) that they, and their loved one, are also recipients of God's fidelity and mercy (Ps 130). Therefore, they, too, have reason to hope.

6. Luke 7:11-17

Readings from the Ambo

The gospel. Luke pairs his unique account of the raising of the widow's son with another story: the healing of the centurion's slave (Luke 7:1-10; also found in Matt 8:5-13). Together, they lead to the question posed by John the Baptist and his messengers (Luke 7:19-20): "Are you the one who is to come, or should we look for another?" Jesus' answer to them is to look at his deeds; they reveal who he is. Together, the stories reveal that Jesus is, at the very least, a prophet, one like Elijah (1 Kgs 17:20-24; see Luke 4:25-27).[31] As the people declare (Luke 7:16): "A great prophet has arisen in our midst," and "God has visited his people."

Application to funerals. Jesus, "moved with pity" (v. 13), consoles the widow of Nain, as Jesus consoles all who mourn. More than that, Jesus raises the widow's son from the dead. In the midst of sorrow, God visits God's people. This is a message that those gathered for the funeral rites are in special need of hearing. Because Jesus is revealed as "the one who

---

31. Luke Timothy Johnson, *The Gospel of Luke*, vol. 3, Sacra Pagina series, ed. Daniel J. Harrington (Collegeville, MN: Liturgical Press, 1991), 81.

is to come" (v. 19), mourners can have faith that just as the widow's son was raised from the dead, so, too, will their beloved one be at the end of time. The focus on consolation and presence recommends the gospel for the vigil; if a preacher wanted to focus on the future hope of resurrection, of Jesus' power over life and death, it could also be used in the funeral liturgy.

Other readings. A number of the Old Testament readings offer words of consolation to the mourners. From Wisdom (OT #2), we hear that our beloved dead "are in peace" (3:3), recipients of God's "grace and mercy" (3:9). We also hear (OT #3) that the just one, whose soul was pleasing to God, is now at rest (4:7, 14). This second reading from Wisdom tries to address the problem of one dying young, arguing that long life should not be equated with God's favor (or short life with God's judgment; see essays 3 and 7); this resonates with the setting of the story in Luke. Isaiah (OT #4) promises that God will wipe away the mourner's tears, and death will be destroyed forever (25:8). Alternatively, the reading from Lamentations (OT #5) can be read as an echo of the widow's lament.

In the gospel passage, Jesus is moved with pity. God's compassion and mercy are mentioned in Psalms 25, 103, and 116. Psalm 103 uses parental imagery to speak of God's compassion (v. 8), and Psalm 116 proclaims, "The Lord keeps the little ones" (v. 6). Therefore, these might be especially appropriate to use with this reading from Luke.

As Ben Sira spoke words of consolation and encouragement, so does Paul to his communities. In his second letter to the Corinthians (NT #10, #11), Paul instructs us not to be discouraged (4:16) because after "this momentary light affliction" eternal glory awaits (4:17-18); that even if earthly life (our "tent") is destroyed, an eternal dwelling awaits in heaven (5:1). In his first letter to the Thessalonians (NT #13), Paul encourages his community not to grieve like those who have no hope (4:13); if Christ rose from the dead, then those who follow him will also share in the resurrection.

Connecting the Bible and the Liturgy

The OCF. The second prayer found in OCF 398 echoes both the lament of the widow as well as the sentiments of the first reading from Wisdom (OT #2). The image of rising from the dead is found in prayers

#8 ("strengthen our belief that your Son has risen from the dead / and our hope that your servant N. will also rise again") and #13 ("raise him/her on the last day"). Prayer #4 ("where there will be no sorrow, no weeping nor pain") reflects the reading from Isaiah (OT #4) and Wisdom (OT #2, "no torment shall touch them"). The second half of the reading from Lamentations (OT #5) speaks of hope; so does prayer #12. A number of prayers (##1, 7, 10, 13) speak of being released or freed from death. The metaphor of "sleep" for death, found in the reading from 1 Thessalonians (NT #13), is also found in prayer #5. If this gospel passage was chosen specifically for the funeral rites for a young person, then prayers #27 and #28 apply. In that same situation, prayers #4 ("brevity of our lives on earth"), #6 (those "left behind" to mourn), and #7 (the bereaved "overwhelmed by their loss") from OCF 399 would be helpful. These prayers also carry a message of hope, reflecting OT #5 (Lam) and NT #13 (1 Thess). Finally, OCF 399 #4 and #5 speak of testing and doubt in the face of death, as does NT reading #11; prayer #1 speaks of tears being wiped away (see OT #4).

The Missal. A number of the prayers listed above (OCF 398, ##5, 8, 12, 13, and 27) have equivalents in the Roman Missal (see collects I.A, B, C, and IV.7). Collect IV.7 is specifically designated for the funeral of one who died young; the language of flourishing in God's "house" or dwelling would suggest that this prayer could be used well with the reading from Isaiah (OT #4) and especially with the readings from 2 Corinthians (NT #10, #11). The prayer after Communion I.C mentions passing over "to a dwelling place of light and peace" and collect III.A.1 (second option) mentions "a place of peace and light" (NT #10, #11). Collect III.A.3 ("for whom the fleeting light of this world shines no more") is appropriate if this is a funeral for a younger person, especially if the reading from Wisdom 4:7-15 (OT #3) is used. The metaphor of sleep for death (NT #13) is found in the prayer over the offerings in Mass III.B.2 and the collect in Mass III.B.3.

God's compassion is mentioned in preface V. The connection between death and sin is also brought out in this preface, which may provide a corrective to trying to "canonize" the deceased. Consolation and the language of earthly dwellings giving way to an eternal dwelling in heaven is found in preface I. This latter theme is also found in both readings from 2 Corinthians (NT #10, #11).

Strategy for Preaching

Scriptural Texts: Wisdom 4:7-15; Psalm 116; 1 Thessalonians 4:13-18; Luke 7:11-17

Liturgical Texts: Collect III.A.3; Prayer over the Offerings III.B.2; Preface V

The preaching scenario envisioned here is the funeral liturgy for one who died young. Therefore, the emphasis on loss, typically the focus of the vigil, continues with greater poignancy into this liturgy. The task of the preacher remains to acknowledge the loss as well as to proclaim hope in the midst of such sorrow. The *focus* of the homily could be to proclaim why hope is possible in such circumstances. The *function* could be to enkindle that hope and encourage those gathered to be a source of consolation for each other.

As mentioned in essay 2, a homily that follows the form of Lowry's Loop is structured in five parts: the bind, the exploration of the bind (which builds dramatic tension), the reversal or "aha" moment, the proclamation of the Good News, and the implications of that proclamation.

The "early" (Wis 4:7) death of a young person, one whose life has been especially "fleeting" (collect), is often experienced as particularly tragic. Not only grief but anger and guilt may be strong emotions being experienced by the mourners; they are afflicted, and human resources are of no avail (Ps 116:10-11). Into this tumult the words of Jesus—"Do not weep"—and Paul—do "not grieve like the rest"—not only ring hollow but can seem harsh and dismissive. The first task of the preacher is to acknowledge that reality and then help guide the assembly to the reasons why Jesus and Paul could make such a claim.

The reading from Wisdom addresses the assumption, at the time the text was written, that an early death was a sign of sinful living. Old age was seen as a reward for virtue. While that is unlikely to be a common assumption today, the preacher must set the Wisdom reading in its proper context. It would be tempting to go to the opposite extreme and use the text to explain an "early" death as God's "rescue" (Wis 4:11) of one who was perfect (Wis 4:13) before one could sin. In recalling the life of the deceased, the preacher needs to avoid the error of presenting this death as either a reward for virtue or a punishment for sin. One cannot explain why someone died. Rather, one can only acknowledge that death is part of our "fallen" existence (preface).

The death of anyone is "precious"—dear, costly, grievous; not pleasing—to God (Ps 116:15). Death is *not* what God desires for us (Ezek 18:23; see also John 10:10). This is the very situation that Christ addressed at the cross. In Christ, we see that God indeed does "keep the little ones" (Ps 116:6). Therefore, Paul can proclaim that Jesus' own death and resurrection means that "those who have fallen asleep" (1 Thess 4:14; prayer over the offerings) will also rise. That's the Good News. We live in the hope that the words Jesus spoke to the young man—"I tell you, arise" (Luke 7:14) will be spoken to the deceased, and to each of us. Therefore, we are able to "console one another" (1 Thess 4:18).

7. Luke 12:35-40

Readings from the Ambo

The gospel. Chapter 12 in Luke's gospel begins with Jesus and his community under threat. Jesus reassures his followers that there is nothing to fear in this world—neither material need nor physical death. It is in this context that Luke places the story of the servants awaiting their master's return. The story stresses preparedness for the final coming of the Son of Man at the Parousia. This coming will be sudden, a surprise. The servant who is ready is blessed, so one should focus on preparation rather than on the anxieties of this life. The full account (through v. 48), including the judgment of the unprepared servant, is not included in the funeral Lectionary. Interestingly, the same account from Matthew's gospel (24:45-51) is not part of the funeral Lectionary at all. Instead, the funeral Lectionary gives us a similar text that also speaks to the theme of preparedness: Matthew 25:1-13 (see essay 3 above).

Application to funerals. With the omission of the second half of the story (Luke 12:41-48), the focus of the reading is more clearly the warning that the coming of the Son of Man will be a surprise, so the listener ought to be prepared. Such an emphasis suggests that this reading is best used at the vigil, especially if death was sudden or unexpected. At the same time, the wider context of Jesus addressing the fears or anxieties of his followers allows the preacher to speak a word of hope in the midst of loss: even bodily death is not to be feared. The good news is that the Master will welcome to the table, the eschatological banquet, those who have been vigilant. After a life of service, they are the ones who will be served. In other words, this passage may also be used in those situations when the deceased was vigilant and well prepared, and so might be appropriate for the funeral liturgy when one emphasis falls on thanksgiving for the life of the deceased.

Other readings. Readings that reflect the idea of preparedness have been mentioned as part of the discussion of Matthew 25:1-13 (essay 3). These include: Wisdom 4:7-15 (OT #3), Daniel 12:1-3 (OT #6), 1 Corinthians 15:51-57 (NT #9), and 1 Thessalonians 4:13-18 (NT #13). The admonition against judgment found in Romans 14:10 (NT #7) may be appropriate if the sudden death was due to suicide or an accident. The lament psalms would be most appropriate.

The image of servants now being served by the master suggests the image of rest. If the preacher wishes to emphasize this metaphor for death, then Wisdom 3:1-9 (OT #2), which states that even though death appears to be an "affliction" or "destruction" the deceased "are at peace," would also be appropriate. The notion of death as "rest" is also found in 2 Maccabees 12:43-46 (OT #7). While not explicitly named, the reading from Isaiah 25:6a, 7-9 (OT #4) suggests the eschatological banquet. The rewarding of a faithful servant can be found implicitly in 2 Corinthians 5:1, 6-10 (NT #11) and Revelation 20:11–21:1 (NT #18); Revelation 14:13 (NT #17) explicitly mentions the reward of "rest" for those who "die in the Lord." If a lament psalm is not selected, then Psalm 23 speaks of the deceased finding "repose" by "restful waters" (v. 2) as well as of a lavish banquet (v. 5; see also Psalm 63:6). If the Isaiah reading is used and a lament psalm is desired, Psalm 42/43 speaks of God's "holy mountain" (43:3).

Connecting the Bible and the Liturgy

The OCF. Liturgical texts from the OCF that reflect the notions of preparedness or the suddenness of death have been discussed in essay 3. These include 398, ## 1, 2, 3, 9, and 42–43 as well as 399, ## 4, 6, 7. If the preacher wishes to focus more on the notion of rest as the reward of a good and faithful servant, then 398, ## 4, 5, and 12 would be appropriate. OCF 399, #3 speaks of the "faithful lives" of those who are God's. The wording of the prayer does not allow for a Pelagian interpretation. God is the one who has graced the deceased first; the life of faith they evidenced gives witness to that grace. If Revelation 14:13 (NT #17) is used, then reference could be made to the concluding rite at the vigil (OCF 81 or 97): "[L]et them rest from their labors for their good deeds go with them."

The Missal. Liturgical texts from the Missal—such as collects I.C (first option), III.A.3, and IV.9, as well as prayer after Communion III.B.9—that reflect the notions of preparedness or the suddenness of death have been discussed in essay 3. Among the prefaces for the dead, prefaces I, IV, and V were also mentioned.

If the preacher wishes to focus more on the notion of rest as the reward of a good and faithful servant, then a number of collects that pray for the deceased to come to a place of rest and peace (II.E., III.A.2., III.A.5.) are suggested. Three prayers over the offerings (III.B.1, III.B.4, III.B.9) make mention of the "reward" or "prize" of eternal life; one (III.B.3) prays for the "repose of the souls" of the deceased and so might be especially appropriate if Psalm 23 was used. Prayer after Communion I.A asks that the deceased "come to the eternal table of Christ" and prayer after Communion I.C asks that he or she come to a "dwelling place of light and peace."

Strategy for Preaching

Scriptural Texts: Revelation 14:13; Psalm 63; Luke 12:35-40

Liturgical Texts: Opening Prayer 399, #3; Concluding Prayer 398, #4; OCF 81

The sudden appearance of the Master suggests the use of this gospel primarily for the vigil. The *focus* of the homily could be to recall the ways the deceased has been a faithful servant, giving evidence of God's grace at work in his or her life. The *function* of the homily could be to comfort those gathered for the vigil by drawing the connection between the deceased's life of faith and Christ's promises. The Master is faithful.

The homily would therefore begin with acknowledging the disequilibrium that those in the assembly are experiencing. Whether the death was in some ways expected (older age, long illness) or truly sudden, it will still have likely caught the mourners by surprise; there will still be grief.

The preacher can then draw out the ways in which the deceased gave evidence in life that he or she belonged to God (399, #3). The preacher can name the ways that the deceased thirsted for God (Ps 63:2) and the ways that, by a life of faith, he or she awaited the Master's coming, vigilant for his arrival (Luke 12:35-40). Such preparations may have been lifelong, evidenced by service ("works") at the family table, at the table of those in need, or at the altar table (Rev 14:13; OCF 81, 97). Or, such preparations may have been more focused and intentional recently in the face of increasing age or illness. Finally, the preacher can point to the Good News: such servants are blessed. They are promised rest (398, #4), a place at the banquet table (Ps 63:6; Luke 12:37) in paradise, where sorrow, weeping, and pain will be no more (398, #4), where a thirst for God will be satisfied (Ps 63). The Master will care for the servant (Ps 63; Luke 12:37).

8. Luke 23:33, 39-43

Readings from the Ambo

The gospel. This and the next gospel pericope include portions of Luke's passion narrative. The next selection will center on the death and burial of Jesus. In this reading, while the crucifixion itself is mentioned, the focus is on the dialogue between Jesus and the two criminals crucified with him, an account unique to Luke. One of the criminals joins in the mocking; the other professes faith and trust in Jesus and in his ability to save. They therefore serve as examples of the two possible responses to Jesus and the Good News.

The language used in this passage deserves some mention. The word translated as "today" (v. 43)—*sēmeron*—is used in Luke's gospel to "signify a special moment of revelation or salvation."[32] It is more than just a temporal reference and should be read with reference to the eschaton (the Day of the Lord) rather than to a literal day. In addition, the term "paradise" is rarely used in the New Testament. In intertestamental texts such as 4 Ezra and Enoch, this Persian term for an enclosed garden came to refer to "an intermediate state of happiness" that the righteous enjoy prior to the final judgment.[33]

---

32. Johnson, *The Gospel of Luke*, Sacra Pagina, 378.

33. Bergant and Karris, *Collegeville Bible Commentary*, 978; Patricia Datchuck Sánchez, *The Passages We Celebrate: Commentaries on the Scriptural Texts for Baptisms, Weddings, and Funerals* (Kansas City, MO: Sheed and Ward, 1994), 200.

Application to funerals. The images of the reality of death are juxtaposed with Jesus' promise to the second criminal, whose cry of "remember me" could be placed on any dying person's lips. On the one hand, the mourners could hear those words addressed to them—pointing to the important role that remembrance plays in grief and in the funeral rites. On the other hand, the cry is addressed primarily to Jesus, and his words of hope and promise could be imagined as spoken to the one who has died. At the same time, Jesus' words are also spoken to all of us: we are all sinners in need of forgiveness. Rather than turn away from Jesus we are invited to place our faith in his power to save. But the choice is ours.

Other readings. The promise of paradise after suffering suggests the readings from Wisdom 3:1-9 (OT #2) and Isaiah 25:6a, 7-9 (OT #4). In Wisdom, affliction, destruction, and chastisement give way to peace in God's presence. In Isaiah, tears are wiped away and any reproach removed. Job (OT #1) expresses the hope reflected in Jesus' promise: he holds that he will see his vindicator, just as the repentant criminal will see Jesus in paradise.

Romans 8:14-23 (NT #5) and 8:31b-35, 37-39 (NT #6) and 2 Corinthians 4:14–5:1 (NT #10) also speak of the glory that will follow present suffering, which cannot separate the believer from the love of God. The second criminal lives the words of 2 Corinthians 5:1, 6-10 (NT #11): "[W]e walk by faith, not by sight" (v. 7). The reading from 1 Corinthians 15:20-28 (NT #8) speaks of Christ being the firstfruits, preceding us in death and resurrection—as he promised he would precede the criminal to paradise.

Although the word, "paradise," is not used, a number of New Testament readings do refer to resurrection life, or life in the world to come. For example, 1 Corinthians 15:51-57 (NT #9) states that both the living and the dead will be changed at the coming of Christ, the corruptible and mortal giving way to the incorruptible and immortal. Philippians 3:20-21 (NT #12) proclaims that "our citizenship is in heaven" (v. 20). First John 3:1-2 (NT #15) promises that "we shall be like him" in the next life.

The image of "paradise" suggests Psalms 23 and 42/43; as well as 122 if the references to "Jerusalem" are not read literally. In Psalm 25, the psalmist pleads with God to remember past compassion and kindness and so bring that same care to bear in the present.

Connecting the Bible and the Liturgy

The OCF. If the reading from 1 Corinthians 15:20-28 (NT #8) is used, it could be paired with prayer #5 from OCF 398, which also refers to Christ as the "firstfruits of all who have fallen asleep." "Paradise" is specifically mentioned in prayers #4 and #6, while prayer #2 mentions a "kingdom of light and peace." Of the Prayers for Mourners (399), prayer #2 mentions "a place of happiness, light, and peace," prayer #3 speaks of "the world to come," and prayer #6 speaks of our hope in "the eternal kingdom" and—of particular note—makes reference to holding the memory of the deceased dear.

The Missal. While the first collect from Mass I.A reflects prayer #5 from 398 in the OCF, the reference to Christ as the "firstborn" is missing. None of the prayers found among the "Masses for the Dead" in the Missal mention "firstfruits" or "paradise." The latter is mentioned in the entrance antiphon for Masses I.B and III.A.1. "Light and peace" are mentioned in the prayer after Communion in Mass I.C and the second collect for Mass III.A.1; light and rest in collect II.E. Preface I for the Dead speaks of "an eternal dwelling" made ready in heaven for those who have died.

Strategy for Preaching

Scriptural Texts: Romans 8:31b-35, 37-39; Psalm 42/43; Luke 23:33, 39-43

Liturgical Texts: Opening Prayer 399, #6; Concluding Prayer 398, #6

The setting of the crucifixion scene would suggest this reading for the vigil, which is the context assumed here. The focus on remembrance, however, is also appropriate for the funeral liturgy, where gratitude for the gift of the life that has been lived is a prominent concern. Regardless of the setting, the *focus* of the homily could be on God's faithfulness. The *function* would be to not only remember the past with gratitude but, by doing so, be able to "remember" the future with hope.

The homily could begin with the preacher acknowledging that the mourners, in their anguish, might be feeling separated from Christ's love (Rom 8:35). There may even be anger: Why did Christ not act on the behalf of the deceased and save him or her (Luke 23:39)?

The preacher might next choose to place the crucified prisoner's plea to be remembered (Luke 23:42) on the lips of the deceased whose vigil is being celebrated. In the first instance, the desire to be remembered might be spoken to the mourners. So, in this part of the homily, the preacher would remember the life of the deceased, helping those gathered to "hold his/her memory dear" in their grief (399, #6). Perhaps the preacher might mention the ways that the deceased both experienced God's presence in this life and mediated that presence to others (Ps 42/43).

Finally, these words could also be envisioned as spoken by the deceased to Jesus. If so, then having Jesus' promise of paradise (Luke 23:43) spoken to the one who has died can provide a word of hope and consolation. Jesus shares the human condition with us, even death. Life is possible only through death, a reality that must be kept in mind in funeral preaching. Christ who has preceded us in death intercedes for us at God's right hand. Therefore, even death cannot separate us from God's love (Rom 8:35). As the friends and family of the deceased, we pray for the fulfillment of this promise (398, #6). So, while it may be normal to be downcast, sighing in grief, we have reason to hope (Ps 42/43). Keeping in mind the points made above about the language used by Luke should help the preacher avoid taking references to "today" too literally and claiming that the deceased is enjoying the beatific vision at that very moment.[34]

9. Luke 23:44-46, 50, 52-53; 24:1-6a (or 23:44-46, 50, 52-53)

Readings from the Ambo

The gospel. The short form of the reading describes Jesus' death and burial; the long form includes the finding of the empty tomb by the women and the annunciation of the resurrection by the angels. Even the long form used in the funeral Lectionary omits some of the details, such as the proclamation of Jesus' innocence by the centurion, the response of the crowd, and the presence and actions of the faithful women (vv. 49, 55-56). Instead, the role of Joseph of Arimathea receives greater attention. He is mentioned in this selection from Luke, but he is absent from the verses chosen from Mark's account of the crucifixion (see essay 5 above). Here, he is presented as a righteous man (though, with the omission of

---

34. For a current discussion on the limits of time-bound language when speaking of life after death, see *Is This All There Is? On Resurrection and Eternal Life* by Gerhard Lohfink, especially chapter 10. The documents from the CDF and ITC also address this issue. Please see the bibliography.

v. 51, other details about him are missing). The emphasis is not on him per se, but on his care of Jesus' body.

As in the account from Mark, Jesus' death is accompanied by darkness; the reference may be to the seeming victory of evil over good, but more likely refers to the signs that would accompany the Day of the Lord (Amos 8:9; also Joel 3:3-4 and Zeph 1:15).[35] The tearing of the veil in the temple, also mentioned in the Markan account, has been interpreted in numerous ways.[36] In the context of funeral preaching, if mention is made of it at all, it could be emphasized that Jesus' death grants all human beings access to God as the division between sacred and profane is overcome.[37] However, a crucial difference between this account and the one found in Mark is that here Jesus prays Psalm 31 instead of Psalm 22: he abandons himself *to* the Father.

Application to funerals. As noted with the similar reading from Mark (essay 5 above), the short form, missing the account of the events at the empty tomb, is better used at the vigil; the longer form could be used at the funeral liturgy. Regardless of which form is used, the preacher could emphasize Jesus' abandonment into his Father's hands. Such abandonment should not be presented as passive acquiescence, as if God is the overpowering cause of suffering. Rather, what Jesus models is active trust in God's mercy and hope that God's words are true. If mourners are feeling that God is the source of suffering, one strategy in preaching would be to acknowledge and then gently challenge this answer to theodicy. The abandonment necessary is to our creatureliness—which includes death—and to the merciful God preached by Jesus, not to a god more akin to the Fates.

Other readings. The theme of abandonment to and trust in God's will is found in Wisdom 3:1-9 (OT #2). The transitory nature of suffering is stressed in 2 Corinthians 4:14-5:1 (NT #10). As mentioned in essay 5, the cross figures prominently in the two readings from Romans 5 (NT #2 and #3). While Psalm 31 is not included in the funeral Lectionary, if the

---

35. Sánchez, *The Passages We Celebrate*, 201.

36. Johnson, *The Gospel of Luke*, Sacra Pagina, 379; see also Bergant and Karris, *Collegeville Bible Commentary*, 978.

37. Margaret Aymer, Cynthia Briggs Kittredge, and David A. Sánchez, eds., *The New Testament*, Fortress Commentary on the Bible (Minneapolis, MN: Fortress Press, 2014), 257.

Office for the Dead is celebrated (in lieu of or in addition to the typical vigil), the OCF allows great flexibility in choosing which psalms will be used (OCF 359). Of the options included in the funeral Lectionary, Psalm 27 refers to God as "refuge" while Psalm 25 prays for rescue. Psalm 143 asks God to teach the petitioner to do God's will.

Connecting the Bible and the Liturgy

The OCF. Among the prayers found in OCF 398, prayer #4 is especially appropriate to use with the Lukan crucifixion account. The prayer begins: "Into your hands, O Lord, we humbly entrust our brother/sister. . . ." In other words, the assembly makes the words of Jesus (and of Psalm 31) their own. Prayers #5–#7 speak of death and the cross, so could also be considered. These prayers, echoing the language found in Paul, might be especially useful if one of the readings from Romans (NT #2, #3) is used. Prayers #1 and #2 from OCF 399 also emphasize the cross and rising from the dead. The preacher could make reference to the prayers of commendation (OCF 175; cf. 202, 231, 404), which speaks of the assembly handing over, commending, the deceased to the care of God. One of the alternate introductions to this prayer (402, #2) echoes this same sentiment (see also the opening invitation in the Rite of Committal with Final Commendation, 224).

The Missal. Reflecting the Pauline readings, both the collect ("underwent death in the flesh") and the prayer over the offerings ("in the Blood of Christ") from II.C would be appropriate. The "mystery of the Cross" is mentioned under III.A.1 (first collect) and Christ's blood in the prayer over the offerings in III.A.5. The first collect found in funeral Mass I.A corresponds to 398, #5.

Pauline language is also found in various prefaces for the dead. In preface II, our corporate personality in Christ, reflecting the Adam-Christ typology in Romans 5:17-21 (NT #3), is stressed while proclaiming that Christ "accepted death" for our sake. Preface III speaks of Christ as life and salvation while Paul's belief that death results from sin finds expression in preface IV. Preface V states that grace and redemption come through Christ's victory (NT #3).

Strategy for Preaching

Scriptural Texts: Wisdom 3:1-9; Psalm 27 (first antiphon); Romans 5:17-21; Luke 23:44-46, 50, 52-53; 24:1-6a

Liturgical Texts: Collect 398 #4; Prayer over the Offerings III.A.5; Preface II; OCF 175; 402, #2

At the funeral liturgy, a homily anchored in this reading from Luke could have God as light in the darkness as its *focus*. The *function*, then, could be to help the assembly move from that understanding to being able to "commend" the deceased to God in hope.

The homily would begin by acknowledging that the mourners find themselves in darkness (Luke 23:44). The death of their loved one has left them "afflicted" (Wis 3:2). Such darkness is part of the human condition; sin and evil seem to have the upper hand (Rom 5:17-18). The darkness is real.

Yet, a light shines in that darkness (Ps 27:1); Christ's obedience has undone Adam's disobedience (Rom 5:17-19; preface). If God is light in the darkness, how has the assembly glimpsed that light in this life? As the prayer of commendation (175A) puts it, "[T]he blessings / which you bestowed upon N. in this life . . . are signs to us of your goodness . . ." So the preacher can name these blessings as evidence that darkness does not have the last word. In particular, the preacher can make mention of how God's love is manifest in the Eucharist; as Christ poured himself out on the cross for our behalf (Luke 23:46), he continues to give himself to us "as the Bread of Life" and blood poured out "as the chalice of salvation" (prayer over the offerings). The deceased, too, experienced this gift in his or her life (402, #2).

Because we have experienced the light in this life (Ps 27:1), we can live in the "sure and certain hope" (175A) of the resurrection. In the end, the tomb is empty (Luke 24:3). Therefore, in the midst of loss, we can have courage as we wait for the Lord, trusting that God is our refuge (Ps 27:1). We can entrust our doubts, fears, and grief to God, knowing that God has pity and will answer (Ps 27:7). More importantly, we can entrust our beloved dead to God (collect), knowing that our God cares for them and they are at peace (Wis 3:3).

10. Luke 24:13-35 (or 24:13-16, 28-35)

Readings from the Ambo

The gospel. The account of the disciples on the road to Emmaus, unique to Luke, serves a number of purposes. To begin with, as in other accounts of Jesus' appearance after the crucifixion, the story is intended to witness to the resurrection. However, Luke is also explicit that the Messiah had to suffer and die in order to be glorified (v. 26); thus, the passage serves to proclaim Luke's particular Christology.[38] Finally, the story also speaks of Jesus' abiding presence in the community ("on the way"—Luke's way of speaking of the Christian life, v. 35; cf. Acts 9:2; 18:25-26; 19:9, 23; 24:14, 22), especially in the "breaking of the bread" (Luke's language for the community's ritual meal; cf. Luke 22:19; 24:30; Acts 2:42, 46; 20:7, 11; 27:35).

Application to funerals. In the context of the funeral rites, this passage might also function on a number of levels. To begin with, the passage makes the claim that the Messiah had to suffer in order to be glorified. The same pattern applies to believers: suffering and death are the path to eternal life.[39] Because Jesus has gone this way before us, we are able to hope.

Like the disciples on the road, the mourners are brokenhearted. Because of their grief, they may not "see" that Christ is present to them. The story shows the risen Christ as initially hidden from the disciples; it is only once their eyes are opened that they are able to recognize his presence. The church still ministers that presence, in word proclaimed and bread broken. Likewise, our beloved dead are also hidden now; but that does not mean that our relationship has ended. It is just being lived out in the mode of silent absence—a sacramental mode—rather than in obvious presence; a mode that requires the eyes of faith to see. Given these emphases on unexpected encounter and ongoing relationship after death, this pericope seems best suited to the funeral liturgy—especially if celebrated in the context of Eucharist.

Other readings. Job 19:1, 23-27 (OT #1) speaks of Job's faith that his vindicator (in some translations, redeemer or defender; the Hebrew is

---

38. Johnson, *The Gospel of Luke*, Sacra Pagina, 20, 395.
39. Fuller, "Lectionary for Funerals," 58.

go'el) lives, whom he will see (vv. 25, 27). In their original context, and given the uncertain manuscript record, the meaning of these verses is obscure. Is the reference to vindication in the present life, or in the life to come? However, in the context of the funeral liturgy, it can be a potent proclamation of faith in Christ, even in the face of death (cf. 1 Cor 15).[40]

The funeral Lectionary offers two readings from 1 Corinthians 15: verses 20-28 and verses 51-57 (NT #8 and #9). Both selections refer to Christ's defeat of death. Another appropriate passage could be Romans 6:3-9 (NT #4). The baptismal imagery could be tied to the eucharistic imagery of the Emmaus account, allowing the preacher to weave a homily that uses the sacraments of initiation as an organizing principle. Like-wise, the claim that we grow into union with Christ through a death like his echoes Luke's theology of death/suffering being the way to glory. Acts 10:34-43 (NT #1) refers to eating and drinking with Christ after the resurrection.

Typically, I would use lament psalms at the vigil and the other psalms at the funeral. Psalm 42/43, with its baptismal imagery and anticipation of seeing God face-to-face, would be appropriate in either setting. Other psalms that would work well at the funeral include Psalm 63, with its reference to thirsting for God, and Psalm 23; its reference to a banquet connects well to the meal at Emmaus. If the preacher wanted to empha-size encountering God's presence here and now, Psalm 116 would work as well.

Connecting the Bible and the Liturgy

The OCF. The liturgical imagery of the Emmaus story suggests the communion of saints, an image found in a number of prayers in OCF 398: ##1, 2, 3, 7, and 13. Prayer #9 echoes the sentiments of Preface I for the Dead: "To you, O God, the dead do not die, / and in death our life is changed, not ended." The Invitation to Prayer at the vigil (OCF 71 or 87) speaks of the continued relationship between the bereaved and the deceased: "[W]e believe that all the ties of friendship and affection which knit us as one throughout our lives do not unravel with death." If baptis-mal imagery is being used (NT #4), then the homilist could allude to the

---

40. Fuller, "Lectionary for Funerals," 38–39.

sprinkling rite and associated symbols used at the start of the funeral liturgy (OCF 83–84, 160–161, 185–186). The Universal Prayer refers to the deceased as one of the baptized and as having been fed at the eucharistic table (OCF 401, #1, #3). If this gospel is used at the vigil, OCF 399, #4 refers to the abiding relationship between the bereaved and the deceased: "But for those who believe in your love / death is not the end, / nor does it destroy the bonds / that you forge in our lives." It is interesting to note that the prayer refers to God as the source of these relationships, another way that God's abiding care and presence is manifest.

The Missal. There are a number of collects in the Roman Missal that refer to the communion of saints (see II.B; III.A.1, 2, 3; and III.B.2, 9). If Romans 6:3-9 (NT #4) is used, a connection could be made to the prayers found under section I.D. In the prayer over the offerings, the petition is made that just as the deceased was once "cleansed in the waters of baptism" so now might their sins be washed away "in the Blood of Christ"—an evocative way to connect baptism and Eucharist. The prayer after Communion speaks of the deceased being "cleansed by the paschal mysteries"—which we celebrate sacramentally. Specific connection could also be made to the words of Preface I for the Dead, as noted above. The inserts for Eucharistic Prayers II and III (Missal 105, 115) mention the deceased being united with Christ "in a death like his"—a reference to Romans 6:5 and baptism.

Strategy for Preaching

Scriptural Texts: Job 19:1, 23-27; Psalm 42/43; Romans 6:3-9; Luke 24:13-35

Liturgical Texts: Prayers I.D.; Preface I for the Dead; OCF 71, 160–61

As mentioned above, the Emmaus account lends itself to preaching in the context of the funeral Mass. The *focus* of such a homily could be Christ's abiding presence to the church, especially in the sacraments. The *function* of the homily could be to help mourners not only recognize that abiding presence but also see that, because of that presence, death does not have the final word regarding their loved one.

I imagine that this homily could be structured using Paul Scott Wilson's Four Pages. In the first page, "Trouble in the Bible," the preacher would name the sense of loss and bewilderment experienced by the two disciples in the aftermath of Jesus' death. Even given the testimony of the women and the finding of the empty tomb (Luke 24:22-24), they are "slow of heart to believe" (v. 25). Is their grief that overwhelming? All the two on the road can do is find solace in one another's company—as the bereaved themselves are doing.

In the second page, "Trouble in the World," the homilist could place the assembly on that same road. Just like the disciples, they are reeling from loss. What was once known and stable has now been thrown into chaos and confusion. For some, even faith might be questioned. It is into this situation that Jesus speaks.

In the third page, "God's Action in the Bible," Christ's presence "on the way" and "in the breaking of the bread" is proclaimed. Far from being the end, death is Christ's way to glory. The cross makes resurrection life, and Christ's abiding presence, possible. The disciples are overcome, their hearts burning, so they have to share this good news with the others; it is this same good news that is proclaimed to those gathered for this funeral.

In the final page, the grace, or God's activity, mentioned in page three will need to be named as present in the life of the deceased as well as in the lives of the bereaved. To begin with, the deceased was "cleansed in the waters of baptism" (prayer over the offerings I.D). The preacher could refer to the introductory rites and the strong baptismal imagery that is part of the funeral liturgy (OCF 160–61). In baptism, the deceased was also buried with Christ; the death of baptism meant a sharing in Christ's life here and now (Rom 6:4). Such a sharing, like the Eucharist, is a foretaste of life in Christ after death, and in the fullness of time, when Christ's presence will no longer need to be hidden or mediated. As with Christ, it is the path of suffering and death that leads to true glory. As one of the baptized, the deceased became part of Christ's Body—a body manifest in the liturgical assembly, and in the Eucharist. The homilist could then give thanks to God for the ways the deceased was sent from the liturgy to be Christ's presence to others, to proclaim the Good News in word and deed.

While it is true that the bereaved no longer experience the presence of their loved one as they did before, this does not mean that he or she is completely absent. The liturgical texts proclaim that in death, life is changed, not ended (preface) and that the "ties of friendship and affection which knit us as one throughout our lives do not unravel with death"

(OCF 71). More than that, we are part of the same body in baptism, a unity deepened in the Eucharist. The same eyes of faith that allow us to encounter Christ in word and sacrament allow us to hold to that "sure and certain hope" (OCF 175A) that for our beloved, their sins washed away in the Blood of Christ, death is not the end. While the bereaved still live in the "not yet" of life here, with its incompleteness, its pain and sorrows, they can be helped to hope that just as we experience Christ's presence in hidden ways now, we will experience the fullness of that presence in glory.

11. John 5:24-29

Readings from the Ambo

The gospel. The discourse found in John 5:19-30, a portion of which makes up this selection from the funeral Lectionary, along with the two healing stories that precede it (the healing of the official's child, John 4:43-54, and the healing at Bethesda, John 5:1-18), center on the theme of the power of Jesus' word.[41] He speaks, and the son is healed and the crippled man walks. In this reading, the one who "hears" Jesus' word will "live"—will enjoy resurrection life—not just be healed of an illness or affliction. The discourse itself, especially in its entirety, emphasizes the role of Jesus as life giver and judge, who has received life and the power to judge from the Father. Giving life and judging: this is the work that God continues to do, even on the Sabbath. Thus, this section also forms part of the overall argument of chapter 5 in John's gospel: that Jesus was justified in healing on the Sabbath (John 5:17) because of his true, divine identity.

Application to funerals. The Johannine texts place great importance on hearing the voice of the Son of God, and the power of that voice to bring life. At the end of time, this voice will call forth those who have been asleep in death to judgment. The promise of eternal life and of the coming hour—eschatological concerns—would place this reading among those better suited for the funeral liturgy. The readings from the Fourth Gospel speak eloquently of new life in the reign of God. The funeral homily should touch on how that new life was experienced or evidenced by the deceased, on how the reign is present in the mourners' lives, and

41. Bergant and Karris, *Collegeville Bible Commentary*, 988–89.

on the final consummation awaiting us all. The eschatological hour is both "coming" (future) and "now here" (realized) (v. 25). The Son's voice is effective now, as it will be at the end. While there is a definitive judgment (vv. 28-29), the journey from death to life is not a single event. It does not begin when one dies; it takes place moment by moment, deed by deed, as we heed (or not) Christ's voice. The final judgment at the end of the journey reflects what has come before. The assembly gathered for the funeral, as well as the deceased, are all on that same journey; just at different places.

Other readings. Readings that speak to the final judgment have been mentioned in essay 4, including 2 Maccabees 12:43-46 (OT #7); Daniel 12:1-3 (OT #6); Wisdom 4:7-15 (OT #3); Acts 10:34-43 (NT #1); Romans 14:7-9, 10c-12 (NT #7); 2 Corinthians 5:1, 6-10 (NT #11); 1 John 3:14-16 (NT #16); and Revelation 20:11–21:1 (NT #18). Of these, the emphasis on belief found in this gospel passage is also mentioned in 2 Corinthians (NT #11); the language of "passing" from death to life is also found in 1 John (NT #16). The reading from Daniel refers to the dead as "those who sleep in the dust of the earth"—which reflects the gospel's image of the dead. In addition, the preacher might consider using Philippians 3:20-21 (NT #12) or Romans 6:3-9 (NT #4). These readings emphasize newness of life that comes with faith.

The gospel passage speaks of the dead hearing God's voice and then coming out of their tombs to face judgment. First Thessalonians 4:13-18 (NT #13) refers to "the word of command" summoning those who have "fallen asleep" in death. Psalm 25 might be taken as a cry to God to remember compassion in the face of such judgment. The psalmist in Psalm 122 rejoices in being called to the Lord's house, Jerusalem. The second antiphon for Psalm 130 expresses trust in God's word. Judgment is explicitly mentioned in Psalm 143.

Connecting the Bible and the Liturgy

The OCF. Any of the general prayers found in OCF 398 would reflect the themes of this and the following gospel passages from John. With this reading, those prayers referring to judgment are especially appropriate: #3, #9, and #12 (see essay 4 above). If the reading from Romans 6 is used (NT #4), then prayers that make reference to baptism (such as # 9 and #10, which speak of being "cleansed" from sin) could be considered. Prayer #7 refers to baptism this way: "[B]y the sacrament of the resurrection / you have sealed us as your own." In addition, the preacher may wish to make reference to the reception of the body (OCF 83–84, 160–161, 185–186), including the sprinkling of the coffin (and the words accompanying that action), the placement of the pall, and the presence of the paschal candle. As mentioned in essay 4, if the Maccabean text is used, connections may be made to other liturgical texts from the vigil that emphasize the ongoing relationship between the living and the dead (OCF 71, 87; 399, #4).

The Missal. The metaphor of "journey" (= passing) as a way to speak about death features in the prayers for Mass I.A (second collect, prayer after Communion), which also refer to Christ as a "merciful Judge" (prayer over the offerings). The book of life (see OT #6, NT #18), an image that alludes to both judgment and baptism, is mentioned in collect I.B (second option).

If the reading from Romans 6 is used, in addition to the inserts for Eucharistic Prayers II and III (Missal 105, 115), there are a number of prayers in the Missal that also use baptismal imagery. Under funeral Mass I.B, as mentioned above, the collect (second option) talks about the name of the deceased being "inscribed in the book of life" and the prayers over the offerings and after Communion use the image of sin being wiped away or cleansed (the latter also speaks of death as a journey). Baptism is explicitly mentioned in the prayer over the offerings I.D; the accompanying prayer after Communion states that the deceased has been "cleansed by the paschal mysteries." Other prayers invoking baptismal imagery include: the prayer over the offerings and prayer after Communion II.A, collect II.B ("dew of your mercy"—which could be used with Eucharistic Prayer II), prayer over the offerings, and prayer after Communion II.C, collect III.A.4 (adoption), prayer after Communion III.B.1, and collect III.B.7 ("font of rebirth").

Prayers that refer to the company of saints, especially appropriate if the reading from 2 Maccabees is used, include collect III.A.1 (option two) and collect III.B.9. The notion of death as "sleep in Christ" is found in the prayer over the offerings III.B.2 and collect III.B.3; the reading from Daniel speaks of death this way (OT #6) and the gospel suggests the same view of death (vv. 28-29). Eucharistic Prayer I uses similar language: "Grant them, O Lord, we pray, / and all who sleep in Christ, / a place of refreshment, light and peace" (Missal 95). Preface V for the Dead, with its focus on God's compassion and grace, on Christ's victory, and on the promise of resurrection, puts judgment in proper perspective. Preface III notes that Christ is the resurrection and the life. Preface IV notes that when God gives the sign, the redeemed will be raised to glory; this parallels the call of the Son of God in the gospel reading (John 5:25) and in 1 Thessalonians 4:16 (NT #13).

Strategy for Preaching

Scriptural Texts: Daniel 12:1-3; Psalm 122; 2 Corinthians 5:1, 6-10; John 5:24-29

Liturgical Texts: Collect III.B.3; Prayer over the Offerings I.A; Prayer after Communion I.A; Preface IV; OCF 160–61

The setting for this homily is the funeral liturgy (within Mass). The *focus* of the homily is the power of God's word; the *function* is to foster and strengthen the faith of the mourners in that word.

The preacher can use the image of the "voice of the Son of God" (John 5:25) as an anchoring point throughout the homily. To begin with, at baptism, the deceased was called to journey (prayer after Communion) with, to walk by faith in (NT #11), Christ. The preacher could make use of the baptismal imagery found in the funeral rites to emphasize this point (OCF 83–84, 160–161, 185–186). The preacher can mention how the deceased was fed on that journey at the Eucharist (prayer after Communion) and how he or she sought to "aspire to please" Christ (NT #11) by heeding his voice.

Hearing, the deceased believed, and so is heir to the promise of eternal life (John 5:24). Therefore, what seems like the end is really not. The deceased is asleep in Christ (collect; Dan 12:2). Our faith holds that the same voice that called the deceased into relationship in this life will call once again at the very end (John 5:28-29; preface). Awakened, the dead will stand before a merciful judge (Dan 12:2; 2 Cor 5:10; John 5:28-29, prayer over the offerings). Those who have lived according to Christ's reign here and now (the preacher might offer examples from the life of the deceased) will enjoy the fullness of that reign forever. They will rejoice, hearing the voice of Christ say: "Let us go to the house of the Lord" (Ps 122:1)!

Those, like the mourners, who remain "away from the Lord" (2 Cor 5:6) are heirs of that same promise. They, too, are on that journey from the reign partially realized to its final consummation, just at a different place. They have experienced the power of God's word in the life of the deceased, and in their own lives. Therefore, they can trust in that word. They, too, can rejoice on the way to Jerusalem (psalm). An eternal dwelling awaits (2 Cor 5:1).

12. John 6:37-40

Readings from the Ambo

The gospel. This reading and the next are part of the Bread of Life discourse (John 6:25-59). However, this section, removed from the larger context, makes no mention of the Bread of Life. Rather, the focus becomes much narrower: Jesus will not lose anyone the Father has given him, those who see and believe in the Son, but will raise them to eternal life (vv. 39-40). As in John 5:24-29 (essay 11), the eschatology presented here is both realized (the believer is in the Son's possession) and future (the believer will be raised). Keeping the wider context in mind, it is because Jesus is identified as the Bread of Life, sent by the Father, that he is able to save (vv. 32-35). However, this is not made explicit here.

A key verb in this passage is "to see" (v. 40). As Raymond Brown pointed out, the word used here, *theōrōn*, means to behold, to gaze upon with concentration, to study carefully, even to linger; in other words, to perceive the truth about Jesus.[42] It is spiritual sight that is needed. The one who truly "sees" Jesus has also seen the Father (John 14:9).

Application to funerals. Those who have seen and believed in the Son, in Jesus, will be raised to eternal life. They will not be lost. This promise is a source of hope and consolation for those who mourn the death of a loved one. It is this good news that the funeral preacher is called to proclaim. The preacher can draw out the ways that the deceased "saw" and came to know Jesus: family and friends, the Scriptures and prayer,

---

42. Sánchez, *The Passages We Celebrate*, 209; Francis J. Moloney, *The Gospel of John*, vol. 4, Sacra Pagina series, ed. Daniel J. Harrington (Collegeville, MN: Liturgical Press, 1998), 216.

acts of service, and—keeping the wider context of John 6 in mind—in the Eucharist. The ways that the deceased helped others "see" Jesus can be named with gratitude. The preacher can encourage the mourners: if one has the eyes to see, one realizes that they are not abandoned in their grief, and that they share in the same hope and promise as their loved one. As with the reading from John 5, the promise of future life makes this an appropriate reading for the funeral liturgy.

Other readings. As noted above, "seeing" is a key verb in the gospel passage. Job says he will "see" his vindicator and God (OT #1). Seeing alone is not enough; one must also believe. Paul points out in his second letter to the Corinthians (NT #11) that we are to walk by faith, by true sight, and not by limited, earthly sight (5:7). Those who see and believe will be raised on "the last day"—a reference to the Parousia. We read similar notions in Daniel 12:1-3 (OT #6), 1 Corinthians 15:51-57 (NT #9), and 2 Corinthians 4:14-5:1 (NT #10). In Revelation 21:1-5a, 6b-7 (NT #19), John "sees" a new heaven and earth; the voice from the throne commands, "Behold!" Psalm 63 reads in part: "Thus have I *gazed* toward you in the sanctuary to see your power and your glory" (v. 3).

Connecting the Bible and the Liturgy

The OCF. A number of prayers in the OCF refer to "light" (398, #1, #2, #3; 399, #2), a visual metaphor for eternal life. The dialogue that forms part of the concluding rite at the vigil prays that "perpetual light" would shine on the deceased (OCF 81, 97). The eschatological day of resurrection is mentioned in prayers 398, #3, #9, and #13.

The Missal. In addition to the numerous prayers that make reference to "light" as a metaphor for eternal life (see Masses I.C, II.E, III.A.1, III.A.3, III.A.5, III.B.6), two prayers make specific mention of gazing at (collect III.B.1) or beholding (collect II.D) God forever. Another (collect III.A.4) notes that the human person is created in God's *image.* In Mass I.B, the second collect makes reference to the "book of life" (see OT #6). The first collect there speaks about the eschatological "day of resurrection," as does collect I.D. In preface I, the hope of resurrection is said to have "dawned"—another reference to light.

Strategy for Preaching

Scriptural Texts: Job 19:1, 23-27a; Psalm 63; 1 Corinthians 15:51-57; John 6:37-40

Liturgical Texts: Collect III.B.1; Prayer after Communion I.C; Preface I

The gospel proclaims that those who have seen and believed in the Son are promised eternal life. This emphasis on future hope suggests the funeral liturgy as the setting for this homily, the *focus* of which is Christ's victory over death. The *function* of the homily is to help the mourners see how the deceased, and they, share in that victory—if they also see and believe.

The preacher can begin by naming the loss: the mourners no longer "see" their beloved friend or family member who has died. They feel the "sting" of death (1 Cor 15:55-56). It seems as if he or she is "lost." In fact, that is not an uncommon way to speak of death: the loss of a loved one. Yet, Jesus promises that he will "not lose" anyone given to him by the Father (John 6:39).

It is here that the preacher can unpack what it means to truly see, or gaze, upon Christ (Ps 63:3; John 6:40; collect). The language connotes more than mere superficial glancing. To gaze is to spend time, to be drawn deep into relationship. It is a bridge between persons. The preacher can mention the look between parent and newborn, between spouses as vows are spoken, between the closest of friends. In other words, the preacher can name the ways in which the deceased saw Christ in family and friends, especially those gathered for the funeral, and how those experiences of love helped him or her know God's love, and believe. That first opening of the eyes of faith might have led the deceased to see Christ in other places. For example, the preacher might be able to show how the deceased spent time "gazing" at Christ in the pages of Scripture or in the intimacy of prayer. Or perhaps the deceased was touched by seeing Christ in the faces of the suffering, and so was moved to live a life of service. Given the context of John 6, the preacher might name how the deceased came to "gaze" on Christ in the sanctuary (Ps 63:3), in the eucharistic liturgy, and perhaps in the practice of adoration. In other words, the deceased is shown as one who saw and believed, and so is an heir to the promise, that victory (1 Cor 15:57).

Those in the assembly, too, are invited to share in Christ's promise (preface) and victory: John proclaims that Christ will not lose anyone the Father has given him (John 6:39), while Paul tells the Corinthians that *all* will be changed and clothed with immortality (1 Cor 15:53). How have they seen God's love? In particular, the preacher can name those ways that the deceased helped others "see" Jesus.

Beholding the beatific vision is a common metaphor for eternal life; the collect even asks that the deceased would "gaze eternally on [God]," and Job is confident that one day he will "see God" (Job 1:26). In the meantime, he longs for that day—like the author of Psalm 63. The deceased longed for that day; now the church prays in the "sure and certain hope" (OCF 175A) that that longing is fulfilled, that he or she "may pass over to a dwelling place of light and peace" (prayer after Communion; cf. preface). The mourners might still have the words of Job and the psalmist on their lips, not only with Christ but also with their deceased in mind. The church prays, and proclaims the consoling hope (preface), that those longings would also be fulfilled.

13. John 6:51-58(59)[43]

Readings from the Ambo

The gospel. This gospel selection comes at the end of John's Bread of Life discourse. Here, Jesus identifies himself as the Bread of Life, the true manna from heaven, and promises that those who feed on him will have eternal life. The text functions on two levels, primarily the sapiential and then secondarily the eucharistic. First, recalling that the Johannine community is separating from the synagogue, the text argues that Jesus has replaced the manna of the Law; only he is the true "bread that came down from heaven" (v. 51). "The idea that the Law was consumed and absorbed like food is not foreign to Jewish thought."[44] Those who once fed on the Torah and were nourished by it must now, John argues, eat and

---

43. The final verse number is given as v. 59 in the Lectionary for Mass and v. 58 in the OCF, but the text is the same.

44. Moloney, *The Gospel of John*, Sacra Pagina, 224.

drink the flesh and blood of the Son of Man. The one who totally ingests this new revelation is the one who will live. As Francis Moloney notes:

> The idea of the reception of the revelation of God in and through the Son is not new (cf., for example, 3:11-21, 31-36), but the imagery has been changed by the Passover context. No longer does Jesus speak of "belief in" (cf. 3:12, 15, 18, 36), but of "the one who eats me" (v. 57b: *ho trōgōn me*). The expressions are parallel.[45]

In other words, Jesus is the "bread of wisdom and revelation who nourishes all who come to him in faith."[46] But he is also the one who will give his life, his flesh (body), for the life of the world (v. 51) at Golgotha. The connections to both Passover and crucifixion point to the Last Supper, to the Eucharist. Jesus is adamant that his flesh and blood are true food and drink. The verb translated as "eat" shifts from *phagē* (vv. 51-53; in v. 58 in reference to manna) to *trōgōn* (vv. 4, 54, 56, and 58 in reference to Jesus' flesh). While some argue that the verbs are interchangeable, most point out that the latter refers to a very real and physical experience of crunching, chewing, or chomping on one's food.[47] As Moloney also writes:

> The Eucharist renders concrete, in the eucharistic practice of the Christian reader, what the author has spelled out throughout the discourse. The Eucharist is a place where one comes to eternal life. Encountering the broken flesh and the spilled blood of Jesus, "lifted up" on a cross (vv. 53–54), the believer is called to make a decision for or against the revelation of God in that encounter (vv. 56–58), gaining or losing life because of it (vv. 53–54).[48]

As with the other Johannine readings, there is evidence here of both a realized and a future eschatology: verbs are both in the present and future tenses. One "has life" by feeding on the Son of Man—who remains in the believer—now; and, by doing so, one is promised that he or she will be raised and have life forever.

---

45. Ibid., 222.
46. Bergant and Karris, *Collegeville Bible Commentary*, 992.
47. Moloney, *The Gospel of John*, Sacra Pagina, 221.
48. Ibid., 224.

Application to funerals. Jesus promises that on the last day he will raise up those who feed on him (v. 54). Keeping the above in mind, to "feed" on Jesus should be understood broadly: to believe in him and internalize his teachings as well as to share at the eucharistic table. A preacher could point out the ways that the deceased "fed" on Jesus in his or her life, noting the hope that is possible because of Jesus' declarations in this reading. The preacher may also remind the hearers that they, too, share in a foretaste of eternal life in the Eucharist being celebrated. Christ remains with us now; because he abides, we are promised eternal life. The emphasis on Jesus' promise of resurrected life recommends this reading for the funeral liturgy, especially if celebrated in the context of Eucharist.

Other readings. As noted above, the "Bread of Life" has both sapiential and eucharistic meanings. If the preacher wants to treat the question of wisdom in general, then Wisdom 3:1-9 (OT #2) draws the distinction between the true fate of the dead and what the "foolish" believe. Daniel 12:1-3 (OT #6) notes that "the wise shall shine brightly" in the resurrection. If we take "to eat" as a synonym for "to believe," then the emphasis placed on faith in 2 Corinthians 5:1, 6-10 (NT #11) and 1 Thessalonians 4:13-18 (NT #13) recommends these readings. If the preacher wishes to focus on the eucharistic aspect of the gospel passage, then Acts 10:34-43 (NT #1), with its reference to eating and drinking with Christ after the resurrection, would be appropriate. Romans 5:5-11 (NT #2) mentions being justified by Christ's Blood (v. 9). Psalm 23 refers to the table spread before the psalmist (v. 5). Psalm 63 uses the metaphor of a banquet (v. 5) to refer to the richness of God's presence.

As mentioned in the discussion of the Emmaus account (essay 10), the baptismal imagery found in Romans 6:3-9 (NT #4) combined with the eucharistic imagery here could lead to a homily using these sacraments as a unifying thread. Liturgical texts from the OCF and Missal that include baptismal imagery have been explored in essays 10 and 11 above, and will not be repeated here.

Connecting the Bible and the Liturgy

The OCF. Prayer 398, #1 refers to God's wisdom, and prayer #11 refers to God's word. While none of the prayers found in 398 or 399 refer to the Eucharist, some of the intercessions found as part of the Universal

Prayer refer to the deceased as being baptized and as having been fed at the eucharistic table (OCF 401, #1, #3).

The Missal. A few of the prayers found in the Missal make explicit use of eucharistic imagery. Prayer after Communion I.A refers to the Eucharist as "food for the journey"—especially appropriate if the deceased was able to receive Viaticum. Prayer over the offerings II.C refers to sins being washed away "in the Blood of Christ"—which connects to baptismal imagery as well. The covenantal aspect of Eucharist (and baptism) is found in prayer after Communion III.A.1. Finally, prayer over the offerings III.A.5 explicitly mentions "the Bread of life" as well as "the Chalice of salvation."

The preacher may also want to refer to texts from the eucharistic liturgy itself. In particular, the preacher could mention the "second epiclesis" in Eucharistic Prayers II ("Humbly we pray / that, partaking of the Body and Blood of Christ, / we may be gathered into one by the Holy Spirit") and III ("grant that we, who are nourished / by the Body and Blood of your Son / and filled with his Holy Spirit, / may become one body, one spirit in Christ"), noting that by the action of the Holy Spirit and our sharing in the Eucharist, "the bonds" forged in this life perdure (OCF 71, 87; 399, #4). Or, the preacher could draw out the connection between Eucharist and the proclamation of the paschal mystery ("When we eat this Bread and drink this Cup, / we proclaim your Death, O Lord, / until you come again"), explaining that the Eucharist is also an expression of hope, the hope that the mourners have for the deceased and for themselves. Finally, the preacher could turn to the invitation to communion (Missal 132), noting that those who are called to the supper of the Lamb—in the Eucharist here and at the eschatological banquet—are indeed blessed. The people's response notes that it is only by God's word (see OCF 398, #11) that the healing needed to share in that banquet is possible.

Strategy for Preaching

Scriptural Texts: Wisdom 3:1-9; Ps 23; Acts 10:34-43; John 6:51-59

Liturgical Texts: Collect 398 #11; Prayer over the Offerings II.C; Prayer after Communion III.A.1; Missal—Liturgy of the Eucharist; OCF 71

The homiletic strategy presented here presumes the funeral liturgy within Mass as the setting and uses Paul Scott Wilson's Four Pages as its structure (see essays 5 and 10). The Eucharist serves as the "one doctrine"[49] that helps provide unity to the homily. Adapting Wilson's approach, we begin with "Trouble in the World." The mourners are in a "dark valley" (Ps 23:4); the death of their loved one is an "affliction" that can feel like complete "destruction" (Wis 3:3). The analogous "Trouble in the Bible" is that, as Jesus puts it, the ancestors of those present ate the manna and still died. "God's Action in the Bible" is the sending of Jesus as the Bread of Life, the answer to the mystery of death. As noted above, to eat his flesh and drink his blood has clear eucharistic meanings. But, more broadly, to eat and drink is to heed his teaching, his word (398, #11).

God acts "in the World" through the sacraments. Through baptism, the deceased has been given "a part in [God's] covenant" (prayer after Communion), and been cleansed (prayer over the offerings) or forgiven (Acts 10:43) of his or her sins. But that was just the beginning. The preacher can hold up for the assembly the ways that the deceased "ate and drank" with Jesus (Acts 10:41): at the eucharistic table (Ps 23:5), certainly, but also in the company of loved ones, and in prayer and delving into God's word (398, #11). Having fed on the Son of Man, the deceased remains in Christ and Christ in him or her, and so is promised eternal life (6:51, 53-54, 57-58). As Reginald Fuller notes: "Reception of Holy Communion nourishes the new life begun in baptism, a life of 'abiding in Christ,' a life that cannot be extinguished by physical death, and which will continue to eternity."[50] Those called to the supper of the Lamb—in the Eucharist here and at the eschatological banquet—are indeed blessed (Missal 132). The table spread here (Ps 23:5) foreshadows the heavenly banquet, expressing and sustaining hope (Wis 3:4) in Christ's return ("When we eat this Bread and drink this Cup, / we proclaim your Death, O Lord, / until you come again.") as well as making visible and deepening the unity of the church, living and dead, by the power of the Holy Spirit (see the "second epiclesis" of Eucharistic Prayers II and III, as well as OCF 71, 87). "[T]he eucharist's deepest meaning is a communion of life between the living Lord and the believer . . . this life bond cannot be broken, even by death."[51] That is, indeed, good news.

---

49. Paul Scott Wilson, *The Four Pages of the Sermon: A Guide to Biblical Preaching* (Nashville, TN: Abingdon Press, 1999), 44–47.

50. Fuller, "Lectionary for Funerals," 59.

51. Senior, *Loving and Dying*, 84.

14. John 11:17-27 (or 11:21-27)

Readings from the Ambo

The gospel. The dialogue between Martha and Jesus forms the core of this story. The beginning verses (17-20) help to set the stage for the conversation; these verses are omitted from the short form of the reading. In the past, it might have been safely assumed that members of the assembly would be familiar enough with the story that they could supply those details; that is no longer the case. Therefore, the long form should typically be used.

At the start of the account, it is mentioned that Lazarus has been dead for four days; in other words, he is truly dead. The mourners have gathered and are ministering to the sisters. It is Martha who takes the initiative and goes out to Jesus, while Mary remains behind. Are her first words to Jesus plaintive or accusatory? The text does not give us any clues. She goes on to express one Jewish view of eschatology current in the first century: the dead will rise "on the last day" (v. 24).

Reflecting the Johannine tension between realized and future eschatology, Jesus proclaims that he is both the (future) resurrection as well as source of spiritual life here and now (cf. 3:6; 5:24-25). This life, given to those who believe in Jesus, transcends death (cf. 5:28-29; 6:40, 54). It is debated whether Martha makes a truly novel profession of faith in response, a model of Johannine belief, or if she simply conceives of Jesus as a miracle worker in the context of contemporary messianic hopes.[52]

Application to funerals. The questioning of Jesus in the face of the death of Lazarus echoes the question mourners often ask God from the depth of their loss: Where were you? Therefore, this reading would be used for the vigil. Those words can be spoken with a range of emotions that the preacher would do well to acknowledge. If Martha is seen to reflect imperfect faith,[53] then the preacher can help those in the assembly to see themselves and their struggles in her. Jesus does not abandon or chastise, but continues to abide with Martha. So, too, with the mourners.

Other readings. Mourners come with many questions, as do the authors of the biblical books. For example, the author of Wisdom wonders

---

52. Moloney, *The Gospel of John*, Sacra Pagina, 327–29.
53. Ibid., 330, 338.

about the meaning of death (OT #2), especially of a young person (OT #3). Is death the end? Is living a long life a reward for virtue? Paul wonders if there is anything that can separate us from the love of God (NT #6), whether suffering here and now (see NT #5 and #10) or even death itself. Readings that refer to the resurrection on the "last day" include Daniel 12:1-3 (OT #6); 1 Corinthians 15:20-28 (NT #8); 1 Corinthians 15:51-57 (NT #9); 1 Thessalonians 4:13-18 (NT #13); and Revelation 20:11–21:1 (NT #18).

The lament psalms are appropriate for the vigil, especially if the death raises doubts and questions. In Psalm 25, the psalmist asks that his or her troubled heart be relieved (v. 17). In Psalm 27, the psalmist pleads to be heard and answered, like Martha (v. 7). The notion of pleading to be heard is also found in Psalms 130 (vv. 1-2) and 143 (v. 1).

Connecting the Bible and the Liturgy

The OCF. While many of the prayers in OCF 398 focus on the "soul" and life in heaven, a few speak more specifically to the promise of resurrection. Prayer #5 asks that the deceased "share in the joy of [Christ's] resurrection" and prayer #6 speaks of the deceased's belief "in the resurrection of the dead." Prayer #8 asks that the mourners' belief in Christ's resurrection and their hope in the resurrection of their loved one be strengthened. Prayer #13 asks that the deceased be raised "on the last day to rejoice in [God's] presence for ever." Among the prayers for the mourners (OCF 399), prayers #2 and #3 emphasize passing from death to life. That God's "wisdom is beyond our understanding" is mentioned in #7.

Wisdom 4:7-15 (OT #3) speaks of the deceased being "snatched" away; OCF 398 #1–3 refers to the deceased being "called/summoned out of this world." Similar imagery is found in 1 Corinthians 15:51-57 (NT #9) and 1 Thessalonians 4:13-18 (NT #13). Of course, the preacher will need to be careful not to blame God for actively causing the death of this person.

The OCF provides collects (398) for various situations, including those that might raise more acute questions for the mourners. Prayers #39–41 address the situation of death after a long illness while sudden, accidental, or violent deaths, including deaths by suicide, are attended to in prayers #42–#45. Prayers #27–#28 are for use in the case of the death of a young person.

The Missal. The day of resurrection is mentioned in collect I.B (first option), collect I.D, and the collects and prayers after Communion given under Masses II.A and II.C. Collects that address specific situations are found in section IV, and include prayers for a young person (#7), for one who suffered a long illness (#8), and for one who died suddenly (#9). If 1 Corinthians 15:51-57 (NT #9) or 1 Thessalonians 4:13-18 (NT #13) is used, consideration should be given to preface IV, which prays: "And when you give the sign, / we who have been redeemed by the Death of your Son, / shall be raised up to the glory of his Resurrection." Preface III states that Jesus is "the *life* of the human race, / the *resurrection* of the dead" (emphasis added).

Strategy for Preaching

Scriptural Texts: Romans 8:31b-35, 37-39; Psalm 143; John 11:17-27
Liturgical Texts: Opening Prayer 399, #2; Concluding Prayer 398, #2

Acknowledging that death raises core questions would be an important aspect of preaching at the vigil utilizing this gospel passage. Therefore, Lowry's Loop (see essays 2 and 6) would be an appropriate way to structure the homily. Rather than give facile answers, the readings show that people of faith have always wrestled with making meaning out of death. While the Christian answer is found in the paschal mystery, the homilist should help the mourners "discover" this answer rather than impose it (*function*). Whether their faith is strong, or they are struggling, Jesus abides with the mourners (*focus*).

The homily begins with the "bind"—in this case, acknowledging the loss. The questions raised by the death are named in the second section of the homily. Where was God during the illness or at the death? Why did God seemingly not act? Why did the deceased suffer? Does this mean that the deceased, or the mourners, are not loved by God (Rom 8:35; 398, #2)? The preacher can help the mourners see themselves in Martha, hands outstretched in pleading (Ps 143:1; John 11:21-22). Questioning does not mean a complete lack of faith, but presumes faith enough to approach Jesus; God's faithfulness is still remembered (Ps 143:1). The "clue" to the resolution, or "aha" moment, consists in the preacher emphasizing Jesus' claim that he is the resurrection and the life (John 11:25). In other words, the "answer" to the questions posed by Martha, and by the mourners gathered for this vigil, is not an idea but a person.

The preacher then unpacks the Good News. John proclaims that, indeed, Lazarus will be raised "on the last day" (John 11:24). The preacher can begin by preaching the eschatological hope that the deceased would be welcomed into God's merciful arms in a place of light and peace (398, #2; 399, #2). Nothing can separate us from God's love (Rom 8:35). But John's eschatology is also realized; that love is experienced in this life not only "on the last day." Therefore, the preacher must also name the ways that the deceased and the mourners experienced that "life" here and now. What were the ways that Christ's presence was manifested in the life of the deceased? What were the ways that Christ's presence was manifested in the care given to the deceased by family and friends? How is Christ's presence being experienced by the mourners in the way they are caring for each other in these circumstances? Lowry's Loop ends by anticipating the consequences of the Good News that has been proclaimed. Hopefully, the good news that nothing, not even death, can separate us from God's love (Rom 8:38) and mercy will be a comfort (399, #2) to the mourners. And, hopefully, even in their grief, they will be strengthened to continue being mediators of that love to one another.

15. John 11:32-45

Readings from the Ambo

The gospel. This reading continues the story started in the previous selection. Now, in response to Jesus' summons (11:28), Mary joins her sister. She repeats Martha's cry, and then weeps. Jesus becomes "perturbed and deeply troubled" (v. 33) and also weeps (v. 34). The Greek in verse 33 has been the subject of much debate. The phrase refers to strong emotion, including anger. Why such emotional distress? Perhaps there is sadness and disappointment at Mary, who rather than staying focused on Jesus joins "the Jews" in focusing on Lazarus's death.[54] Martha, too, evidences imperfect faith in questioning Jesus' order to remove the stone. Jesus' summons is again determinative: he calls, and Lazarus comes from the tomb. The

---

54. Ibid., 330.

aftermath of the raising of Lazarus provides an important insight. This action by Jesus is what sets in motion his eventual arrest, crucifixion, and glorification. The sign is not an end in itself, but serves to reveal Jesus' identity and mission, a mission for which he will give his life.[55]

Lazarus is called Jesus' friend, beloved by him (11:3, 36). Therefore, he serves as a "type" or image of the Christian disciple. Like Lazarus, we are called from death and all that binds us to new life. While not in quite the same dramatic fashion, we are called to experience such movement in daily life. Like Lazarus eventually did, we experience that movement definitively at the end of this earthly life.

Application to funerals. Mary's (and Martha's) imperfect faith is understandable in the midst of loss; that mourners also have their doubts—and their grief—is to be expected. Jesus' strong emotion in response is best explained in this context not as a critique of any individual, but because it seems that his unconditional gift of himself as source of life will not be understood or embraced.[56] It is often mentioned that Jesus wept because of grief over the death of his friend,[57] but such a reading is not strictly supported by the text itself. However, the image has been appropriated this way in both preaching and liturgy. For example, the Preface for the Fifth Sunday of Lent, referring to Jesus, reads:

> For *as true man he wept for Lazarus his friend*
> and as eternal God raised him from the tomb,
> just as, taking pity on the human race,
> he leads us by sacred mysteries to new life. (emphasis added)

The preacher will want to tread lightly; he or she will need to acknowledge the real limits of human faith while still using Jesus' strong emotion not to induce guilt but to point out the depths of Jesus' love for all in the assembly. We, too, are Jesus' "friends."

The raising of Lazarus shows both who Jesus is and provides a succinct image of the nature of his mission. Jesus reveals God's saving love—a love that sets the human person free from everything that binds him or her,

---

55. Bergant and Karris, *Collegeville Bible Commentary*, 1000; Senior, *Loving and Dying*, 85.

56. Moloney, *The Gospel of John*, Sacra Pagina, 331.

57. See, for example, Sánchez, *The Passages We Celebrate*, 216.

including sin and death. Reginald Fuller mentions that "untie him and let him go" (v. 44) uses the same language that is used for the forgiveness or remission of sin. "Baptismal release from sin and death is finalized in the resurrection of the dead at the End, and to that too the raising of Lazarus points."[58] The preacher can make fruitful connections to the baptismal imagery and theology used in the funeral liturgy. Liturgical texts from the OCF and Missal that include baptismal imagery have been explored in essays 10 and 11 above, and will not be repeated here.

While the prominent role played by mourners in this account might suggest its use at the vigil, the baptismal imagery and Jesus' defeat of death point to the funeral liturgy as a better locus. One might even consider reading John 11:17-27 (gospel #14) at the vigil and this text at the funeral liturgy, creating a flow from one homily to the next.

Other readings. If the preacher wants to emphasize the image of tears, he or she could use Isaiah 25:6a, 7-9 (OT #4) or Revelation 21:1-5a, 6b-7 (NT #19) to accompany this gospel passage. While none of the psalms in the funeral Lectionary refer specifically to tears, Psalm 42/43 speaks of dwelling on God's holy mountain, where longing gives way to joy (cf. OT #4).

Connecting the Bible and the Liturgy

The OCF. Prayers #10 and #13 in OCF 398 refer to being released or freed from death. The former asks that the soul of the deceased be granted "release from the chains of death" and the latter prays that the deceased be "delivered from the bonds of death." Prayer #11 speaks of consolation, while #4 speaks of weeping being no more. God is referred to as the "ruler of the living and the dead" in 399, #3, echoing Jesus' prayer to the Father. Prayer #5 includes a number of ideas that might be helpful. This prayer asks both for comfort as well as for a strengthening of (imperfect) faith, both elements found in the Lazarus story.

The Missal. Collect I.B (first option) is the Missal's version of OCF 398, #13, and notes that the deceased has been "freed from the bonds of mortality." The same phrase is repeated in prayer after Communion III.A.5. Being raised or rising from the dead is specifically mentioned in

---

58. Fuller, "Lectionary for Funerals," 60.

collect I.A (first option), prayer over the offerings III.A.1, collect III.A.2, and prayer over the offerings III.B.5. Preface I for the Dead mentions consolation and that death is not the end of life; preface III states that Jesus is "the *life* of the human race, / the *resurrection* of the dead" (alluding to the part of the Lazarus story discussed in essay 14).

The raising of Lazarus is the gospel used for the celebration of the third scrutiny as part of the Rite of Christian Initiation of Adults (RCIA). As mentioned above, the Preface for the Fifth Sunday of Lent draws on the image of Jesus weeping for Lazarus as well as his raising Lazarus from the dead to proclaim Christ's full humanity and divinity. The texts of the third scrutiny could provide the preacher with additional images or language to be woven into the homily. For example, we are told that the Father sent the Son "to snatch us from the realm of death, / and to lead us to the resurrection" and that Jesus "by raising Lazarus from the dead . . . showed that [he] came that we might have life / and have it more abundantly" (RCIA 175A). It would be especially appropriate to make reference to these texts if the deceased had at one time been a catechumen.

Strategy for Preaching

Scriptural Texts: Isaiah 25:6a, 7-9; Psalm 42/43; Revelation 21:1-5a, 6b-7; John 11:32-45

Liturgical Texts: Collect I.B (option 1); Prayer over the Offerings III.B.5; Preface III for the Dead

The funeral homily proposed here uses Paul Scott Wilson's Four Pages as its organizing structure. The *focus* of the homily is God's ultimate power over death; the *function* would be to, metaphorically, dry the tears of the mourners by helping them see the story of the deceased in the story of Lazarus.

The homily can begin with the incongruity of Jesus' strong reaction. Why does he weep? On the one hand, death has won a temporary (Isa 25:7; Rev 21:4) victory, so he weeps over the loss of his friend (preface for Fifth Sunday of Lent). On the other hand, he weeps for the mourners, for their incomplete faith. Like Jesus, the mourners gathered for this funeral are weeping over the loss of their beloved. And, like Mary (and Martha), they come with their imperfect faith, their questions and doubts. The preacher should not shy away from that reality.

The good news in the scriptural account is that Jesus acts on behalf of Lazarus; he speaks and the bonds of death (collect) are broken. Lazarus is freed, showing that Jesus is indeed the resurrection and the life (preface). Tears give way to belief (gospel). Jesus "by raising Lazarus from the dead . . . showed that [he] came that we might have life / and have it more abundantly" (RCIA 175A). God promises that those who thirst (Ps 42:2-3) will receive from life-giving waters (Rev 21:6). The deceased, as one of the baptized, is heir to that promise, a promise experienced in this life (as the preacher might describe) as well as after death. We pray that he or she, "[f]reed from bonds of mortality" (collect), unbound like Lazarus, would be raised again to life and have a place at Christ's right hand (prayer over the offerings) in the new Jerusalem (Rev 21:2). God's ultimate victory and power over death is not just for the one who has died but for the mourners as well. Reunited on that holy mountain, all tears will be wiped away, and all will rejoice and be glad (Isa 25:8; Ps 43:4; Rev 21:4). In the Eucharist celebrated, and in the life of faith shared, we enjoy a foretaste of that victory. The veil (Isa 25:7) is lifted and our thirst (Rev 21:6) is slaked, our tears dried, at least temporarily.

16. John 12:23-28 (or 12:23-26)

Readings from the Ambo

The gospel. We read in the verses before this pericope that some Gentiles ("Greeks," perhaps converts to Judaism) want to "see" Jesus. The hour has come; the nations are gathering (Isa 52:15; John 12:19, 32). While Jesus will be killed, his death is also his glorification, his being "lifted up" and exalted. Thus he can say that to give up his life, like a grain of wheat, is necessary if an abundant harvest is to follow. The servant must follow the Master, even through death. To let go of one's life in self-gift, like Jesus, is to gain it. The believer who follows in this manner will be with the Son of Man, and will be honored by his Father.

The long version of the reading adds verses 27-28: although troubled, Jesus asks the Father not to save him but to help him fulfill the mission for which he was sent. Jesus is always dependent on the Father and follows the Father's will; therefore, God has been glorified and, through the events that are unfolding, will be glorified.

Application to funerals. The dying grain promises new life; the "hour" promises glory. In their original context, these words would have comforted those facing exclusion or death because of their decision to follow Christ. In the context of the funeral rites, they also serve to uphold those who are afraid or doubting in the face of the death of a loved one. The promise of Jesus, that through his being lifted up those who believe and join him in self-sacrificial love will also have eternal life, applies to the deceased and those gathered for the funeral as much as they applied to the Johannine community. Buried with Christ we rise with him.

The homilist can draw out the implications of this passage for the whole of Christian life. The gospel claims that "life's beauty is found in giving, a giving that is a type of death".[59] While for some that may mean a literal sacrifice of one's life, for most it will mean a daily dying to sin and selfishness. Such daily dying prepares one for the final "letting go" in hope at the end. Jesus provides the model for the Christian facing death: prayerful trust in the Father. The homilist can mention not only how the deceased evidenced these attitudes but can also encourage the assembly to live in like manner. The future orientation of the reading, as well as its encouragement of trustful relinquishment, would lead me to use the reading for the funeral liturgy rather than for the vigil. The presence of "outsiders" (Gentiles) in the verses leading up to this passage also affords the preacher an opportunity to address the diversity often encountered at a funeral.

Other readings. The good news that Jesus gave his life so we, too, might have life is proclaimed by Paul in his letter to the Romans (NT #2, #3, #4, #7). Romans 6:3-9 (NT #4) also makes the point that we are joined to Christ "through a death like his" (v. 5). The notion that Jesus' crucifixion is his exaltation or glorification is a core aspect of John's theology of the passion, and this connection between suffering and "glory" is also made explicit in Romans 8:14-23 (NT #5) and 2 Corinthians 4:14–5:1 (NT #10). The latter reading notes that "momentary light affliction" will give way to "glory beyond all comparison" (v. 17). In his letter to the Philippians, Paul reminds us that by being conformed to Christ's death (3:10) we will also be conformed to Christ's "glorified Body" in the resurrection (3:21; NT #12). In his first letter, John makes the claim that to give one's life

59. Senior, *Loving and Dying*, 87.

in love for others is to gain it (1 John 3:14-16; NT #16). That the dead would be glorified is alluded to in Wisdom 3:1-9 (OT #2)—"they shall shine . . ."—and Daniel 12:1-3 (OT #6)—"the wise shall shine brightly in the splendor of the firmament." Second Maccabees 12:43-46 (OT #7) speaks of "the splendid reward that awaits those who had gone to rest in godliness." If the preacher makes reference to the Gentiles seeking Jesus, he or she may want to include Isaiah 25:6a, 7-9 (OT #4) and/or Acts 10:34-43 (NT #1) among the readings; they make the point that God is the God of all the nations and shows no partiality.

A number of the psalms might work well with this gospel passage. Psalm 23 claims that after sojourning through the "dark valley," one is greeted with an extravagant banquet; and even in that dark valley, one is never alone (vv. 4-5). Like the gospel, Psalm 63 specifically refers to God's "glory" (v. 3). Psalm 103 also uses agricultural imagery to speak of the transitory nature of life (vv. 15-16): "Men's days are like those of grass; like a flower of the field he blooms; the wind sweeps over him and he is gone. . . ."

Connecting the Bible and the Liturgy

The OCF. In 398, prayer #13 specifically mentions burial, which the preacher could connect to the image of the grain falling to the ground. The preacher may also want to look at the texts in the rite of committal, where, for example, the grave is referred to as a "sign of hope" (218A, 405, #1). Prayer 399, #2 states that Jesus willingly gave himself up to death so that all might be saved. If evening prayer from the Office for the Dead were to be used, then reference could be made to Christ's kenotic love as expressed in the canticle from Philippians 2:6-11 (388).

The Missal. If the preacher wanted to focus on the image of the grain, collect I.B (option one), which explicitly mentions burial, could be used. Collect I.C (option two) would also be appropriate, referring in poetic fashion to the grain germinating: "through the ending of present things / open up the beginning of things to come."

The gospel passage speaks of the Son of Man, and the Father's name, being glorified. Some prayers refer to the glory of the Father or Son: prayer after Communion I.D, collect II.A, and prayer over the offerings III.A.3. Other prayers ask that the deceased share in the glory of Father and Son;

as John notes, "where I am, there also will my servant be" (12:26). These include: prayer over the offerings I.C, collect I.D, prayer over the offerings II.A, collect III.A.2, and collect III.B.2. Prayer after Communion II.C refers to the glorification of both Christ and the deceased.

Christ's self-sacrifice is mentioned in prayer after Communion I.D ("who was sacrificed for us and rose in glory"), in collect II.C ("willingly underwent death in the flesh"), and in prayer over the offerings III.B.6 ("your Son, though innocent, was slain for us"). Romans 6:5 states that "if we have grown into union with him through a death like his, we shall also be united with him in the resurrection." Our imitation of Christ's death is alluded to in two prayers. Collect I.D asks that the deceased "may, when the day of resurrection comes, be united with [God] in glory." Collect III.A.2 refers to the deceased being "conformed to Christ"—a reference to Philippians 3 (see NT #12).

Preface II for the Dead ("Christ died so that we might live") proclaims: "For as one alone he accepted death, / so that we might all escape from dying; / as one man he chose to die, / so that in your sight we all might live for ever." The inserts to be used in Eucharistic Prayers II and III during Masses for the Dead also stress being united with Christ in a death like his so as to join in the resurrection. The texts (Roman Missal 105, 115) read:

> Remember your servant N.,
> whom you have called (today)
> from this world to yourself.
> Grant that he (she) *who was united with your Son in a death like his,*
> *may also be one with him in his Resurrection.* (emphasis added)

Strategy for Preaching

Scriptural Texts: 2 Maccabees 12:43-46; Psalm 103; 1 John 3:14-16; John 12:23-28

Liturgical Texts: Collect I.C; Prayer over the Offerings I.C; Prayer after Communion II.C; Preface II for the Dead; Inserts for Eucharistic Prayers II and III (Missal 105, 115)

The *focus* of this funeral homily is the paschal mystery: to love is to die, and to die is to live. The *function* is to help the mourners see how that mystery was lived out in the life of the deceased, and how it is present in their own lives as well.

To love is to die. That's why the mourners experience grief and loss. They have loved; and now they are experiencing a form of death. In love, they have gathered to pray for the deceased (2 Macc 12:43). To love is to die. The preacher can name the ways the deceased died to self in loving service (1John 3:16; John 12:25) to others: to family, in the church, to the wider community. The preacher can also mention that these "little deaths" helped prepare the deceased for larger losses, perhaps illness or the decline that comes with growing older, as well as for that final relinquishment in death itself.

But to die is to live. That is the mystery writ large in creation. Generations of stars had to die to eventually create carbon, the basis of life on our planet. Species have had to die off to eventually allow for human persons to evolve. Fall gives way to winter, which makes spring possible (Ps 103:15-16). Seeds must die in order to germinate and produce fruit (John 12:24).

To die is to live. That is also the story of Jesus (John 12:27). Having followed the Father's will and died to life in this world, he has been glorified. The deceased became part of this story at baptism, having gone through a "death like his" (Missal 105, 115; cf. preface). Now, "the ending of present things / open[s] up the beginning of things to come" (collect). The dying grain promises new life; the "hour" promises glory (John 12:28; prayer over the offerings; prayer after Communion). This is as true for the mourners as it is for the deceased.

17. John 14:1-6

Readings from the Ambo

The gospel. In John's gospel, the Last Supper is followed by a long last, or farewell, discourse (chaps. 14–17). The overall function of this discourse is to prepare the disciples for Jesus' departure. At the end of the supper, Judas has departed on his errand of betrayal, Jesus has given the new commandment of loving one another, and he has predicted Peter's denial. It is in this context that he says to his disciples: "Do not let your hearts be troubled" (*tarassō*—the same word used in John 11:33 and 12:27; see essays 15 and 16, above).

This section of the discourse begins with Jesus calling the disciples to have faith in him and in the Father; the emphasis on belief will also be found in the verses (John 14:7-14) that immediately follow this passage. The mix of realized and future eschatology in verse 3 is lost in translation; but the point is made that in the time between Jesus' departure and return, he remains present.[60] Thomas's question (v. 5) may reflect that the disciples are unwilling to accept the full implications of Jesus' departure; their faith is faltering. At the same time, his question allows Jesus another opportunity to make clear that he is the way *to* the Father because he is the definitive revelation *of* the Father (the truth: 1:14, 17; 5:33; 8:32, 40, 44-46; the life: 1:4; 6:33, 35, 48, 63, 68; 8:12; 10:10; 11:25).[61] The only way to oneness with the Father is through faith and trust in Jesus; through a person, not anything we do.

Application to funerals. Mourners may need to hear words of comfort from Jesus' lips: "Do not let your hearts be troubled." This reading, therefore, is recommended for the vigil. The preacher can, in the course of the homily, speak Jesus' words to the bereaved—repeating it like an antiphon. Rather than false consolation, these words are based on the promises found in the other readings and in the paschal mystery that leads to the promised reign. Jesus is the one who has gone before us. He is the way, the source of life and truth, whose passage assures our own.[62]

The image of death as a homecoming can be powerfully comforting. To view death this way is possible only because we believe in Jesus as the way home; we trust his promise to abide always with those who are his own.[63] "Christ has prepared a 'room' for the believer in the intermediate state which follows death, just as he found 'room' to dwell in him through the Paraclete while he lived on earth, and will find him a room in his consummated kingdom."[64]

Other readings. The image of a dwelling place features in Revelation 21:1-5a, 6b-7 (NT #19) as well as in the readings from 2 Corinthians (NT

---

60. Moloney, *The Gospel of John*, Sacra Pagina, 394.
61. Ibid., 395.
62. Sánchez, *The Passages We Celebrate*, 221.
63. Senior, *Loving and Dying*, 87.
64. Fuller, "Lectionary for Funerals," 61.

#10, #11), which refer to "a dwelling not made with hands, eternal in heaven" (5:1). Paul, in his letter to the Philippians (NT #12), reminds us that "our citizenship is in heaven" (3:20). Isaiah (OT #4) makes mention of place: God's mountain (25:6-7). The psalmist petitions to "dwell in the house of the Lord all the days" of his or her life in Psalm 27:4. Moving in procession "to the house of God" is mentioned in Psalm 42:5. Jerusalem, and the "house of the Lord," are central to Psalm 122.

Connecting the Bible and the Liturgy

The OCF. Among the prayers for the dead (398), ##1, 3, 10, 12, and 13 use images of welcome and place, which have an affinity for the gospel's mention of "many dwelling places" (John 14:2). Prayer 399, #6 refers to departing "this earthly dwelling" for an eternal kingdom.

Jesus goes before the disciples; but his departure does not sever ties with them. Therefore, texts that refer to the mourner's ties to the deceased enduring may be appropriate. For example, 399, #4 (= 72) proclaims that "death is not the end, / nor does it destroy the bonds / that [God] forge[s] in our lives." We read something similar in the Invitation to Prayer at the vigil (OCF 71): "[A]ll the ties of friendship and affection which knit us as one throughout our lives do not unravel with death." In addition, 398, #9 proclaims that "in death our life is changed not ended."

The image of heaven as a dwelling place, and death as a homecoming, suggests this gospel for the funeral of a parent or spouse, with whom one has spent a lifetime creating a home. In that case, the preacher ought to consider using prayers specifically designated for parents, a married couple, or a spouse. For example, prayer 398, #30 refers to "our heavenly home" and #33 speaks of sharing table "where the saints feast together in [God's] heavenly home."

The Missal. Both the metaphor of journey (Jesus as the way; being taken) and of place figure prominently in this gospel passage. Some of the prayers in the Missal, such as prayers after Communion I.A and I.B, emphasize the idea of journey. Others, like collect II.E, emphasize place ("place of refreshment, of blessed rest and resplendent light"). A number of prayers weave both metaphors together. For example, the second collect in Mass I.A reads: "[G]rant that he/she may be *led* to our true *homeland*" while collect III.B.1 asks that the deceased "*pass over* into the *realm* of heaven." The prayer after Communion for Mass I.C asks that the deceased "*pass over* to a *dwelling place* of light and peace." Preface I for the Dead reads: "Indeed for your faithful, Lord, / life is changed not ended, / and, when this earthly dwelling turns to dust, / an eternal dwelling is made ready for them in heaven."

Jesus' statement that there are "many dwelling places" where he is going evokes the idea of the communion of saints. If death is a home-coming, there is a family awaiting us. A number of prayers ask that the deceased become part of this "company" of saints in heaven. These can be found in Masses II.B (collect, prayer over the offerings), II.D (prayer after Communion), III.A.1 (both collects), III.A.2 (collect, prayer after Communion), III.A.3 (collect, prayer over the offerings), and III.B.9 (collect).

Strategy for Preaching

Scriptural Texts: Philippians 3:20-21; Psalm 27; John 14:1-6

Liturgical Texts: Opening Prayer 398, #30; Concluding Prayer 398, #3; OCF 71, 87

The *focus* of this vigil homily is Jesus as the way to the Father; the *function* is to ease the troubled hearts of the mourners by reminding them that they, as well as the deceased, are promised a place in the Father's house. The homily is structured along the lines of David Buttrick's method in his work *Homiletic: Moves and Structures*.

The preacher can begin with Jesus' own words—"Do not let your hearts be troubled"—and then acknowledge that those are hard words to hear at a funeral, when hearts are quite troubled. But Jesus does not speak those words lightly. The three "moves" that follow explore why these words are, indeed, appropriate.

In the first move, the emphasis is on Jesus' departure: "I go and prepare a place for you" (John 14:3). In this kingdom, this house, there are many dwelling places, room for all the saints at table, a place of light, peace, refreshment (OCF 398, #3, #30; Ps 27:1; John 14:2). Our true citizenship is there (Phil 3:20). Stories of separation from the life of the deceased could be recalled, and the ways that love was mediated in spite of absence could be mentioned. Sharing at table has a way of overcoming such absence. At the family table, stories and memories are shared. At the eucharistic table,

Christ's presence is mediated sacramentally. Christ has gone before us to prepare a place for us, and for our loved one. But we are not separated from him, or from our loved one who has died. The bonds of family (398, #30; cf. 71, 87) endure. Don't let hearts be troubled: a place is ready for the deceased, and for the mourners.

In the second move, Christ's promised return is recalled. We feel the absence of our loved one, as the disciples would feel Jesus' absence. Into that absence, Christ speaks: "I will come back . . . and take you to myself" (John 14:3). For the mourners, there is the hope that such a reunion will include the deceased. The hope is founded on faith (John 14:1) that Christ has the power to subject even death to himself (Phil 3:21). Stories of how the deceased sought out and attended to the needs of the mourners in the past could be recounted. The preacher proclaims that the mourners, and the deceased, are not forgotten. God's care is even manifested in the love and support found in the community gathered for the funeral. Don't let hearts be troubled: Christ will return for the deceased, and for the mourners.

"I am the way." Jesus not only shows us the way, but goes before us and *is* the way. Here, the preacher can mention the ways that the deceased, especially as a parent, showed "the way" to his or her children. How did they live the faith? The preacher can hold up that while apart from their loved one, while waiting (Phil 3:20), the mourners might feel lost, like Thomas (John 14:5). However, they have also been promised the way, the same way that the deceased walked. Don't let hearts be troubled: Christ is the way (John 14:6).

18. John 17:24-26

Readings from the Ambo

The gospel. As the previous selection marked the beginning of Jesus' farewell discourse, this passage marks the end. It is also the end of Jesus' High Priestly Prayer to the Father (chap. 17). Jesus has completed his mission; he has made the Father known. The disciples now share in the same bond of love shared between the Father and the Son. The Son abides in them; thus, they can make the Father known as well by the way they love one another. Remaining in this bond of love, the disciples (and all those whom the Father gives to the Son) are the subject of Jesus' prayer for final union with him in glory (17:5), in that place that existed "before the foundation of the world" (v. 24). All this will come to pass because the Father is righteous and just (v. 25). John explains that Jesus' abiding presence (v. 24) and his promise of continued revelation (v. 26) are possible only through the gift of the Paraclete (14:26; 16:13).

Application to funerals. Jesus prays that those given to him will be with him. The future orientation of this reading would argue for its use at the funeral liturgy. One of the emphases of the funeral liturgy is prayer for the dead. The homily, grounded in this reading, can speak to that practice by presenting (as in essay 10 above) the continuity of the relationship between the living and the dead in ways that resonate with contemporary sensitivities. As Donald Senior notes, "Jesus' final intense prayer matches the yearning of our hearts."[65]

Other readings. In this gospel passage, Jesus prays that those the Father has given him would always be with him. Therefore, the readings listed in essay 17 above that speak of "place" might also be appropriate. Prayer for the dead is explicitly mentioned in 2 Maccabees 12:43-46 (OT #7).

The love shared between Father and Son, and therefore now shared with those who believe in Jesus, is the focus of 1 John 3:14-16 (NT #16). One could speak of this love in terms of "adoption," and the believer being a child of God. If the preacher wanted to stress this aspect of the divine relationship, then 1 John 3:1-2 (NT #15) or Romans 8:14-23 (NT #5) would be appropriate. Romans 8:31b-35, 37-39 (NT #6) proclaims that nothing can separate the believer "from the love of Christ" (v. 35). The love of father for children as an image of God's compassion for God's people is mentioned in Psalm 103:13.

Connecting the Bible and the Liturgy

The OCF. Prayers that use images of welcome and place have been reviewed in essay 17. While no prayers in OCF 398 mention that the deceased is a child of God, prayer #3 does refer to the deceased as a child of Abraham, and #4 references the "tender love" with which God embraced the deceased in this life. Prayer #2 asks: "Are you not the God

---

65. Senior, *Loving and Dying*, 88.

of love who open your ears to all?" If we are with Christ, both before and after death, then indeed life changes but does not end (#9). Among the prayers in OCF 399, #1 refers to the mourners as God's "family" and #4 (= 72A) refers to disciples of Jesus as "the children of God." This prayer also expresses the hope that "death is not the end, / nor does it destroy the bonds / that you forge in our lives," a sentiment also expressed in the vigil's Invitation to Prayer (OCF 71, 87).

The Missal. As also mentioned in essay 17, a number of prayers use "place" as a metaphor for the next life or ask for the deceased to be included among the saints, those who are the "children of God" who even now abide in and with Christ. However, only collect III.A.4 refers to adoption as a child of God explicitly. Prayer after Communion III.B.5 refers to the mourners (rather than the deceased) as God's children. God's love is only mentioned in prayer over the offerings I.C. This prayer, however, does weave together a number of themes found in the gospel passage from John, as it asks that God's departed servant

> may be taken up into *glory* with your Son,
> in whose great *mystery of love* we are all *united*. (emphasis added)

Preface I for the Dead echoes prayer 398, #9 (see above).

Strategy for Preaching

Scriptural Texts: 2 Maccabees 12:43-46; Psalm 103; 1 John 3:1-2; John 17:24-26

Liturgical Texts: Collect III.A.4; Prayer over the Offerings I.C; Prayer after Communion III.B.5; Preface I for the Dead; OCF 71

The *focus* of this funeral homily is the bond of love between Father and Son, while the *function* of the homily is to help the mourners see that they, and their beloved deceased, are included in that bond, a bond that transcends death. A homily preached following the method of Paul Scott Wilson might begin by acknowledging the loss, recalling in gratitude what the mourners might miss the most about the one who has died. Sadness (preface) is normal. Next, the preacher could speak about the context of the gospel reading. The disciples are in mourning as they anticipate Jesus' crucifixion. It is into that sense of loss that Jesus speaks. Here, at the end of the discourse, he prays that the bond of love that he shares with the disciples (and, in turn, they share with the Father) will endure; that they will be with him always (John 17:24). The nature of their relationship might change, but it will not end.

This is the same hope that the mourners have: that in death, life changes but does not end (preface) and that the bonds we share endure (OCF 71). The preacher can proclaim that by baptism, the deceased (and those present) are children of God (1 John 3:1; collect; prayer after Communion). The Father's love and compassion (psalm) brought the Son safely through death; therefore, we hope that the same love will lead us to eternal life (1 John 3:2). In Christ, all are united in a "great mystery of love" (prayer over the offerings). This enduring bond is expressed in prayer for the deceased (2 Macc 12:43-44) as well as the support shown one another.

19. John 19:17-18, 25-30(39)

Readings from the Ambo

The gospel. The Lectionary for Mass adds nine verses to the passage originally chosen for the OCF, which ends with Jesus' death on the cross. The longer version includes the piercing of Jesus' side with the resultant flow of water and blood, as well as the handing over of Jesus' body for burial. The selection omits verses 19-24, which details the placing of the inscription identifying Jesus as "the King of the Jews" and the division of Jesus' clothes by the soldiers.

The account begins with Jesus carrying his own cross. Simon of Cyrene (Matt 27:32; Mark 15:21; Luke 23:26) is missing; Jesus is in complete control. Jesus' placement in between the other two condemned men suggests a "royal retinue";[66] this follows John's view of the crucifixion as an enthronement and Jesus' being "lifted up" on the cross as his being lifted up in glory.

The address of Jesus to his mother and to the "disciple whom he loved" has been interpreted in myriad ways. Some focus on what seems to be Jesus' concern that she be cared for after he is gone. Others see a connection to the account of the wedding at Cana: the "hour," which had

66. Moloney, *The Gospel of John*, Sacra Pagina, 507.

not yet come then (2:4), has now arrived (17:1); and Mary—addressed as "Woman" in both instances—is witness to both events. Others make connections to both Genesis (3:15) and chapter 12 in Revelation. Raymond Brown sees the passage as John's way of addressing the problem of how Jesus' natural family was related to the new family created by discipleship (cf. Mark 3:31-35; Matt 12:46-50; Luke 8:19-21).[67] That the disciple took Mary into his home "from that hour" (v. 27) has a double meaning. On the one hand, there is the literal, temporal meaning: from that moment, she was under his care. More importantly, the "hour" is Jesus' "hour." As Moloney notes: "Because of the cross and from the moment of the cross a new family of Jesus has been created."[68]

Jesus' thirst is more than a physical sensation. Just as he "thirsted" for the faith of the Samaritan woman (John 4:4-42), he now thirsts for the consummation of his task: the glorification of the Father and the sending of the gift of the Spirit. His drink is given him on a sprig of hyssop, recalling the hyssop used to sprinkle the lintels with the saving blood of the sacrificed lambs prior to the Exodus (Exod 12:22-23). Jesus' "exodus" (John 13:1) is now finished, his task brought to perfection; as his last act, he gives the gift of *the* Spirit (*to pneuma*), not *his* Spirit, to the new community of faith formed at the foot of the cross.[69]

That blood and water flowed from Jesus' side has also been interpreted in various ways. On the one hand, the point is made (versus Docetists) that Jesus truly died a physical death. At the same time, a sacramental reading is also reasonable: the gift of the Spirit is followed by the gift of baptism and Eucharist. Through these gifts, Jesus remains present in the community, even though he is physically absent.

Joseph retrieves the body and Nicodemus brings a tremendous amount of spices. What is missing from the pericope is the account of the burial itself (John 19:40-42). The passion, which started in a garden (18:1), now ends in a garden (19:41). Jesus is buried like a king, which is how he has been identified at numerous points in this story.[70]

---

67. Raymond E. Brown, *The Death of the Messiah*, vol. 1 (New York; London: Yale University Press, 1994), 1025.

68. Moloney, *The Gospel of John*, Sacra Pagina, 504.

69. Ibid., 509.

70. Ibid., 510; Bergant and Karris, *Collegeville Bible Commentary*, 1013.

Application to funerals. Many of the approaches discussed in previous essays are suggested by this final selection as well. As with the other crucifixion accounts included in the funeral Lectionary (especially the short forms of gospels #5 and #9; see above), the stark reality of death suggests this reading for the vigil. However, the Johannine stress on death as glorification may be too much of a contrast with the grief being experienced in some situations; the homilist will need to be careful not to move to hope/praise too quickly, leaving the mourners behind. Therefore, this account of the passion—such as the long form of the accounts mentioned above—may also work well at the funeral liturgy. That being said, this reading from John has unique features when it comes to preaching at the funeral rites. The sacramental imagery invites the preacher to make connections to baptism and the Eucharist. The emphasis on Jesus' abiding presence in the nascent church also invites the preacher to draw out how the community, currently gathered at the cross of grief, is also called to care for one another—as the Beloved Disciple cared for Mary.

Readings and prayers that might be used to accompany an account of the passion have been discussed in essays 5, 8, and 9. Those readings and prayers that refer to baptism or Eucharist, or use such sacramental imagery, have been discussed in essays 10, 11, 13, and 15. Readings and prayers that echo John's theology that Jesus' death is his glorification have been explored in essay 16. The bond that abides between believers even in death has been mentioned in essays 10 (especially the notion of the communion of saints) and 18. They will not be repeated here.

There are two unique features of John's passion account that I will emphasize in this essay. First, there is Jesus' comment that he "thirsts." The connections to the story of the Samaritan woman present a number of possibilities for funeral preaching, as discussed below. Second, his death on the cross is associated with his giving of the Spirit.

Other readings. The image of "thirsting" is prominent in Psalms 42/43, 63, and 143. The latter also mentions God's "good spirit" (v. 10). It might be said that the author of Lamentations is thirsting for peace, longing for God (OT #5). In Revelation 21:6, God promises "life giving water" "to the thirsty" (NT #19).

The Paraclete, or Holy Spirit, is named explicitly in Acts 10:38 (NT #1), Romans 5:5 (NT #2), and Romans 8:14, 16 (NT #5). In the reading from Romans 5, the Spirit is described as having been given to those who follow Christ. One of the gifts of the Spirit is wisdom, which provides a true view of death—as opposed to the foolish mentioned in Wisdom 3:2 (OT #2). The Paraclete continues Christ's abiding presence "in the land of the living" (Ps 116 antiphon).

Connecting the Bible and the Liturgy

The OCF. If the connection between the Spirit and wisdom is made, then prayers 398, #1 and 399, #7 are appropriate. The sacrament of confirmation is often referred to as being "sealed" with the Spirit, making 398, #7 a fitting selection as well. The idea of thirsts being slaked is reflected in the description of heaven as a place of refreshment (398, #3).

The Missal. The continuing work of the Holy Spirit might be addressed by making reference to the second epiclesis in Eucharistic Prayers II and III (see essay 13).

In John 19:28, Jesus says, "I thirst." As noted in the Preface for the Third Sunday of Lent, Jesus ardently thirsted for the faith of the Samaritan woman. In like manner, Jesus thirsted for the faith of the deceased, and thirsts for the faith of those gathered. Baptismal imagery, and language concerning the catechumens' thirst for Christ, are found in the prayers used as part of the first scrutiny (RCIA 154), which may be helpful to the preacher as well. Two prayers from the Missal might also be used if the preacher chose to focus on the image of thirsting. Collect II.B asks God to send the "lasting dew" of his mercy on the deceased; if this prayer is used, a further connection to Eucharistic Prayer II, which likens the Holy Spirit's descent on the gifts to the dewfall (Missal 101), could be made. Collect II.E refers to heaven as a place of "refreshment."

Strategy for Preaching

Scriptural Texts: Lamentations 3:17-26; Psalm 143; Revelation 21:1-5a, 6b-7; John 19:17-18, 25-39

Liturgical Texts: Collect II.B; Preface I for the Dead; Eucharistic Prayer II

The *focus* of this funeral homily is God's "thirst" or desire to be in relationship with not only the deceased but with each of the mourners.

The *function*, then, is to proclaim that that desire transcends even death, and to invite the mourners deeper into that union.

The preacher might begin by giving voice to the loss the mourners are experiencing. Using the image of "thirsting," the preacher could note that the mourners are longing, or thirsting, for their loved one; for answers or meaning in the midst of loss; for comfort, consolation, and peace (Lam 3:17); even for God (Ps 143:6). Next, recalling the life of the deceased, the preacher could speak about the ways he or she "thirsted"—what was it that he or she was most passionate about, that gave life meaning and direction? Perhaps it was the relationships with those who have gathered for the funeral? Or perhaps there was a social cause or program to which the deceased volunteered? How did he or she "thirst for living water" (RCIA 154A), for Christ, whether as a catechumen or a lifelong Christian? Or, like the Samaritan woman, did he or she "thirst" to share the Good News with others (John 4:39)? How might have the deceased "thirsted" to see God face-to-face, perhaps in the context of increasing age or illness?

It would be easy to dismiss Christ's "thirst" on the cross as purely physical. However, John intends something else here. Just as he "thirsted" for the faith of the Samaritan woman (John 4:4-42; cf. Preface for the Third Sunday of Lent), Christ thirsts at the cross to complete the mission for which he was sent: to give glory to the Father and to send the gift of the Spirit. And, he thirsts for the faith of the deceased and the mourners as well. Therefore, the preacher can proclaim that Christ is the one who refreshes, who slakes our thirsts. "To the thirsty I will give a gift from the spring of life-giving water" (Rev 21:6). It is in baptism that the believer's thirst is first quenched. But more: Christ sends the Holy Spirit like the dew (collect; Eucharistic Prayer II), with mercy for the deceased (collect) and guidance (Ps 143:10) in the midst of loss for the mourners. Through the Spirit, God dwells with humanity now; in that same Spirit, life in the new Jerusalem is possible (Rev 21:2). Therefore, the mourners can hope (Lam 3:21) in the one who hears their prayers (Ps 143:1) and who wipes away their tears (Rev 21:4).

Summary

These final tables summarize the correlations between the gospel readings and the texts from the OCF (table 9) and the Roman Missal (table 10). As with the previous tables, if the reference is boldface then that text is part of the preaching strategy presented for that essay.

Table 9: Summary of Correlations between the Gospel Reading and Texts from the OCF

Gospel (Essay) #	OT #	NT #	Psalm #	398 #	399 #	Other
1	1,2, 4,**6**	8,14,17, 18,19	1,5,**6**	3,5,7,9	1,2,5, 7	175
2	2,**4**	1,5,6,10, 13,15,19	1,9	4,5,12, 39,40,41	4,6	175
3	3,6	7,**9**,13	2	1,2,3,9, 42,**43**,44, 45	4,6,7	71/87
4	3,4,6	1,7,11, 16,17,18, 19	2,3,6,7	3,4,5, 9,12,	4	**71/87** 81/97
5	**5**	2,3	**9**	**2**,5,6, 7,12	1,2,4, **5**,6	
6	2,**3**,4, 5	10,11,**13**	2,6,7	1,2,4,5,7,8,9 10,12,27,28	1,4,5, 6,7	
7	2,3,4, 6,7	7,9,11, 13,**17**,18	1,4,5	1,2,3,**4**, 5,9,12	3,4,6, 7	**81/97**
8	1,2,4	5,6,8,9, 10,11,12, 15	1,2,**4**,8	2,4,5,6	2,3,6	
9	2	2,3,10	2,3,10	4,5,6,7	1,2	**175** **224/402.2**
10	1	1,4,8,9	1,4,5,7	1,2,3, 7,9,13	4	**71/87** **83-84** 175; 401

Gospel #	OT #	NT #	Psalm #	398 #	399 #	Other
11	3,**6**,7	1,4,7,**11**,12,13,16,18	2,**8**,9,10	3,7,9,10,12	4	71/87 **83-84**
12	**1**,6	**9**,10,11,19	**5**	1,2,3,9,13	2	81/97 175
13	**2**,6	**1**,2,4,11,13	**1**,5	1,7,9,10,**11**	4	**71/87** 83-84 401
14	2,3,6	4,5,**6**,8,9,10,13,18	2,3,9,**10**	1,**2**,3,5,6,7,8,9,10,13,27,28,39,40,41,42,43,44,45	**2**,3,7	83-84
15	**4**	**19**	**4**	4,10,11,13	3,5	
16	2,4,6,**7**	1,2,3,4,5,7,10,12,**16**,	1,5,**6**	13	2	218A 405
17	4	10,11,**12**,19	3,4,8	1,**3**,9,10,12,13,**30**,33	4,6	**71/87**
18	4,7	5,6,10,11,12,**15**,16,19	3,4,**6**,8	1,2,3,4,9,10,12,13	4,6	**71/87**
19	2,**5**,6,7	1,2,3,4,5,6,10,12,16,**19**	1,4,5,6,7,**10**	1,2,3,5,6,7,12,13	1,2,4,7	71/87 83-84 401

Table 10: Summary of Correlations between the Gospel Reading and the Texts from the Missal

Gospel (Essay) #	Mass for the Dead	Preface for the Dead	Other
1	I.A; I.B; **III.A.1; III.B.2;** III.B.3; III.B.9	I,V	
2	I.C; III.A.1; III.A.3 III.B.2; III.B.3; **IV.8**	I,IV	
3	I.C; III.A.3; III.B.9; IV.9	I,IV, V	
4	**I.A;** I.B; III.A.1; III.B.2; III.B.3; **III.B.9**	V	Eucharistic Prayer (EP) I,II,III
5	I.A; II.C III.A.1; III.A.5	III,IV, V	
6	I.A; I.B; I.C; III.A.1; **III.A.3; III.B.2;** III.B.3; IV.7	I,II, **V**	
7	I.A; I.C; II.E III.A.2; III.A.3; III.A.5 III.B.1; III.B.3; III.B.4; III.B.9; IV.9	I,IV, V	
8	I.A; I.C; II.E; III.A.1	I	
9	I.A; II.C; III.A.1; III.A.5	II,III, IV,V	
10	**I.D;** II.B III.A.1; III.A.2; III.A.3 III.B.2; III.B.9	I	EP II,III
11	**I.A;** I.B; I.D; II.A; II.B; II.C; III.A.1; III.A.4; III.B.1; III.B.2; **III.B.3** III.B.7; III.B.9	III,**IV**, V	EP I,II,III
12	I.B; **I.C;** I.D; II.D; II.E III.A.1; III.A.3; III.A.4 III.A.5; **III.B.1;** III.B.6 III.B.7	I	
13	I.A; I.D; II.A; II.B; **II.C** **III.A.1;** III.A.4 III.A.5; III.B.1		**EP II,III** **RM132**

Gospel (Essay) #	Mass for the Dead	Preface for the Dead	Other
14	I.B; I.D; II.A; II.B; II.C III.A.4; III.B.1; III.B.7 IV.7; IV.8; IV.9	I,III, IV	
15	I.A; **I.B** III.A.1; III.A.2 III.A.5; **III.B.5**	III	Preface: Lent Sun 5 RCIA 175
16	I.B; **I.C**; I.D; II.A; **II.C** III.A.2; III.A.3 III.B.2; III.B.6	I,II	**EP II,III**
17	I.A; I.B; I.C; II.B; II.D; II.E III.A.1; III.A.2; III.A.3 III.B.1; III.B.9	I	
18	I.A; **I.C**; II.B; II.D; II.E III.A.1; III.A.2; III.A.3; **III.A.4**; III.B.1; **III.B.5**; III.B.9	I	
19	I.A; I.B; I.C; I.D II.A; **II.B**; II.C; II.D; II.E III.A.1; III.A.2; III.A.3 III.A.4; III.A.5 III.B.1; III.B.2; III.B.5 III.B.7; III.B.9	I,II,III, IV,V	**EP II,III** Preface: Lent Sun 3 RCIA 154

Bibliography

Ritual Books

The Lectionary for Mass, 2nd ed., 1998–2000.
Order of Christian Funerals (OCF), 1989, 1985.
Rite of Christian Initiation of Adults (RCIA), 1985.
The Roman Missal, Third Edition, 2010.

Catechisms

Catechism of the Catholic Church, 2nd ed., 1997.
United States Catholic Catechism for Adults, 2006.

General Biblical Commentaries

Aymer, Margaret, Cynthia Briggs Kittredge, and David A. Sánchez, eds. *The New Testament*. Fortress Commentary on the Bible. Minneapolis, MN: Fortress Press, 2014.

Bergant, Dianne, and Robert J. Karris, eds. *The Collegeville Bible Commentary: Based on the New American Bible with Revised New Testament*. Collegeville, MN: Liturgical Press, 1989.

Brawley, Robert L. "Luke." In *The New Testament*. Edited by Margaret Aymer, Cynthia Briggs Kittredge, and David A. Sánchez. Fortress Commentary on the Bible. Minneapolis, MN: Fortress Press, 2014.

Brown, Raymond E. *An Introduction to the New Testament*. New York: Doubleday, 1997.

———. *The Death of the Messiah: From Gethsemane to the Grave, a Commentary on the Passion Narratives in the Four Gospels*. Vols. 1 and 2. New York; London: Yale University Press, 1994.

Donahue, John R., and Daniel J. Harrington. *The Gospel of Mark*. Edited by Daniel J. Harrington. Vol. 2. Sacra Pagina Series. Collegeville, MN: Liturgical Press, 2002.

Flanagan, Neal M., OSM. "John." In *The Collegeville Bible Commentary*. Edited by Dianne Bergant and Robert J. Karris. Collegeville, MN: Liturgical Press, 1989.

Harrington, Daniel J. *The Gospel of Matthew*. Edited by Daniel J. Harrington. Vol. 1. Sacra Pagina Series. Collegeville, MN: Liturgical Press, 2007.

Johnson, Luke Timothy. *The Gospel of Luke*. Edited by Daniel J. Harrington. Vol. 3. Sacra Pagina Series. Collegeville, MN: Liturgical Press, 1991.

Kodell, Jerome, OSB. "Luke." In *The Collegeville Bible Commentary*. Edited by Dianne Bergant and Robert J. Karris. Collegeville, MN: Liturgical Press, 1989.

Moloney, Francis J. *The Gospel of John.* Edited by Daniel J. Harrington. Vol. 4. Sacra Pagina Series. Collegeville, MN: Liturgical Press, 1998.

Nowell, Irene. *Sing a New Song: The Psalms in the Sunday Lectionary.* Collegeville, MN: Liturgical Press, 1993.

Rybolt, John E. "Wisdom." In *The Collegeville Bible Commentary.* Edited by Dianne Bergant and Robert J. Karris. Collegeville, MN: Liturgical Press, 1989.

Van Linden, Philip, CM. "Mark." In *The Collegeville Bible Commentary.* Edited by Dianne Bergant and Robert J. Karris. Collegeville, MN: Liturgical Press, 1989.

General Homiletics

Buttrick, David. *Homiletic: Moves and Structures.* Philadelphia: Fortress Press, 1987.

Craddock, Fred B. *As One Without Authority.* Revised. St. Louis, MO: Chalice Press, 2001.

Hilkert, Mary Catherine. *Naming Grace: Preaching and the Sacramental Imagination.* New York: Continuum, 1997.

Long, Thomas G. *The Witness of Preaching.* Louisville, KY: Westminster John Knox Press, 1989.

Lowry, Eugene L. *The Homiletical Plot: The Sermon as Narrative Art Form.* Expanded edition. Louisville, KY: Westminster John Knox Press, 2001.

Wallace, James A. *Preaching to the Hungers of the Heart: The Homily on the Feasts and within the Rites.* Collegeville, MN: Liturgical Press, 2002.

Wilson, Paul Scott. *The Four Pages of the Sermon: A Guide to Biblical Preaching.* Nashville, TN: Abingdon Press, 1999.

The Funeral Lectionary / Preaching at Funerals

Agnoli, Francis L. "'First of All, Do No Harm'—Lament in the Development of a Gentle Funeral Homiletic." DMin thesis. Aquinas Institute of Theology, St. Louis, MO, 2009.

Fuller, Reginald H. "Lectionary for Funerals," *Worship* 56, no. 1 (1982): 36–63.

Hughes, Robert. *A Trumpet in Darkness: Preaching to Mourners.* Fortress Resources for Preaching. Philadelphia: Fortress Press, 1985.

Krieg, Robert A. "The Funeral Homily: A Theological View." *Worship* 58, no. 3 (May 1984): 222–39.

Sánchez, Patricia Datchuck. *The Passages We Celebrate: Commentaries on the Scriptural Texts for Baptisms, Weddings, and Funerals.* Kansas City, MO: Sheed and Ward, 1994.

Schmitz, Barbara G. *The Life of Christ and the Death of a Loved One: Crafting the Funeral Homily*. Lima, OH: CSS Publishing, 1995.

Senior, Donald, CP. *Loving and Dying: A Commentary on the Lectionary Texts for Weddings and Funerals*. Kansas City, MO: Celebration Books, 1979.

Turner, Paul. *Light in the Darkness: Preparing Better Catholic Funerals*. Collegeville, MN: Liturgical Press, 2017.

Wallace, James A., ed. *Preaching in the Sunday Assembly: A Pastoral Commentary on* Fulfilled in Your Hearing. *Commentary and Text*. Collegeville, MN: Liturgical Press, 2010.

Grief / Pastoral Care

MacDonald, Coval B. "Loss and Bereavement." In *Clinical Handbook of Pastoral Counseling*. Vol. 1. Expanded ed. Edited by Robert J. Wicks, Richard D. Parsons, and Donald Capps. New York: Paulist Press, 1993.

Maciejewski, Paul K., Baohui Zhang, Susan D. Block, and Holly G. Prigerson. "An Empiric Examination of the Stage Theory of Grief." *JAMA* 297, no. 7 (February 21, 2007): 716–23.

Volkan, Vamik D., and Elizabeth Zintl. *Life After Loss: The Lessons of Grief*. New York: Charles Scribner's Sons, 1993.

Theology

Congregation for the Doctrine of the Faith. "Letter on Certain Questions Concerning Eschatology." May 17, 1979.

International Theological Commission. "Some Current Questions in Eschatology." December 1991.

Lohfink, Gerhard. *Is This All There Is? On Resurrection and Eternal Life*. Translated by Linda M. Maloney. Collegeville, MN: Liturgical Press, 2017.

Pontifical Council for Promoting Christian Unity. *Joint Declaration on the Doctrine of Justification*. October 31, 1999.

Pope Francis. *Gaudete et Exsultate*. Apostolic Exhortation. March 19, 2018.